Louder than Words

Lawyers, Communities and the Struggle for Justice

A Report to the Rockefeller Foundation

by Penda D. Hair
March 2001

Copyright © 2001 the Rockefeller Foundation
450 Fifth Avenue, New York, NY 10018-2702
212-869-8500
Web site: www.rockfound.org

ISBN   0-89184-050-8

Hair, Penda D.

Louder than words: lawyers, communities and the struggle for justice: a report to the Rockefeller Foundation/by Penda D. Hair.

p. cm.

"March, 2001"

ISBN   0-89184-050-8

1. Lawyers—United States.   2. Civil rights—United States.

I. Rockefeller Foundation.

342.73087

Table of Contents

Advisers

Convened under the direction of Dayna L. Cunningham, Associate Director, Working Communities Division, the Rockefeller Foundation

Theresa Fay-Bustillos, Vice President of Global Community Affairs and Executive Director of the Levi Strauss Foundation, Levi Strauss & Co.

Douglas I. Foy, President, Conservation Law Foundation

Lani Guinier, Professor of Law, Harvard Law School

Alan Jenkins, Deputy Director, Human Rights and International Cooperation, the Ford Foundation

Geraldine P. Mannion, Chair, Special Projects, Carnegie Corporation of New York

Ceasar McDowell, Associate Professor and Director, Center for Reflective Community Practice, Department of Urban Studies and Planning, Massachusetts Institute of Technology

Clyde E. Murphy, Executive Director, Chicago Lawyers' Committee for Civil Rights Under Law, Inc.

Karen K. Narasaki, Executive Director, National Asian Pacific American Legal Consortium

William P. Quigley, Professor of Law, Loyola University, New Orleans, School of Law

Constance L. Rice, Co-Director, Advancement Project

Catherine Samuels, Director, Program on Law and Society, Open Society Institute

Mark Soler, President, Youth Law Center

Susan P. Sturm, Professor of Law, Columbia Law School

Gerald Torres, H.O. Head Centennial Professor of Real Property Law and Vice Provost, University of Texas at Austin, and Director, Texas LEADS

Brenda Wright, Managing Attorney, National Voting Rights Institute

Contributors: Zenobia Lai, Andrew Leong and Chi Chi Wu (authors of the article excerpted in Chapter 6)

About the author: Penda D. Hair is Co-Director of the Advancement Project

Foreword From the Rockefeller Foundation

Actions speak louder than words. The words of our Founding Fathers—espousing the principles of fairness, justice and freedom—have served as a beacon of hope and attainment for countless generations. Yet, even today, many of our nation's policies and practices marginalize and exclude people because of race, ethnicity, language and income. Unfortunately, discrimination still exists.

LOUDER THAN WORDS: Lawyers, Communities and the Struggle for Justice, is a valuable contribution to the ongoing struggle to combat racial exclusion in the United States.

The Rockefeller Foundation is committed to supporting work to bring about racial justice and is pleased to introduce this Report.

Authored by Penda Hair of the Advancement Project, LOUDER THAN WORDS is the product of a multiyear examination of the civil rights field. The report uncovers important developments in the practice of civil rights law that respond to changes in the law and public opinion, and that build on the best traditions of the civil rights and other social movements. Many issues are featured, from community-based organizations working to address poor corporate citizenship, to major national institutions taking on unfair practices of large public agencies. They reaffirm that race and ethnicity remain front and center in the struggle for justice.

What is new? Importantly, the field of racial justice is evolving and the work is widespread. Through experience and innovation, seasoned civil rights practitioners and newcomers alike are connecting more closely with community organizations to seek accountability from public institutions. They are building popular support, and often bridging political and racial lines, to seek and sustain social and economic fairness.

The Foundation would like to thank Penda Hair, whose valuable insights contained in this report come from more than 20 years of civil rights lawyering and a tireless commitment to racial justice. Her report would not have been possible without the guidance and inspiration from an extraordinary group of advisers from the academic, advocacy, legal and philanthropic fields. We would like to convey our gratitude to the advisory committee, as well as the civil rights and community leaders who reviewed drafts of the report and provided incisive and critical perspectives.

They are continuing the heroic work of the civil rights pioneers in the never-ending struggle for justice.

Dayna Cunningham

Executive Summary

Claiming the Promise of Justice

The civil rights movement shattered the foundations of legalized racial hierarchy in the United States, ending officially sanctioned segregation and discrimination—the first step in dismantling the pervasive structure of inequality in this country. But the work of the civil rights movement is not finished. Despite remarkable progress, widespread discrimination persists, and many forms of exclusion rooted in race have not been addressed by anti-discrimination strategies. These structures continuously re-create racial inequality.

In 1997, the Rockefeller Foundation undertook a three-year investigation of advocacy in the field of civil rights. The goal was to reveal emerging patterns in the field, illustrate the variety of roles and approaches lawyers have taken in this type of work, identify the capacities needed to be effective and to make meaningful change, and highlight a range of successful strategies for addressing issues of race and ethnicity.

This report presents six case studies that reveal how the field of racial-justice lawyering is transforming itself in response to major changes in the landscape.

One case details lawyers' and others' creative response to a court ruling ending affirmative action at the University of Texas. In another, community-service organizations and lawyers successfully take on a case of modern-day slavery for undocumented garment workers. One case demonstrates new techniques in dealing with traditional voting-rights claims in Mississippi; another describes a creative campaign for fairness in public transit spending in Los Angeles. A case study that began as an employment-discrimination fight in Greensboro, North Carolina, ended in a citywide dialogue about responsible corporate citizenship. The final case study involves a multifaceted community effort to preserve one of the last remaining parcels of open space in Boston's congested Chinatown. Two of the case studies highlight the role of national civil rights organizations in racial-justice innovation.

PATTERNS OF DISCRIMINATION, STRATEGIES FOR ADVANCING JUSTICE
Our racial past infuses the present. In today's struggles for justice, those enslaved may be Asian, the bus riders Latina and some in the power structure may be people of color. The patterns seem remarkably familiar, as the problems addressed in the case studies show:

- In 1946, the University of Texas (UT) Law School refused to admit blacks, leading to a Supreme Court decision that struck down racial exclusion. Fifty years later, the U.S. Court of Appeals in HOPWOOD V. UNIVERSITY OF TEXAS ruled in favor of white applicants, striking down UT Law School's modest affirmative-action program. In the fall of 1996, only four black students enrolled in UT Law School's entering class. However, the innovative Ten Percent Plan for UT admissions, created by a collaboration of academics, lawyers and civil rights groups, is expanding the numbers of African-American and Latino Students. It is also changing the profile of success at UT. African-American and Latino "ten-percenters" entering

The struggle continues: The 1965 Selma to Montgomery march followed years of voting-rights organizing in Alabama. Violent reaction to the march impelled Congress to pass the Voting Rights Act, which provided unprecedented protection for minority voters and placed certain jurisdictions with histories of egregious voting-rights violations under Justice Department supervision. Once under the eye of the Justice Department, these jurisdictions are required get preapproval of any changes in their voting systems (left).

UT's freshman class are outperforming their white counterparts admitted under traditional criteria. The Plan's focus on top performers in public high schools also creates incentives to improve disadvantaged schools at the K–12 levels.

- The 13th Amendment to the Constitution, ratified in 1865, prohibits slavery and involuntary servitude within the United States. But 130 years later, 71 Thai garment workers were found enslaved behind barbed wire in the El Monte suburb of Los Angeles. They were imprisoned for many years and forced to sew name-brand clothes for major labels in the fashion industry. The lawyers went beyond in-court representation, collaborating with activists to make sure the workers obtained housing, food and the skills they needed to take control of their own lives. The advocates were effective in making the egregious El Monte situation the centerpiece of a successful industrywide effort to prevent exploitative labor practices. In the process, the workers successfully overcame cultural and language barriers to forge a coalition of Thai and Latina garment workers who have become forceful advocates for garment-industry reform.

- In 1957, in the midst of voting-rights activism across the Mississippi Delta, Emmitt Till, a young black man from Chicago, was kidnapped off the streets of Tallahatchie County, Mississippi, and murdered by white segregationists. In 1992, 70 percent black Tallahatchie County had never elected an African-American to the powerful Board of Supervisors or to any other county office. With relentless community organizing and effective assertion of Voting Rights Act claims, two African-American supervisors won election in Tallahatchie County. The number of African-American officials elected statewide also doubled, fueling broad civic engagement around education reform and other quality-of-life issues.

- In 1955, an African-American seamstress named Rosa Parks ignited the civil rights movement when she refused to give up her bus seat to a white person. Forty years later in 1995, bus service for poor riders of color remained appallingly unequal in Los Angeles. The Metropolitan Transit Authority voted that year to raise fares for the dilapidated city bus service, choosing to spend billions on lavish rail lines to predominantly white suburbs. Civil rights lawyers teamed up with highly organized bus riders. Combining sophisticated use of data, engagement with the arts, skilled community organizing, strategic political connections and savvy media relations, as well as a groundbreaking lawsuit, together they convinced the transit agency to reroute millions of dollars to improve bus transportation.

- In the 1960s, Nelson Johnson was one of the college students who joined sit-ins at Woolworth's lunch counter in Greensboro, North Carolina, that sparked a nationwide student sit-in movement. In 1992, Kmart opened a huge distribution facility in the outskirts of Greensboro. It paid the largely African-American work force lower wages than in majority-white distribution facilities, and tolerated serious mistreatment of the workers. Some of the Kmart workers were members of the Faith Community Church, where the Rev. Nelson Johnson now serves as pastor. Old-fashioned protest, a community-focused vision of justice and timely, strategic assistance from attorney James Ferguson, a giant of the civil rights bar, enabled the workers to win a union contract with increased wages and protections. At the same time, the ministers and workers engaged the entire city in a new kind of dialogue about the meaning of racial and social justice and helped pass a living-wage ordinance.

- The first large group of Chinese laborers came to Massachusetts in 1870 as cheap labor to break a shoe-factory strike. Many eventually settled in Boston. Joined later by Chinese-Americans fleeing rising nativism on the West Coast, they created a flourishing Chinatown community. Starting in the 1950s, "urban renewal" policies led to freeway construction, large hospital development and the siting of a "combat zone" for "adult" businesses in Chinatown. In 1993, when the city proposed development of a parking lot on one of the last remaining open parcels of land in Chinatown, a coalition of residents and activists rallied to stop it. Taking democratic decision making as its core value, the coalition launched a relentless organizing campaign against the decision to approve the garage. Working with a group of young visionary legal-services lawyers, the coalition mobilized residents for administrative hearings, conducted a community-wide referendum and held press conferences and cultural events to stimulate public involvement among marginalized immigrant groups. As a result, it opened up the neighborhood decision-making process and won a decisive victory to preserve the community space.

The case studies reflect the broad range of issues, constituencies, geographic settings, lawyer roles and visions of racial justice that characterize an emerging field of work—racial-justice innovation. Racial-justice innovation begins with the premise that societal structures—market and political structures, and social and cultural institutions and practices—are the primary cause of racial exclusion. It goes beyond popular notions that explain racial exclusion in terms of individual prejudice as the reason why some whites treat minorities differently. Under this common line of reasoning, curing racism requires treating everyone the same—in a "colorblind" manner. But the emphasis on colorblindness merely obscures societal structures that exclude minorities. As these cases illustrate, addressing racial exclusion requires more far-reaching strategies that build alliances, that encourage participation by all relevant parties, and that strengthen democratic involvement in making changes that address the fundamental causes of racism.

FINDINGS

1. RACE AND ETHNICITY REMAIN FRONT AND CENTER.

In all of the cases in this report, race remains central to the work. Creative lawyers explore the experiences of each racial or ethnic group and, where possible, combine claims of different racial groups without abandoning the particular history, needs and interests of individual groups. For racial-justice lawyers, approaches that deny or mute the goal of racial justice are neither feasible nor desirable.

2. RACIAL-JUSTICE ADVOCATES FACE UP TO THE COMPLEXITIES OF RACE AND CLASS.

Racial exclusion often is symptomatic of broader, structural unfairness that, while impacting more heavily on racial minorities, also affects large numbers of disadvantaged whites. The Los Angeles transit case included white bus riders in the class of the plaintiffs, even though the cause of action was discrimination against people of color. On the other hand, people of color with power and resources were among the defendants in the case. Similarly, garment workers' advocates helped create a powerful coalition between Thai and Latina workers, overcoming not only language and cultural barriers, but also suspicion stemming from the fact that the sweatshop operators are often Asian.

3. RACIAL-JUSTICE LAWYERS EXPAND AN APPROACH TO RACE TO INCLUDE EFFORTS THAT DEEPEN DEMOCRATIC PARTICIPATION AND VALUES.

While enforcement to end and remedy discrimination remains critically important, racial-justice lawyering is expanding to address problems of equity as well as democratic participation and values. Racial-justice advocates reach high and dig deep into the systems and structures that cause exclusion. In the Los Angeles garment-workers case, lawyers took on the major corporate players who benefited from sweatshops, rather than just the employers who directly oppressed workers.

Most racial exclusion cannot be overcome without mobilizing and enlivening local democracy; that is, the full participation and voice of all members and segments of society. Where public and private institutions become more racially inclusive and more accountable to community concerns, they reinforce local democracy. In this context, marginalized communities can use the processes of local democracy to challenge the structures that isolate and impoverish them. Lawyers can become problem solvers by facilitating access to unresponsive institutions and providing legal leverage against unfair practices.

4. RACIAL-JUSTICE LAWYERS ARE ADOPTING A PROBLEM-SOLVING, COMMUNITY-BASED APPROACH.

Racial-justice lawyering is evolving as part of a comprehensive problem-solving effort, where lawyers are one group among many players in a community who have a role. They involve community members directly and meaningfully to develop theories, strategies and pleadings. In this way, they build their clients' confidence and competence to take on public issues.

The approach also helps lawyers serve community members' interests in a holistic way. These types of relationships require intensive communication in which listening is an important task for lawyers.

In the Los Angeles bus-riders' case and the Mississippi voting-rights work, a sophisticated organized constituency sought out lawyers to undertake litigation as part of a larger advocacy campaign. These groups did not act as simply clients but demanded control of decision making and worked closely with the lawyers to chart litigation strategies and tactics.

The added efficacy of this type of racial-justice lawyering springs from local lawyers rooted in communities. They have long-term relationships with the constituencies they represent as well as ongoing relationships with religious, political and civic leaders. They understand the context in which the issues play out and are on hand when they become "hot." This requires not just good legal skills, but the ability to listen and communicate in ways that build trusting relationships with a broad array of individuals and groups, including partnerships that cross ideological and political lines.

5. THE VENUES FOR RACIAL-JUSTICE LAWYERING EXTEND BEYOND THE COURTROOM.

While the threat of litigation remains a crucial means to gain leverage, the courtroom is only one of many venues where justice can be won. The cases in this report highlight how lawyers play key roles in efforts to advance the cause of justice and improve the lives of people of color. Civil rights work has always included myriad strategies, but with the groundbreaking victories in the courts, litigation became its most prominent tool.

Today's racial-justice lawyers use many of the same strategies that corporate lawyers use on behalf of their clients: data collection and analysis, media relations, and negotiation are all part of a comprehensive problem-solving strategy. Because of this expanded view of racial justice—one that seeks to change structures and practices which perpetuate racial and ethnic exclusion—lawyers from other fields, including labor law and immigration have joined the ranks of those who followed the path of pioneering litigators like Thurgood Marshall.

6. IT IS POSSIBLE TO GALVANIZE PUBLIC OPINION TO SUPPORT RACIAL JUSTICE.

The case studies illustrate that, while still difficult, it is possible to mobilize broad public support on behalf of racial equity. Central to these cases are lawyers as problem solvers who, joining forces with their clients and broader coalitions, have been able to overcome resistance and discrimination in ways that address not just individual and group remedies, but go to the heart of structural barriers for a more equitable society.

7. RACIAL-JUSTICE LAWYERING REQUIRES A NATIONAL, REGIONAL AND LOCAL INFRASTRUCTURE.

This report highlights six cases of racial-justice lawyering. They are examples of the type of work that can be found across the country. In describing each case, local conditions and circumstances are highlighted. But in every instance, local victories would not have been possible without the precedent and the victories of the national civil rights organizations that created the legal infrastructure of rights and protections for racial justice. The institutional infrastructure for racial-justice work is not fixed or rigid, but changing and adapting to shifting circumstances and conditions. Its strength lies in its interconnections and its resiliency.

RECOMMENDATIONS FOR FUNDERS

1. RACIAL-JUSTICE LAWYERING DESERVES SUPPORT AT ANY AND ALL POINTS IN THE INSTITUTIONAL INFRASTRUCTURE.

Foundation support is needed to continue to build and expand the kind of work that takes on racial injustice while deepening public understanding of the nature and causes of racial exclusion. These cases illustrate that it is possible to achieve more equitable solutions for everyone while remedying injustices that disproportionately disadvantage people of color.

2. RACIAL-JUSTICE LAWYERING CAN STRENGTHEN PHILANTHROPIC EFFORTS ACROSS A RANGE OF PROGRAMS.

Creative approaches to racial justice can help create broader constituencies for equitable policies in foundation areas such as education, health and community revitalization. When used strategically, in conjunction with other social-change strategies, racial-justice lawyering can be a powerful tool to expand community engagement, mobilize public will and promote social policy.

3. FUNDING FOR ORGANIZATIONAL CAPACITY IS NEEDED.

Funding for racial-justice innovators should be structured to build organizational capacity and permit creation of broad networks and development of sophisticated techniques. This requires flexible, longer-term funding that includes support for training and knowledge development.

4. STRATEGIC FUNDING OF NATIONAL, REGIONAL OR LOCAL GROUPS CAN HAVE A BIG IMPACT.

Funders should not view support for national and local groups as an either-or choice; rather, funders should support opportunities that have the greatest chance of amplifying results. National groups continue to be vital to maintaining civil rights protections in the courts as well as in the U.S. Congress and state legislatures. Local groups are the foot soldiers of racial-justice lawyering, working for comprehensive and inclusive solutions in communities around the country. Support for local advocacy and organizing should be supplemented with support for problem-solving legal strategies that:

A. Connect race and democracy,

B. Respect community members' judgments,

C. Focus on broader community interests,

D. Work with communities to improve their understanding of the legal process,

E. Build trust,

F. Build partnerships, and

G. Let community leaders speak for themselves.

CONCLUSION

It really boils down to this: that all life is interrelated. We are all caught in an inescapable network of mutuality, tied into a single garment of destiny. Whatever affects one directly, affects all indirectly.

—Dr. Martin Luther King Jr.

The successful strategies examined in this report hark back to the early days of the civil rights movement. Dr. King preached about the importance of a community framework, and racial justice. Lawyers are heeding his words. They are developing strategies that promote understanding of this truth, that injustice affects all members of our communities, not just the direct victims. And they are pointing the way to a network of mutuality that is more equitable and democratic.

Introduction

This country's aspirations are reflected in phrases like "created equal" and "justice for all." Yet, its practices have not measured up to these lofty principles. This report lays out actions that can speak "louder than words" in transforming America's economic, social and political system so that it truly reflects our democratic ideals.

Lawyers played a critical role in the progress made toward racial and social justice during the latter part of the 20th century. The civil rights movement successfully challenged many of the most blatant contradictions between democratic ideals and exclusionary practices in U.S. society. In the process, it dismantled more than three centuries of legalized segregation.

But even with the most egregious legal barriers formally removed, discrimination on the basis of race and ethnicity remains prevalent. It is important to note that many racial barriers are the product, or legacy, of government action or inaction. For example:

- *Racially disparate enforcement efforts by the Environmental Protection Agency.* A recent study showed that penalties at Superfund sites with largely white populations were about 500 percent higher than penalties at sites with largely minority populations. The disparity was not class-based: on average, sites in white population areas with the lowest median incomes received higher penalties than sites in more affluent minority population areas.[1]

- *Failure of state and federal authorities to enforce and strengthen legal protections for low-wage and immigrant workers.* Existing legal protections for low-wage workers are insufficient to prevent dangerous labor abuses in a highly competitive global market. Despite the proliferation of exploitative sweatshops that ignore minimum-wage and overtime restrictions, state and federal authorities consistently refuse to provide adequate resources for enforcement agencies, and lawmakers consistently fail to enact more stringent protections.[2]

In addition to widespread, overt discrimination, deeper, more structurally based forms of racial exclusion persist.[3] These are embedded within the rules and functions of markets; they are woven into the processes of public and private institutions; they permeate the very values and belief structures of the society.[4] As a result, they continuously create and re-create poverty and racial disparities. These barriers are more difficult to see and prove than the injustices confronted by the early civil rights movement.

Professor Gerald Torres, an adviser for this report, notes that, "Jim Crow racism was a real, big target. How you attack the manifestations of racism in American culture today is more complicated, more difficult. But a lot of that's because of the successes of the civil rights movement."[5]

[1] Alan Jenkins, "See No Evil," **The Nation**, June 28, 1999.

[2] Dayna Cunningham, telephone interview with Stewart Kwoh, Executive Director, Asian Pacific American Legal Center (April 7, 2000).

[3] For the purposes of this Report, structural exclusion refers to subtle and overt forms of racial disadvantage and prejudice including market, political and social mechanisms, that are influenced by gross disparities in wealth, income or value which can be traced to historic racial disadvantage, or, conversely, to historic racial advantage.

[4] See, e.g., Susan Sturm, A Structural Approach to the Law of the Workplace (working draft, Oct. 1999).

[5] Adviser meeting, Dec. 15, 1997.

The United Farmworkers' 1965 grape boycott began as a local strike in California's Coastal Valleys region. The fledgling National Farmworkers Association, founded by Cesar Chavez (left) and Dolores Huerta to represent Mexican-American farmworkers, paired with the Agricultural Workers Organizing Committee (AWOC) whose largely Filipino membership had recently gone on strike. The "Great Grape Boycott" lasted five years, unionized thousands of farmworkers and rallied millions in a nationwide support coalition of unions, church groups and students. It ultimately won higher pay, health coverage, pension benefits and other contract protections for tens of thousands of largely Mexican-American migrant workers.

Advocates on the front lines of the fight for racial and social justice find themselves exhausted from defensive battles against much-better financed and coordinated opposition. The federal courts led the way in creating the modern civil rights infrastructure. But the Supreme Court's cutbacks in areas such as voting rights, affirmative action and criminal justice, as well as lower-court rulings like the HOPWOOD decision, which eliminates affirmative action in Texas higher education, make litigation a less-reliable tool than in the past.

In this environment, many have questioned whether the strategies of the civil rights and anti-poverty movements still work. Some even wonder whether the goals of those movements have lost their moral force. Also, with the changes in policymaking wrought by devolution, state and local initiatives have gained far greater importance. Without intervention, such policies are likely to create new inequities and perpetuate old ones.

The changed landscape raises questions about the most viable strategies for civil rights legal advocacy, such as:

- How to define the problems that require redress?

- What kinds of cases will advance the struggle for justice?

- What kinds of mechanisms, relationships and capacities are necessary now?

- What are the implications for lawyers? For funders?

6 Narration from "So Goes A Nation: Lawyers and Communities," a video produced by New York Lawyers for the Public Interest and Fordham University School of Law

This Report is the result of a three-year study undertaken for the Rockefeller Foundation of the field of civil rights lawyering. It explores changes in the field and seeks to better understand, and bolster, the diverse capabilities needed to advance racial justice.

Our investigation has yielded a sense of both urgency and hope. Creative, visionary new approaches are urgently needed because the plight of many Americans, of all races and ethnic backgrounds, is dire. Despite unprecedented economic prosperity, low-income communities are "more vulnerable than at any time since the Great Depression."[6] The prisons are overflowing with people of color whose dreams of opportunity have proved illusory and whose abilities and talents to contribute to our national life are squandered. In this light, we approached this project heeding the recommendation of Professor William Quigley, an adviser to the project:

> There must be an explicit willingness to go beyond the assumptions, tactics and solutions of the past. Imagination, daring and creativity must be an explicit part

of the agenda. No person, no institution, no strategy should be immune to re-examination, re-evaluation and, if appropriate, change if that effort advances the cause of justice.

While media focus has been on setbacks and racial division, we found throughout the nation examples of creativity, vitality and success in civil rights practice. The spirit of innovation, excitement and hope is palpable. Often operating below the radar screen of public awareness, civil rights lawyers have broadened their techniques of advocacy beyond their traditional role of in-court litigation. They have thought creatively about long-term, sustainable approaches to racial justice and are working hand in hand with communities to forge positive change. Many of today's most effective strategies are rooted in the best traditions of civil rights practice and are being adapted to succeed in today's changed circumstances.

In each of six case studies presented in this Report, lawyers played a crucial role in the successful effort to advance racial justice and improve the lives of people of color and the poor. The lawyers were innovators and problem solvers, bringing a range of skills and techniques to serve the goals of the communities that were their clients.

For civil rights lawyers and activists who are not familiar with these approaches and who are operating with limited resources, it may seem impossible to pursue innovative new strategies without neglecting the urgent work of enforcing and defending existing laws and remedies. Yet, the advisers concluded from their own experience on the front lines, that in the long run, broadening the strategies will help save and strengthen the infra-structure of legal protections. Advisers used the label "triage" as a shorthand descrip-tion of much on the current docket of civil rights lawyers. They used the term "transformation" to describe strategies that focus on changing the underlying structures that produce inequality. The advisers concluded that in many situations, it is possible to do "triage" work in a "transformative" way—using a current crisis to make progress toward a long-term vision. For example, in Texas, creative thinkers were able to address the immediate problem—a court ruling that would result in exclusion of Latino and African-American students from elite state colleges—in a manner that plants the seeds for the transformation of the entire university system.

Adviser, Bill Quigley, expressed the need for a vision in compelling personal terms:

> I was disturbed at the conclusion of the last meeting because of the tension between...putting out fires and changing the world....I know that there are other things out there I should be doing in addition to fire fighting. But I am pulled into the fire fights because there are so many people asking me to help them, and I frequently lose track of what my goals are and in what direction I am trying to go. Redefining a vision of justice would give us a set of criteria upon which to evaluate our effort. It will also help me retarget my efforts and give us a sense of where it is that we should be going.

It is hoped that this Report will inspire attorneys and activists embroiled in the fire fights and help them to incorporate new ideas into their ongoing daily work.

In 1963, the March on Washington (right) was the largest human-rights demonstration in U.S. history. Labor and civil rights leaders organized the multiracial march around three demands: passage of laws against segregated public accommodations, anti-job discrimination laws, and job training and placement services for racial minorities.

CASE STUDIES

From Triage to Transformation

Chapter 1

This school for Mexican American children was a makeshift facility housed in an old church (right). Anglo children from the same district were transported to city schools by bus.

When affirmative action was effectively banned in Texas college admissions, three Texas lawyers teamed up with a coalition of academics and activists and forged a powerful idea to reward hard work and success in high school and use the segregation of Texas high schools to promote racial diversity in admission to the state's flagship universities.

Their idea, the Ten Percent Plan, guarantees a seat at the flagship Texas public colleges and universities to all students from all high schools in the state who graduate in the top 10 percent of their class. In the process, it gives exceptional students of color, even from the most segregated and under-funded high schools, the opportunity for the kind of college education that historically has been denied them. In addition, the Ten Percent Plan reintroduces the potential for racial diversity at Texas flagship universities. And it may inspire community groups throughout Texas, now that their local high schools can field students for those elite universities, to take new interest in how these powerful institutions operate.

Chapter 1
From Triage to Transformation:
The Texas Ten Percent Plan Helps Restore Racial Diversity to the College Campus

Key Lessons Learned

- Build on the legacy of social-justice activism. Tap into existing civil rights infrastructures and resources to strengthen racial-justice efforts. These resources include Latino and black intellectuals—many the products of inclusive affirmative-action policies—and Latino and African-American elected officials who hold office in part because of the Voting Rights Act.

- Think creatively and expansively about possible remedies, keeping in mind that racial exclusion often is an indicator of broader kinds of social exclusion. Remedies that encompass broader issues of class, while remaining sharply focused on race, have the potential to build powerful cross-racial alliances and expand the scope of change.

- Engage a diverse set of community constituents to generate innovative ideas and translate them into policy proposals. Use community-advocacy strategies to build public will.

In its second year, the Ten Percent Plan returned Latino and African-American undergraduate student admissions at UT/Austin to pre-Hopwood levels (left). At Texas A&M, minority admissions are increasing more slowly.

Starting in the 1930s, the NAACP challenged segregated education in Maryland, Missouri and Texas as the first steps of a nationwide campaign. The campaign's goal was to eliminate segregation at all levels of the public education system. Parents and children (above) protest public school segregation in St. Louis, Missouri.

[1] Kimberly Gentile, **The Daily Texan**, Aug. 25, 1999, p. 1.

[2] The HOPWOOD case is discussed in detail below.

[3] Professor Torres served as one of the advisers to this Report.

[4] G. Torres interview, Aug. 25, 1999.

Overview

The Daily Texan headline blares: "UT Minority Enrollment Bounces Back."[1] A colorful chart graphically illustrates that three years after the HOPWOOD decision[2] invalidated affirmative action in admissions at the University of Texas (UT), the incoming freshman class will have the same percentages of African-American and Latino freshmen as in 1996, before HOPWOOD took effect. UT Law Professor Gerald Torres[3] helped design the Ten Percent Plan, a program that is largely responsible for the rebound in minority enrollment.

Torres is one of a small group of activists, scholars and lawmakers who conceived the Ten Percent Plan and shepherded it through the Texas Legislature. Skeptics from both the left and right expressed doubts that the Ten Percent Plan would work. Torres and his fellow Ten Percent Plan supporters have labored quietly to ensure that the doors to higher education stay open for minority students.

Torres remains a firm supporter of affirmative action, viewing it as an important tool to remove barriers and to open up opportunities for minorities and women. He notes with dismay that the president of Students for a Colorblind Society is claiming that the Ten Percent Plan's success means affirmative action is unnecessary. Torres is proud of Texas' efforts to cope with the HOPWOOD ruling, but notes that the Ten Percent Plan has contributed to diversity in the freshman class only because of the state's "rock-solid segregated housing patterns." The persistence of residential segregation is a reminder of how far Texas and the nation still have to go to achieve a truly "colorblind society."

Texas still has far to go in achieving real equity and fairness in access to its most prestigious state universities. According to Torres, "There is no reason for the pre-HOPWOOD number—4 percent African-American and 14 percent Latino at UT/Austin—to be the baseline.[4] African-Americans represent 12 percent of Texas high-school graduates and Latinos represent 29 percent. Texas has the second largest African-American and Hispanic populations in the United States.

Without the Ten Percent Plan, the situation in Texas would undoubtedly be much worse, as shown at the law- and graduate-school level, where the Plan does not apply. The state's flagship law school, UT Law School, enrolled only nine African-Americans in fall 1999, compared to 31 before HOPWOOD.

Torres and others have creatively struggled to cope with the loss of affirmative action, but they do not believe that prohibiting affirmative action is good policy. Thus, they watch with dismay as Florida Governor Jeb Bush has used a variation on their idea to promote ending affirmative-action programs in that state. While a "Percent Plan" might be useful as one element of an effort to increase fairness and merit in Florida university admissions, it should not be substituted for affirmative action.

The Ten Percent Plan

Texas, like California, is poised to become a "majority minority" state early in the 21st century.[5] But the two states have responded differently to their racially diverse, multilingual populations. When California's economy floundered in the early 1990s, conservative activists blamed immigration and affirmative action. Such racial finger-pointing and immigrant scape-goating fired the political climate for the passage of the anti-immigrant Proposition 187 in 1994, the anti-affirmative action Proposition 209 in 1996, and the anti-bilingual education Proposition 227 in 1998.

In Texas, however, Houston voters, with major involvement from civil rights and corporate leaders, rejected an anti-affirmative-action ballot initiative in November 1997.[6] Key business and political figures recognize that the state's growing immigrant population is due credit for contributing to the vibrant Texas economy. Moreover, they recognize that the population and work-force growth (at both ends of the economic spectrum) reflect the immigration patterns that have historically defined Texas, with the growth merely picking up steam in the late 20th century. Additionally, leaders across the political spectrum recognize that political stability is tied to spreading economic opportunity.

In spite of a political and business climate more supportive of racial inclusion, the federal court dealt the state a major setback in the 5th Circuit's[7] 1996 HOPWOOD V. TEXAS decision invalidating the affirmative-action component of the admissions program at the University of Texas School of Law. HOPWOOD sent shock waves through the higher education and civil rights communities. In the wake of the decision, a coalition of attorneys, academicians and activists went into action. The coalition included: Professor Torres; Albert (Al) H. Kauffman, San Antonio Regional Counsel with the Mexican American Legal Defense and Educational Fund, Inc. (MALDEF); and David Montejano, Director of the Center for Mexican American Studies (CMAS) at the University of Texas. They came up with a solution that is broadly inclusive—guaranteed admission to any Texas public university for all high-school students who graduate in the top 10 percent of their class. Known as the "Ten Percent Plan," it immediately garnered widespread, bipartisan political support, working its way through the Texas Legislature in a matter of months with the leadership of the Latino and African-American legislators and the support of some of the most conservative legislators in the state.[8] The first class of "ten-percenters" entered the public university system in August 1998.

The Ten Percent Plan is not a universal antidote that alone can ensure fairness, diversity and equal opportunity in public higher education. But, in the aftermath of affirmative-action losses, the plan offers the potential for reintroducing a measure of fairness into the admissions process for all Texas university applicants. At the same time, it maintains the ability to attract a highly accomplished and diverse student body to the state's flagship campuses.

[5] Latinos comprise just over 28 percent of the population of Texas, while African-Americans make up almost 12 percent. Population Estimates and Projection Program, Texas State Data Center, Feb. 1998.

[6] The City of Houston stands alone in rejecting an anti-affirmative-action proposal placed on the ballot. Voters in the state of Washington adopted an anti-affirmative-action ballot initiative in Nov. 1998.

[7] 78 F. 3d 932, reversing and remanding, 861 F. Supp. 551 (W.D. Tex. 1994), cert. denied, 518 U.S. 1033 (1996) (HOPWOOD I). See, also, HOPWOOD v. TEXAS, 999 F. Supp. 872 (W.D. Tex. 1998) (HOPWOOD II), on appeal, No. 98-5056 9 (5th Cir.).

[8] The political history of the passage of this legislation is rich and deserves a much fuller treatment than is possible here. There are some powerful lessons of leadership and horse trading that emerge from its telling. The role of the Mexican American Legal Defense and Educational Fund, Inc. (MALDEF), in this story cannot be underestimated.

The Ten Percent Plan also sharpens the focus of racial inclusion. The objective is to reward achievement and academic excellence across the board and to recognize students historically ignored despite their strong performances.

The Plan has also validated the intuition of its crafters that the new selection criteria would change the relationship of higher education to primary and secondary education. Universities have a higher stake in ensuring that high-school students come to them well prepared, regardless of their economic circumstances.

The irony is that the Ten Percent Plan is successful because of the unfortunate reality of segregated high schools.

Educating for a Menial Job

Throughout Texas, for much of this century, African-American schoolchildren attended public schools that were officially segregated by race. In Houston, Dallas and Austin, federal courts found that the schools remained intentionally segregated at least until 1967, 1970 and 1980, respectively.[9] Latino students also suffered segregated schooling. The unspoken assumption was that, "children of Mexican descent, seen both as outsiders and members of a dominated race, were never expected to participate fully in American life."[10] "Thus, they were provided a limited education in resource-poor Mexican-American schools...[that] reproduced a low-skilled work force and kept [them] in a state of economic underdevelopment."[11] Elementary and secondary public education in Texas remains substantially segregated even today, with African-Americans and Latinos suffering unequal educational opportunities from kindergarten on.

In 1973, the Supreme Court held in San Antonio v. Rodriguez[12] that the U.S. Constitution does not require a state to provide equal educational opportunity to all its school children—a case arising out of Texas. In 1983, a group of Latino parents, children and educators, represented by the Mexican American Legal Defense and Educational Fund, Inc. (MALDEF), brought the Edgewood lawsuit challenging inequalities among local school systems under the state constitution. The funding system for public schools, dependent on the local tax base, resulted in inadequate educational opportunity for students in scores of schools across Texas. The expenditure gap was most pronounced in the Edgewood Independent School District, with its predominantly Mexican-American student population. In the 1985 to 1986 school year, Edgewood spent $2,112 per student in its schools, the least amount in a state where other school districts were spending as much as $19,333.[13] The Texas Supreme Court in the Edgewood case ordered Texas to move toward a more equitable funding system for public K—12 education.[14] However, implementation of the court order has been slow and contentious. It will be a number of years before the full educational impact of this ruling will translate into increased student opportunities and achievement.

[9] See, Ross v. Houston Independent School District, 699 F. 2d 218, 220-23 (5th Cir. 1983); Price v. Austin Independent School District, 729 F. Supp. 533, 535 (M.D. Tex. 1990); Tasby v. Woolery, 869 F. Supp. 454, 456-57, 477 (N.D. Tex. 1994).

[10] Jorge Chapa and Vincent A. Lazaro, "Hopwood in Texas: The Untimely End of Affirmative Action," in Chilling Admissions, at 52 (G. Orfield and E. Miller, eds, 1998); David Montejano, Anglos and Mexicans in the Making of Texas, 1836-1986 (University of Texas Press,1987).

[11] Mario T. Garcia, Mexican Americans: Leadership, Ideology and Identity, 1930-1960 (Yale University Press, 1989), at 53.

[12] 411 U.S. 1 (1978).

[13] Chapa and Lazaro, supra, at 51, 54, citing Edgewood Indep. Sch. Dist. v. Kirby, 777 S.W. 2d 391 (Tex. 1989) (Edgewood I).

[14] Edgewood I, supra. See also Edgewood Indep. Sch. Dist. v. Kirby, 804 S.W. 2d 491 (Tex. 1991) (Edgewood II); Carrolton-Farmers Branch Indep. Sch. Dist. v. Edgewood Indep. Sch. Dist., 826 S.W. 2d 489 (Tex. 1992) (Edgewood III); Edgewood Indep. Sch. Dist. v. Meno, 917 S.W. 2d 717 (Tex. 1995) (Edgewood IV).

A Higher Educational System With a History of Discrimination

The State of Texas continued to operate a segregated system of public higher education until well into the 1980s. Its flagship universities, the University of Texas at Austin (UT/Austin) and Texas A&M, remained predominantly for whites. African-Americans were channeled to financially starved Southern University and Prairie View A&M. Latinos were effectively segregated to south Texas colleges that were not part of the UT or A&M systems.[15] In 1975, the student body at UT/ Austin was less than 2 percent African-American and 6 percent Latino.[16] The minority enrollment numbers at Texas A&M were even lower.[17]

During the Reagan administration, the Office for Civil Rights (OCR) of the U.S. Department of Education found that Texas still had not desegregated its university system.[18] In June 1983, the state adopted, and OCR approved, a desegregation plan that included affirmative action.[19] The result was a gradual increase in overall minority enrollments so that by 1996, the last year of affirmative action prior to its elimination by Hopwood, Latinos comprised 14.5 percent of entering freshmen at UT/Austin while African-Americans totaled 4.1 percent.[20]

The University of Texas Law School also has an ignoble racial history. Thurgood Marshall and the NAACP Legal Defense and Educational Fund, Inc. (LDF), sued UT Law School in 1947 in one of a series of carefully calculated lawsuits that led to the frontal attack on "separate but equal" in Brown v. Board of Education. When LDF demanded admission of Heman Sweatt, a black man, the state hastily established "a law school for blacks...in the basement of a petroleum company building in downtown Austin, [consisting] of three medium-sized rooms, one smaller room and a toilet."[21] The Texas courts ruled that this unaccredited entity—with no other students, no library, no full-time faculty, no moot court, law review or scholarship fund—was equal to UT/Austin's law school. The U.S. Supreme Court reversed the lower court in 1950,[22] paving the way for the 1954 Brown decision.

Laying the Groundwork

Prior to the Hopwood decision, national, state and local civil rights organizations had spent many years battling the inequalities and discrimination that characterized Texas' public education system. In addition, national civil rights organizations had been discussing strategies to oppose and pre-empt anti-civil-rights and anti-affirmative-action efforts, whether in the form of initiatives such as Proposition 209 in California or legal challenges like Hopwood. These efforts, on national and local levels, ultimately laid the groundwork for the passage of the Ten Percent Plan.

Hostile classmates in registration line with Heman Sweatt (left).

[15] Hopwood II, supra, at 556.

[16] UT/Austin, Office of Institutional Studies, Fall Enrollment Totals by Ethnic Background, 1972-1975.

[17] See, Fact Sheet: Minorities at Texas A&M University, Feb. 1998.

[18] Hopwood I, 861 F. Supp., at 555-56.

[19] Ibid., at 556.

[20] Danielle Holley and Delia Spencer, "The Texas Ten Percent Plan," 34 Harv. Civ. Rts. Civ. Lib. L. Rev., at 245, 252 (1999).

[21] Jack Greenberg, Crusaders in the Courts (Basic Books, 1994), at 64.

[22] See, Sweatt v. Painter, 339 U.S. 629 (1950).

In 1982, MALDEF participated in the OCR review process to ensure that Latino interests were considered and incorporated into the desegregation plan. In 1991, representing the League of United Latin American Citizens (LULAC), GI Forum and Movimiento Estudiantil Chicano de Aztlan (MEChA), and an organization of Mexican-American college students, MALDEF filed a case against the state of Texas alleging discrimination against Mexican-Americans in undergraduate, graduate and professional schools. Although the Texas Supreme Court ultimately reversed the lower court's decision and ruled in favor of the state,[23] two important results followed. First, the state directed some additional funding to public schools in low-income communities. Second, in the process of preparing the case, MALDEF and its San Antonio staff attorney, Al Kauffman, met with and gathered support from several community groups and professional organizations, including the Texas Association of Chicanos in Higher Education, the Mexican-American Bar Association, and the Mexican-American Physicians Association. Eventually, each of these groups would testify on behalf of the Ten Percent Plan.[24]

Simultaneously, as part of a proactive strategy to combat unequal opportunity and access in education, Kauffman worked with these groups to develop policies that would take funding disparities into account and equalize opportunities in higher education. Consequently, when the opportunity arose to collaborate with others on the Ten Percent Plan legislation, MALDEF and Kauffman were ready to assume an active role, providing guidance about how the Ten Percent Plan legislation would fit into broader national and state strategies to alleviate disparities within public education.

LDF had tried to avoid the HOPWOOD disaster by advising UT Law School to modify its affirmative-action program to comply more closely with Supreme Court decisions, but these efforts were unavailing. To address its history of discrimination and to create a diverse environment for learning about the law, UT Law School adopted an affirmative-action program, along with the rest of the university in 1983. The admissions process, including the affirmative-action component, was modified on several occasions over the next 10 years. By the time Cheryl Hopwood and three others sued in 1994, the law school had modified its affirmative-action program in ways that had moved it to the far edge of compliance with Supreme Court authority.

LDF moved to intervene in the HOPWOOD case on behalf of African-American students. It sought to prove that some form of affirmative action was justified to remedy discriminatory features of the admission system, which used a mechanical formula, the Texas Index, heavily weighting LSAT scores. UT Law School's admissions criteria did not appear to be closely tied to the goal of selecting high-performing students of any race, and those procedures had a particularly disadvantageous impact on minority applicants. Experts retained by LDF demonstrated that the Texas Index was inversely correlated to performance for African-American students. LDF ultimately was denied formal party status in the case. This informa-

[23] See, RICHARDS V. LULAC, 868 S.W. 2d 306 (Tex. 1993).

[24] Venu Gupta interview with Al Kauffman, Dec. 3, 1999.

tion was not admitted into evidence and thus was not considered in the decision.[25] However, LDF succeeded in gaining broader public attention to the problems that resulted from rigid use of standardized test scores, an issue that would reappear in the Ten Percent Plan debate.

THE HOPWOOD RULING

The federal trial court in HOPWOOD struck down the particular rigid form of affirmative action used by the UT Law School. But importantly, the trial court held that a flexible, narrowly tailored affirmative-action program would be constitutionally permissible to remedy discrimination and produce a diverse student body, given "the pervasive nature of past discrimination in the higher education system."[26] In a highly controversial decision, the U.S. Court of Appeals for the 5th Circuit not only upheld the invalidation of the Law School's specific, inflexible version of affirmative action but also used very strong language suggesting that it would outlaw any consideration of race in applicant evaluation. The court concluded that, "the use of race to achieve a diverse student body," can never pass constitutional scrutiny, finding that the contrary conclusion by the Supreme Court in the BAKKE case is no longer good law.[27]

In a series of decisions in the 1980s and 1990s, the Supreme Court has tightened the requirements and made it more difficult for governments and private institutions to use affirmative action. These rulings have been roundly criticized by civil rights advocates as threatening to turn back the clock on racial inclusion. A number of lower courts have struck down affirmative-action plans, finding them either too inflexible or not based on sufficient proof of past or current discrimination. But federal courts have continued to uphold flexible affirmative-action plans that admit only qualified applicants. Among federal court decisions, HOPWOOD is at the extreme anti-affirmative-action end of the spectrum, flouting even the Supreme Court's own precedent by adopting requirements so strict that many commentators view it as an absolute bar to affirmative action.[28]

In the first class admitted to the University of Texas after HOPWOOD, the number of African-American freshmen dropped 34 percent, while the number of Latino students fell 4.3 percent. At Texas A&M University, African-American student enrollment dropped 29 percent, and Latino student enrollment dropped 13 percent.[29] A total of only four African-Americans and 26 Mexican-Americans entered the UT Law School Class of 1997, down from 31 African-Americans and 42 Mexican-Americans in 1996.

SEARCHING FOR A SOLUTION IN THE AFTERMATH OF THE HOPWOOD DECISION

In the summer of 1996, Torres, Kauffman and University of Houston Law Professor Michael Olivas began working with a group of Latino scholars and students to develop a strategic response to HOPWOOD.[30] The group's immediate task was one of triage: to stanch the flow of minority students. While overturning HOPWOOD was a prime objective of the group, it also

[25] See, HOPWOOD, 78 F. 3d at 965, and note 62.

[26] See, HOPWOOD, 861 F. Supp., at 572.

[27] See, HOPWOOD, 861 F. 3d, at 944, 948.

[28] The Supreme Court declined to review the HOPWOOD case, 518 U.S. 1033 (1996).

[29] Holley and Spencer, supra, at 251.

[30] This group also included UT/Austin Professors Ricardo Romo (Vice Provost), Jorge Chapa (Lyndon Baines Johnson School of Government), Susan González-Baker (Department of Sociology) and David Montejano (Director of the Center for Mexican American Studies), and UT/Austin students Óscar de la Torre and Mariela Olivares. David Montejano, "On HOPWOOD," The Continuing Challenges," in Reflecionales 1997: New Direction in Mexican-American Studies (Neil Foley, ed., 1997), at 139, 153, note 12.

31 MALDEF's Al Kauffman proposed that the Legislature develop additional evidence or findings that might allow affirmative action to be reinstated. HOPWOOD left open the possibility that proof of a pattern of recent discrimination might permit affirmative action but indicated that such findings must be made by the Legislature, not by the University. The Legislature enacted a bill in March 1997, requiring a study of the state's history of discrimination. The state comptroller recently released the findings; the exhaustive and compelling documentation may prompt the Legislature to reconsider affirmative action. The state is also still litigating HOPWOOD, which remains pending in the courts. See, HOPWOOD II.

wanted to develop an educationally sound model for university admissions that would ensure both diversity and inclusion of highly qualified students who could contribute to the learning environment and become the next generation of Texas leaders.

The Task Group, as it called itself, simultaneously pursued two avenues for addressing HOPWOOD: 1) legal approaches that might eventually result in the reinstatement of affirmative action,[31] and 2) alternatives to traditional affirmative action.

The challenge for the Task Group was to devise a formula that would recognize outstanding minority and other students who had managed to excel despite an educational system fraught with inequality and lack of opportunity. In its research, the Task Group looked at the pattern of admissions to UT/Austin. The findings were remarkable. Out of more than 1,500 public high schools statewide, 50 to 75 schools were providing 90 percent of the students who were admitted to UT/Austin. This small group of high schools lacked not just racial diversity but geographic and economic diversity. The confluence of racial, class and geographic disparities generated by the traditional admission process led to the idea for the Ten Percent Plan. The Task Group also discovered that from 1983 until 1988, UT/Austin had implemented an admissions policy that granted automatic admission to the top 10 percent of the state's high-school graduates.

THE POWER OF AN IDEA

One day as they arrived for a meeting at the Center for Mexican American Studies (CMAS), Task Group members found copies of a typed, five-sentence proposal waiting on the table. It was the idea for the Ten Percent Plan, and from the moment they read it, group members were taken with it. The proposal was unsigned, but everyone assumed that Professor David Montejano, CMAS director, was the author.

The idea of admitting the top 10 percent from every school was compelling. In an examination of data on 1996 high-school graduates, the Task Group found a pool of students eligible for automatic admission that compared favorably to the pre-HOPWOOD African-American and Latino enrollment percentages at UT/Austin.[32] Because of the high degree of segregation in Texas public schools, the Plan offered the potential of maintaining, or even expanding, the existing, fairly low levels of diversity at flagship schools.

32 In 1996, Latinos comprised 16.2 percent of the state's top 10 percent graduates and 14.5 percent of the UT/Austin freshmen while African-Americans were 5.8 percent of the top ten-percenters and 4.1 percent of the UT entering class.

33 E.g., Douglas S. Massey and Nancy A. Denton, American Apartheid: Segregation and the Making of the Underclass (Harvard University Press, 1993).

While not racially explicit in operation, the Ten Percent Plan exposed deep truths about race. Public school segregation results from continuing patterns of residential segregation as well as, in some places, white residents' withdrawal from public education into private schools. As scholars have exhaustively documented, residential segregation is not the result of chance but derives from a host of segregative governmental policies, as well as private racial discrimination. Racial segregation itself imposes disadvantage. Thus, to address the state's history of racial discrimination,[33] it makes sense to use segregated-school geography to allocate a scarce resource, such as admission to flagship campuses.

The truly transformative feature of the Ten Percent Plan is that it addresses race in a fundamental way, while at the same time including whites and creating the potential for a cross-racial alliance. Adviser Bill Quigley concludes, "It isn't an end run around affirmative action [but] truly...an expansion of affirmative action, an expansion of opportunity."[34]

The Ten Percent Plan also appealed to the Task Group because of its transformative potential to redefine merit in the context of college admissions and its ability to build multiracial support for greater diversity and fairness in the admissions process. "It addresses the broader inequities that lead UT/Austin to see few of the brightest kids of any color from the state's poorer counties."[35] Task Group member Torres says: "We based our argument on essentially two factors. One is that the best predictor of success is success—if kids have been successful, they'll continue to be successful. The second is that we wanted to create a different incentive structure in the high schools. We wanted to reward hard work."[36]

The Task Group knew that some would view the Ten Percent Plan as unfair because some high schools offered a more rigorous curriculum than others did. The Task Group welcomed a public dialogue on this issue. Professor Torres explained: "You can't punish the children for the failure of the Legislature to satisfy its constitutional mandate to equalize education in Texas high schools."[37]

The Task Group also anticipated that some would argue that educational inequities meant that ten-percenters would be ill-equipped to survive the competitiveness and heavy educational workload of a flagship university. The group analyzed data from previous years and concluded that the grit and determination that defined ten-percenters would enable most of them to overcome any educational disadvantages. The data showed that during the 1980s, ten-percenters who tested low on the Scholastic Aptitude Test (SAT) nonetheless obtained grades only slightly below the average for the entire class. Even if a significant number of ten-percenters initially struggle at the state's flagship universities, Ten Percent Plan supporters expected that such circumstances would enhance public support for real remedies for the core problem—the appalling inequities in the state's system, particularly gross underfunding of K–12 education at many minority schools.[38]

ADVANCING THE TEN PERCENT PLAN

The Task Group used its knowledge of the state's history and culture—its tradition of fierce independence and populism—to discuss the Ten Percent Plan in terms that would resonate. One compelling argument was that Texas did not want to emulate California with its political hostility toward immigrants and people of color.

The Task Group drew on Texas pride in explaining the decision to de-emphasize standardized tests. They made arguments such as: "Imagine a boy from [poor and predominantly white] Levelland. He puts his shoulder to the wheel and works hard, listens to his teachers

[34] Adviser meeting, Dec. 15-16, 1997.

[35] William E. Forbath and Gerald Torres, "The 'Talented Tenth' in Texas," **The Nation**, Dec. 15, 1997, p. 20.

[36] Adviser meeting, Dec. 15-16, 1997.

[37] Ibid.

[38] Indeed, it appears that the Ten Percent Plan has spurred the flagship universities to take new responsibility for the performance of the state's K–12 public schools. "University administrators who once thought themselves above the public education debate have realized that, to a great extent, the fates of the public schools and the universities are closely intertwined." Editorial, **The New York Times**, Nov. 27, 1999, A14.

Vast disparities in funding for Texas public schools are both a cause and a consequence of racial segregation. The obstacle course for children at predominantly white and wealthy Eanes Elementary School (above). A common area at Putegnat Elementary, Brownsville, serving a largely Latino community (below).

A lavoratory at Plano East Senior High School (above). Edgewood High School lavatory (below). Although Texas has over 1,500 public high schools, before the Ten Percent Plan 90 percent of UT/Austin's students came from the 50 to 75 "elite" public high schools like Plano East.

[39] Forbath and Torres, supra, at 21.

[40] Ibid.

[41] Ibid.

[42] As recently as 1990 there were only four Mexican Americans in the 80-member California Assembly and three in the 40-member Senate. In Texas...Mexican-American legislators have comprised a sizable number since the 1970s. In the recent 1997 legislative session...28 of 150 House seats and seven of the 31 Senate seats were occupied by Mexican-American officeholders. African-Americans added another 14 House members and two Senate members. Montejano, "On HOPWOOD," supra, at 133, 148-50.

[43] For a detailed description of the legislative history of the Ten Percent Plan, see, Holley and Spencer, supra. See, also, Montejano, "On HOPWOOD," supra.

[44] Hearings on H.B. 598 before the House of Representatives, 75th Legis. (Texas 1997) statement of Charlie Howard, state representative House district 26.

[45] See, Montejano, "On HOPWOOD," supra, at 148 (refers to footnote 36).

[46] Adviser meeting, Dec. 15-16, 1997.

and graduates first in his class. Why should some bureaucrats in Princeton, New Jersey (home of the Educational Testing Service, manufacturer of the SAT), be able to tell him he's not good enough to go to the University of Texas?"[39] Professors Forbath and Torres explain: "[E]ven their creators concede that the SAT really measures what a student has learned far more accurately than his or her aptitude for learning. The Educational Testing Service...is just the kind of centralized social bureaucracy that conservatives, in most contexts, love to hate.[40] The Task Group contrasted the New Jersey bureaucrat at ETS with "a standard of merit even more deeply rooted than the SAT: working hard, getting good grades and doing very well what's expected of you."[41]

A crucial factor in gaining passage of the Ten Percent Plan was the presence in the Texas Legislature of a large block of Latinos and African-Americans, many of whom owed their election to the Voting Rights Act. Several had been there for many years and had earned key committee positions. While the black and Mexican-American caucuses were not large enough to form a majority, they possessed sufficient numbers to block bills favored by other legislators. This gave them political power to negotiate and gain votes for passage of the Ten Percent Plan. "I do not want to underestimate the role that the civil rights movement had in producing this cohort of legislators," says Professor Torres. "If people had not struggled for civil rights in the past generations, [the Ten Percent Plan] could not have happened."[42]

When the Ten Percent Plan came before the Legislature, Rep. Irma Rangel and her staff took the lead in moving it through the House, while Sen. Gonzalo Barrientos served as point person in the Senate. Representative Rangel, the first female member of the Texas House, had served for 25 years and had risen to the position of Chair of the House Higher Education Committee. She hails from Kingsville, Texas, and her district lies in the predominantly Mexican-American "Valley" in south Texas.

Representative Rangel held hearings at which several members of the Task Group testified.[43] Two white Representatives from affluent suburban districts argued in opposition to the bill. One of them, Rep. Charlie F. Howard, argued that if an applicant was a "white Caucasian, from a middle-income suburb and both of your parents went to college," he or she would have almost no possibility of being admitted.[44] However, other conservative white lawmakers rejected this inflammatory rhetoric. Representative Rangel brought into her legislative coalition one of the state's most conservative lawmakers, Teel Bivens, the powerful Chair of the Senate Higher Education Committee. Senator Bivens believed the Plan's emphasis on hard work and grit would appeal to his mostly white constituents. In addition, Senator Bivens needed Representative Rangel's cooperation on his other legislative priorities.[45]

At one point, the Speaker of the House requested a meeting, which Task Group members suspected might result in a request to delay the bill for another two years. Praising Representative Rangel's strategic skill, Professor Torres describes the meeting as "pure political theater."[46] She assembled nine Mexican-American experts—sociologists, demographers, political scientists, lawyers and historians. When the Speaker and his colleagues said, "we need to study this," Representative Rangel stood up, waved her arm expansively, slowly pointing to the assembled group of the state's leading Mexican-American academics. Then, turning to the Speaker, she said decisively, "we've studied it." The Speaker dropped the idea of a delay, and Professor Torres wryly noted, "we never had to say a word."[47]

[47] G. Torres interview, Sept. 9, 1997.

REACHING OUT TO UNLIKELY ALLIES

Before publicly proposing any specific admission criteria to be included in the bill, the Task Group met with Terrell Smith, the attorney who had represented lawsuit plaintiff, Cheryl Hopwood. Coincidentally, Smith had moved to a new position, as Legislative Counsel to Texas Gov. George W. Bush. During the HOPWOOD litigation, Smith had stressed that he and his client objected to the use of race in admissions but would support consideration of class or economic circumstances. Task Group members wanted to determine whether Smith was really serious about supporting class-based criteria for admissions. This outreach to a HOPWOOD opponent worried some affirmative-action supporters. However, Representative Rangel describes the pragmatic decision to meet with the governor's counsel, a conservative and an opponent of affirmative action, by saying: "I heard a rumor that the Governor has the veto."[48]

[48] Rep. Irma Rangel interview, Sept. 9, 1997, Austin, Texas.

In presenting the Ten Percent Plan to Smith, the Task Group believed that Governor Bush had higher political ambitions and sought a positive relationship with the state's large Latino community. Smith seemed swayed by the Task Group's emphasis on the importance of diversity to "the mission of a public university system and the standing of Texas in a global economy."

After the meeting with Smith, word came back that if the Ten Percent Plan were enacted, Governor Bush would not veto it. While this position was not an endorsement of the concept, it was enough of a positive signal for Representative Rangel to start moving the bill forward in the Legislature. Three years later, Governor Bush embraced the Ten Percent Plan as his bill.

THE TEN PERCENT PLAN AS ENACTED

The Ten Percent Plan was incorporated as one element of a multifaceted bill to revamp the admissions system for Texas public colleges and universities. The bill passed the Texas House of Representatives by a nonrecorded vote,[49] which observers report was close and largely along partisan lines.[50] When the bill reached the Senate, sponsorship by Republican Teel Bivens helped produce an overwhelming vote in favor of it. House Bill 588 was signed into law by Governor Bush in May 1997, with an effective date of September 1, 1997.

[49] Holley and Spencer, supra, at 258-59.

[50] Montejano, supra, at 147 (refers to footnote 42).

[51] Texas Educ. Code. Ann., § 51.802 (West 1998).

[52] Texas' other public universities are less competitive and, even before the Ten Percent Plan, top 10 percent graduates were virtually certain to meet the entrance requirements for these schools.

The law mandates that each Texas public university or college admit as a first-time freshman any in-state applicant who graduated in the preceding two years and who ranked among the top 10 percent of his or her class.[51] The university may ask the applicant to submit a standardized test score for evaluation and placement purposes, but such scores cannot bar admission. While the plan applies to all Texas public universities, in reality it is likely to make a difference in admission decisions only at the state's two most selective campuses—UT/Austin and Texas A&M.[52]

[53] Texas Educ. Code. Ann., § 51.803(b) (West 1998).

[54] Texas Educ. Code. Ann., § 51.805(b) (West 1999). The law apparently allows the universities to choose which factors they will weigh and how important each of the factors will be in the admissions decision.

[55] Adviser meeting, Dec. 15-16, 1997.

[56] The first year of operation was 1997-1998 leading to a fall 1998 entering freshman class in which the percentage of African-American and Latino students increased slightly at UT/Austin but decreased slightly at A&M. But the first year's implementation of the Plan by university administrators was deeply flawed. The Plan was launched under a tight timetable with little advertising or other efforts to inform students about it. See, Holley and Spencer, supra.

[57] See, Susanna Finnell, "The HOPWOOD Chill," in Chilling Admissions, supra, at 71-72. African-American enrollment at UT/Austin reached a peak of 5.3 percent in 1994 and had fallen to 3.2 percent even prior to HOPWOOD. Latino enrollment peaked at 15.0 percent in 1996. See, also, Holly and Spencer, supra, at 252.

[58] Longhorn Scholarship awards are $4,000 per year, renewable for four years. The program also is being expanded to junior colleges serving the original Longhorn High Schools.

[59] See, e.g., David A. Sanchez, "Texas Ten Percent Solution May Not Add Up to Progress," **Houston Chronicle**, Jan. 25, 1998, p. 4.

Another provision of the bill requires the institution to determine whether applicants may require additional preparation for college-level work, or if they would benefit from a program that would provide services, support and assistance to increase students' chances of remaining in school.[53] The institution may require a student to attend enrichment courses, or an orientation program, the summer before his/her freshman year. Any student not required to enroll in available enrichment courses may do so voluntarily.

During the Task Group's initial research and brainstorming, MALDEF's Kauffman took the position that "merit" to attend a selective public university encompasses a broader range of criteria and accomplishments than test scores and grades. He proposed a list of 18 criteria to govern admission decisions—criteria that reflected academic achievement and potential, the value a student would bring to the learning environment and obstacles the applicant had overcome. Some of these factors are bilingual proficiency, attendance at a school under a desegregation plan and the parents' level of education. The Kauffman criteria were fused with the Ten Percent Plan to become Section II of the bill, which governs admission of applicants who do not make the top 10 percent.[54] According to Torres, the Kauffman factors are very significant because they apply to every unit in the university. Unlike the Ten Percent Plan, which is limited to incoming freshmen undergraduates, all graduate programs must consider the criteria set out in Section II.[55] The law also includes a reporting requirement under which institutions must reveal their actual admissions process and criteria for public scrutiny.

ASSESSING RESULTS THUS FAR

While the first year's results were disappointing,[56] the second year returned Latino and African-American freshman admissions to the pre-HOPWOOD percentages at UT/Austin. At A&M, minority admissions increased but not back to the 1996 levels. But regaining the pre-HOPWOOD level of diversity does not signify full success in attaining equitable access to the flagship universities. Even before HOPWOOD, minority enrollment was low and had started to decline, possibly because the litigation chilled admission officials from admitting black and Latino students.[57] UT/Austin has taken additional steps to ensure that the opportunities provided by the Ten Percent Plan become a reality for students across the state. For example, newly created Longhorn Scholarships are available to top ten-percenters from high schools that have not traditionally sent graduates to UT/Austin.[58] Sixty-four Longhorn Scholarships were awarded to members of the class entering in 1999, and increased to more than 100 for the class of 2000.

One of the most common reservations about the Ten Percent Plan is that those students who were poorly served by the Texas system of public education in primary and secondary grades will be insufficiently prepared for college and may fail.[59] Ten Percent Plan supporters have consistently cautioned against stereotyping students from financially starved, lower-performing high schools as likely to fail. Such students would not have gotten as far as they have without an extraordinary commitment to hard work and the pursuit of excellence—attributes that will overcome most academic challenges they confront at the university level.

Professor Torres and his organization, Texas LEADS, are working with university administrators to monitor any problems encountered by ten-percenters, and thus far, no serious academic concerns have emerged. Indeed, the first year's performance of students admitted under the Ten Percent Plan suggests that the state's faith in the ability of these students to succeed is justi-

Abuse of Children in South Dakota Juvenile Facility

In 1996, South Dakota Govenor Bill Janklow supported a "tough" approach to youthful misbehavior, and particularly favored boot camps. Accordingly, the Department of Corrections redirected the state funding away from community-based programs to expand the State Training School at Plankinton and its boot-camp program.

Few of the young people at Plankinton were charged with serious crimes: at least 30 percent were CHINS (Children in Need of Supervision), i.e., charged with truancy, curfew violation and disobeying parents, and most of the others were charged with minor offenses such as shoplifting. In addition, the weight of punitive policies fell disproportionately on Native American youth. Although Native American youth constitute about 10 percent of the adolescent population of South Dakota, they comprise about 40 percent of youth in the State Training School.

On July 21, 1999, 14-year-old Gina Score collapsed during a forced run in blistering heat at the girls' boot camp at Plankinton. She lay on the ground for more than three hours while staff yelled at her and refused her water or assistance. She eventually became unconscious. When she was finally admitted to a hospital, her body temperature was 108 degrees. She never revived and doctors pronounced her dead an hour later. Govenor Janklow blamed "rogue employees" for the abuse and affirmed his commitment to "tough" policies.

Subsequent investigations uncovered abusive practices in the boot camp and other programs at the State Training School. Parents of children at the facility feared for their children's safety, but also were afraid that criticizing the governor and his policies would bring retaliation on their children.

The Youth Law Center (YLC), a Washington, D.C.-based public-interest law firm with two decades of juvenile justice-reform experience, was asked to investigate the situation at Plankinton. Three attorneys from the Center visited the state several times, interviewing children in the facility, children who had been released and parents.

Parents in the Sioux Falls area began organizing, forming the Parents Who Care Coalition. Some parents traveled for hours, from small towns and Indian reservations, to meet with YLC attorneys at a church in Sioux Falls. They learned about the policy- and resource-allocation choices made by the governor, wrote letters to the largest-circulation newspaper in the state, and vocally supported reform measures before the state legislature.

On February 24, 2000, youth at the institution, represented by the Youth Law Center and a local law firm, brought a civil rights class action against the state for abusive practices and conditions at Plankinton. The practices include male staff stripping girls to their underwear or completely naked and putting them spread-eagled in four-point restraints; locking young people in isolation cells for 23 hours a day, for weeks and sometimes months at a time; and reading and censoring for "negative comments" all mail that youth send to their families. The Parents Who Care Coalition and the attorneys announced the filing of the lawsuit at a press conference, and the litigation was covered by the local and national press.

In this effort, the Parents Who Care Coalition and the attorneys have worked closely and strengthened each other. The parents provided information that was central to the attorneys' investigation of the facility and formulation of the legal claims. The attorneys, in turn, provided crucial support as the coalition was forming, and the filing of the litigation gave the coalition credibility and clout with public officials and the press.

For information about Youth Law Center's report on sentencing disparities among juvenile offenders, check the Web site: www.buildingblocksforyouth.org.

60 Only 1 percent of ten-percenters failed to return after the first semester, compared to 3 percent of other freshmen. See, Implementation and Results of H.B. 588 at the University of Texas at Austin, Preliminary Report No. 2, Dr. Bruce Walker, associate vice president and director of admissions (July 1, 1999).

61 Adviser meeting, Dec. 15-16, 1997.

62 Ibid.

63 See, Sanchez, supra.

fied. At UT/Austin, top 10 percent students outperformed their peers at every SAT score range level and in every college within the university, including competitive majors such as engineering. And, so far, the retention rate for the first group of ten-percenters is significantly above that for other freshmen.[60]

Task Group members stress the need to develop and maintain support systems to ensure that ten-percenters from disadvantaged high schools have a real opportunity to succeed at the flagship campuses. Their slogan for the plan is "10 percent admission, 100 percent graduation."[61] Realization of the 100 percent goal would positively impact on all students—UT/Austin's current overall graduation rate is only 66 percent.[62] The ultimate goal for Texas LEADS is to use the Ten Percent Plan as an impetus to improve K–12 public education for all students.

IMPACT OF THE PLAN ON THOSE WHO JUST MISS THE CUT

The Ten Percent Plan has been criticized for possibly hurting middle-class minority students who attend high-quality, integrated high schools, but do not graduate in the top 10 percent at these competitive schools. The argument is that the Ten Percent Plan replaces some well-prepared minorities admitted under affirmative-action plans with poorly prepared minority students from disadvantaged, segregated high schools.[63] Some critics stress that wealthier minorities are the most likely to succeed at elite universities, thus providing sustainable integration. Preliminary data do not support the prediction that minority students admitted under the Ten Percent Plan will not succeed. And, in any event, given that affirmative action is not currently a legal option for public university admissions in Texas, the critics have not identified a better response to HOPWOOD than the Ten Percent Plan.

It is HOPWOOD, and not the Ten Percent Plan, that dealt well-educated, middle-class minorities a blow. It is too early to gauge the extent of the impact of HOPWOOD and the Ten Percent Plan on this group. The Ten Percent Plan allows universities to extend the automatic-admission program to the top 25 percent of high-school graduates. If universities exercise this option, they will pick up a substantial number of additional minority students attending integrated schools. Also, the Section II factors that must be considered for students not qualified for automatic admission may work to the benefit of middle-class minorities. For example, two of the factors, bilingual proficiency and admission to a comparable out-of-state institution,[64] could offer a competitive edge to middle-class minorities who did not graduate in the top 10 percent. Finally, not all agree that it is preferable to admit wealthier minority students over lower-income minority students. One of the transformative aspects of the Ten Percent Plan is its class-based redistribution of opportunities.

64 Proof of admission to comparable college or university outside of Texas (including universities that still use affirmative action) is among the possible admissions criteria for those not automatically admitted under the Ten Percent Plan.

CONSTITUENCY BUILDING AT THE LOCAL LEVEL

Under the prior admission system, access to the flagship campuses was effectively restricted to a few geographic areas. Of the approximately 1,500 high schools in Texas, more than 1,100 sent no entering freshmen to UT/Austin in the fall of 1997. The top two feeder schools were Plano High School (outside of Dallas), where students are 81 percent white and property value is $362,159 per pupil, and Westlake High School (Austin), which is 89 percent white and has a per-pupil property value of $429,026.[65]

[65] Holley and Spencer, supra, at 267-68.

Communities whose members felt no connection with the flagship universities now have the assurance that their top graduates will be automatically admitted to these often-distant institutions. Parents, students, teachers and community leaders could have a real stake in how these universities function. The Ten Percent Plan thus has the potential to foster communitywide engagement in the operation of the state's system of higher education, as well as improving local public schools.

Ten Percent Plan supporters are now focusing their efforts on empowering parents and students to participate in education policymaking at all levels. In 1999, Texas LEADS held successful public conversations on educational quality in several communities across the state, including Austin, San Antonio, El Paso and Houston. Texas LEADS is now developing a pilot parental-involvement project to be implemented in a middle school[66] that traditionally has not sent large numbers of students to UT/Austin or Texas A&M. This project will focus on the links between quality public education, college participation and a strong democracy. The goal is to expand the role and involvement of parents in their children's education and in school policymaking, ultimately leading to greater parental involvement in policymaking at all levels of the education system, from kindergarten to graduate schools.

[66] Research shows that it is middle school where curriculum and other decisions are made which highly influence whether a student will attend college.

Broader Implications

STRIVING TOWARD TRANSFORMATION

The Ten Percent Plan has rather quickly achieved its "triage" goal. It not only halted the decline in minority admissions. It brought the numbers back up. That alone makes it laudable as an example of creative, transactional lawyering. Even more, the Ten Percent Plan's advocates accomplished this goal in a manner that paves the way for more fundamental transformation.

The Ten Percent Plan illustrates the power and the possibilities of remedies that consider race as a lens on broader unfairness. Professors Lani Guinier and Susan Sturm suggest that the increased visibility and scrutiny of current admissions policies and their underlying components—likely byproducts of the affirmative-action losses—will provide valuable information about ways in which nonminorities also suffer the blows of structural inequality.[67] The Texas Legislature's response to HOPWOOD is one of the first and most promising examples of how a rollback in affirmative action can serve as the "miner's canary," alerting society to the ways traditional admission programs can be exclusionary for many qualified students. At both UT/Austin and Texas A&M, the admission process prior to HOPWOOD relied heavily on standardized tests, disproportionately favoring students with above-average family incomes. The freeze on affirmative action in Texas caused the Legislature to re-examine the universities' reliance on standardized test scores. Ultimately, it concluded such tests were an unnecessary component of the admission decision for top ten-percenters and should be given less weight for applicants not in the top

[67] Susan Sturm and Lani Guinier, "The Future of Affirmative Action: Reclaiming the Innovative Ideal," 84 Calif. L. Rev. 953, 957-997 (1997).

10 percent of their high-school graduating class. With the elimination of the SAT as the primary factor in the admissions process, white students from poor, rural counties stand to benefit along with Mexican-Americans and African-Americans.

If fully implemented, the Ten Percent Plan would change the economic makeup of the flagship campuses. Professors Forbath and Torres opine: "[T]he end of affirmative action may erode...elitism, in ways that many liberals and progressives...could find discomforting. We have grown accustomed to the melding of exclusivity and inclusivity embodied by affirmative action and conventional...college-admission standards, although this system often chooses middle-class minorities (especially African-Americans, less so Latinos) and relatively affluent white students as well. HOPWOOD forced champions of diversity to take account of broader inequities."[68]

Taking on the Overuse and Misuse of Standardized Tests

The Ten Percent Plan is one example of a growing effort by civil rights advocates to eliminate or reduce the weight given to standardized tests in college and graduate-school admissions, as well as challenging unfair "high-stakes" testing at the K–12 levels. As a matter of education policy, the Task Group sought to de-emphasize the role of standardized test scores in university admissions.[69] Many in the broader education community agree that some current admission practices—including ranking applicants on the basis of small, insignificant differences in scores, using test scores mechanically and giving test scores heavy weight—are legally vulnerable and educationally unjustified.

The SAT and other so-called intelligence tests have a sorry history of entanglement with eugenics theories of superior and inferior races. African-Americans, Latinos and women all score lower on average on these tests than white males. The SAT has long been criticized as culturally biased and merely a test of middle-class vocabulary. Proponents of the SAT say that it is a reliable predictor of who will succeed in college. Yet, the SAT is designed to predict only the student's first-year performance in college and bears only a weak relationship to that limited measure of success. Courts have rejected the contention that the SAT is a valid measure of achievement.[70]

Supporters of the SAT also contend that the test gives college admission offices the ability to compare students from different high schools on a standardized basis. Those who oppose rigid use of the SAT counter that it is unfair to compare students from the most privileged high schools to those whose public schools offered them far less educational opportunity.

The Task Group drew on the pioneering scholarship of Law Professors Lani Guinier and Susan Sturm. Guinier and Sturm suggested that setbacks in the battle for affirmative action should spur on the civil rights movement, compelling it to focus on underlying structural inequities, such as the misuse of standardized tests. They point out limitations in the SAT as a predictor of college performance and the negative impact of such tests on lower-income students of all races. Indeed, standardized test scores are more related to the student's family income than they are to success in college.[71]

[68] Forbath and Torres, supra, at 20.

[69] In a similar development, Texas A&Ms medical school dropped use of the Medical School Admissions Test—the medical analog to the SAT—for students selected who successfully complete special undergraduate premed programs. See, Mary Ann Roser, "To Draw Minorities, A&M Drops Test," **Austin-American Statesman**, Feb. 4, 1998.

[70] A full discussion of the debate over the SATs and other standardized tests in university admissions is not possible here. For further information, see, Nicholas Lemann, The Big Test; The Secret History of American Meritocracy (Farrar, Straus & Giroux, 1999); James Course and Dale Trusheim, The Case Against the SAT (University of Chicago Press, 1988). SAT scores have not been shown to predict grades after the first year, even though college is a multiyear experience and the later years are where the student's creativity and interest in a particular field can flourish.

[71] See, Sturm and Guinier, supra, at 968-80, 987-92.

Both affirmative action and the Ten Percent Plan employ a less mechanical, more equitable approach to defining merit. Affirmative action recognizes the critical importance to a democracy of educating students from all segments of society. It incorporates the potential contributions a student will make to his or her classmates, to the educational environment and to society at large.[72] The Ten Percent Plan frames admissions in terms of the mission of public universities to produce leaders from all segments of the state's population and a student's success in overcoming educational obstacles and the mission of public universities to produce leaders from all segments of the state's population.

Spreading the "Percent Plan" Innovation

Other school systems have started to consider their own versions of the Ten Percent Plan. However, developments in California and Florida demonstrate that such efforts should proceed with caution and must not be used as an excuse to end affirmative action. New "percent plans" should be carefully tailored to local circumstances and developed with broad-based consultation and input.

Texas enacted the Ten Percent Plan after vigorously defending affirmative action in the courts. Affirmative-action supporters backed the Ten Percent Plan as the best alternative in light of HOPWOOD. In Florida, affirmative action has been under attack by the same anti-civil-rights groups that generated Proposition 209 in California. Though affirmative action is fully permissible under

[72] See, William G. Bowen and Derek Bok, Shape of the River: Long-Term Consequences of Considering Race in College and University Admissions (Princeton University Press, 1998); Lemann, supra.

The Texas Ten Percent Plan has prompted UT/Austin to set up programs to improve retention and graduation rates of high-performing public high-school students attending UT.

73 The elimination of affirmative action in university admissions would also adversely affect the opportunities of students of color and women to enroll in certain graduate programs. The Executive Order also ends affirmative-action efforts that seek to ensure fair access to state contracting opportunities by women- and minority-owned disadvantaged businesses.

74 Use of a percent plan in conjunction with affirmative action is likely to help the affirmative-action program survive constitutional scrutiny, by strengthening the program's compliance with the Supreme Court's "narrow tailoring" requirement.

75 See, e.g., "Analysis of Governor Bush's One Florida Initiative," **Americans for a Fair Chance** (March 2000), at 8-17. This memo's analysis also points out serious deficiencies in Florida's plan to replace affirmative action in government contracting. Ibid., at 2-6.

76 The lack of seats in the UC system, in comparison with the pool of qualified students, calls attention to a fundamental problem. California's disinvestment in its education system over the past 20 years has resulted in a serious lack of capacity to meet the college needs of the state's residents. Consequently, university seats in the California system have become a very scarce resource, prompting fierce competition and enormous social tension over how those slots are awarded.

current Florida law, an initiative similar to Prop 209 was attempted for inclusion on the Florida ballot. In this highly charged political climate, Florida Gov. Jeb Bush proposed a "Twenty Percent Plan" as a substitute for, rather than a supplement to, affirmative action. With the announcement of the Twenty Percent Plan in November 1999, Governor Bush simultaneously signed an Executive Order wiping out all consideration of race and gender in public university admissions.[73]

Gov. Jeb Bush's anti-affirmative action Order has prompted a firestorm of protest, including a sit-in by two African-American state representatives at the Lieutenant Governor's office and several student-led demonstrations. The "percent plan" concept developed in Texas was never intended by its creators to replace affirmative action in jurisdictions where affirmative action is legally permitted. Instead, in the vast majority of states where this remedy remains an option for public entities, a percent plan could be used in tandem with affirmative-action measures. Such a dual system would preserve the flexibility to consider race to serve a compelling governmental interest not accomplished by a percent plan or other non-race-specific measures.[74]

The Florida Twenty Percent Plan has also been criticized on the grounds that its design is flawed.[75] Despite vigorous protests, Governor Bush, his cabinet and the state university system have acted to eliminate affirmative action in university admissions.

The University of California (UC) system has adopted a "Four Percent Plan." This plan is not likely to significantly increase African-American and Latino representation at the flagship schools such as UC, Berkeley. Though 4 percent is too low to make a large difference, the plan is limited to this figure because of the lack of capacity in the UC system.[76] Also, in contrast to the Texas plan, both the Florida and the California plans guarantee admission only into the university system as a whole, not to the applicant's choice of institution. Thus, neither the Florida Twenty Percent Plan nor the California Four Percent Plan will address segregation within the state university system, nor restore diversity to the flagship campuses.

Whatever the final results in Florida and California, the brief experience thus far highlights some important lessons. First, racial-justice advocates must always be alert to the risk that even innovations like the Ten Percent Plan can be misused. While racial-justice advocates cannot prevent such misappropriation of their ideas, they must be vigilant in monitoring and responding to mischaracterizations.

Second, Florida's Twenty Percent Plan and California's Four Percent Plan show that efforts to replicate the Ten Percent Plan must be flexible enough to incorporate local circumstances. Texas' Ten Percent Plan was developed after detailed analysis of the state's demographics, its patterns of "feeder schools" to the flagship universities, the state's culture and other local factors. Two of the factors that led to success in Texas—broad community input and creative, multidisciplinary research and analysis—appear to have been ignored in Florida.

CHALLENGING THE MYTH THAT AFFIRMATIVE-ACTION ROLLBACKS PRODUCE RACIALLY FAIR ADMISSION SYSTEMS
Even prior to the passage of Proposition 209, the Board of Regents of the University of California adopted SP1, a resolution prohibiting the consideration of "race, religion, sex, color,

ethnicity or national origin as criteria" for admissions purposes.[77] Unlike Texas, California did not respond to the loss of affirmative action by reconsidering its dependence on test scores. Instead, UC, Berkeley, has increased the importance of factors that favor those who already have benefited from above-average K–12 educational opportunities or have the resources for expensive test-preparation courses. In addition to heavy reliance on standardized tests, the new Berkeley criteria award an extra grade point to students who earn A's in Advanced Placement (AP) courses, resulting in grade-point averages that exceed 4.0.[78] This practice puts poor and minority students at a disadvantage, since AP courses are widely available in high schools with predominantly white and wealthy students but are scarce in schools serving minority students.[79] When SP1 took effect for undergraduate admissions for the fall of 1998, "[t]he number of students in groups officially deemed underrepresented at the [UC, Berkeley] campus—African-American, Latino, Chicano and American Indian—dropped nearly 55 percent from the prior fall's admission, according to campus figures.[80]

Civil rights advocates, including MALDEF, NAACP LDF, the Asian Pacific American Legal Center, the ACLU of Northern California and the San Francisco Lawyers' Committee, responded to Berkeley's new, exclusionary admission system with a class-action lawsuit.[81] The suit alleges that Berkeley's practices, including heavy weighting of AP courses to which minority high-school students do not have equal access, violate the 14th Amendment to the U.S. Constitution and Title VI. The case also charges that UC, Berkeley, engages in "unjustified reliance upon standardized-test scores," assigns "unjustifiable weight" to SAT tests and relies on "educationally insignificant" differences in test scores.[82]

Although the context is different, like the Texas Ten Percent Plan, the Berkeley case uses a controversy over university admissions to turn the spotlight on the unequal opportunities provided by public schools at the K–12 levels. Since the filing of the suit, the large disparities in availability of AP courses has been widely reported in the media. By compiling impeccable data and strategically challenging the current structure in the courts, administrative agencies[83] and the media, civil rights advocates are helping to expose the fact that many college admission systems actually reward privilege rather than merit. At the same time, they are challenging the legitimacy of those privileges, contending that public education systems must mitigate, rather than reinforce, existing inequalities.

CONCLUSION

The Texas Ten Percent Plan has simultaneously fostered both diversity and excellence in the student bodies of the state's flagship campuses. It has made the admission process smarter and fairer and, in the process, turned the spotlight on the need to address the vast inequities at the K–12 level.

[77] Prior to the implementation of resolution SP1, UC undergraduate programs utilized admissions criteria that included consideration of racial, ethnic and gender background.

[78] See, RIOS V. THE REGENTS OF THE UNIVERSITY OF CALIFORNIA, ET. AL., First Amended Complaint for Declaratory and Injunctive Relief, No. C.99-0525 SI (N.D. Ca. 1999).

[79] Ibid., at 13.

[80] "Cal Hit With Race-Bias Suit," **San Francisco Examiner**, Feb. 2, 1999, AI, 10.

[81] RIOS, First Amended Complaint, supra.

[82] Ibid., at 11.

[83] Several of these civil rights legal organizations have filed discrimination complaints against members of the UC system with the U.S. Department of Education, Office for Civil Rights and the Department of Labor, Office of Contract Compliance.

chapter

2

Client-Centered Lawyering

Marchers mourn the deaths of 146 fire victims at the Triangle Shirtwaist Factory on March 25, 1911 (right). Many of the workers were women, and most were recent Italian and European-Jewish immigrants. They sought a better life in the United States, but instead found horrific working conditions and cruel poverty. Unfamiliar with the language, they were easy targets for exploitation. Anyone who complained risked losing her job. When the fire broke out on the factory's ninth floor, many were trapped because few fire-prevention measures had been taken; doors were locked to prevent theft and the fire escape did not reach the ground.

On August 2, 1995, 71 Thai garment workers in El Monte, California, were found enslaved behind barbed wire, watched by armed guards in an illegal sweatshop. For seven years, scores of immigrant workers had been imprisoned in this compound, forced to sew clothing under the labels of some of the largest and most well-known U.S. garment manufacturers and retailers. The El Monte prisoners labored virtually round the clock for negligible compensation, and were subjected to ceaseless mental and physical cruelty. The notorious practices discovered in the El Monte slave shop generated enormous public outrage and media coverage.

Several public-interest organizations, including the Asian Pacific American Legal Center of Southern California, had identified sweatshops as a serious civil rights issue. The El Monte raid provided an opening for effective organizing and advocacy, not just on behalf of the formerly enslaved workers, but for all abused garment workers in this country. By joining together, the workers and these groups have provided momentum toward a larger movement against the exploitation of workers.

Chapter 2
Client-Centered Lawyering: Garment Worker Advocacy In Los Angeles

Key Lessons Learned

- Frame issues carefully to account for cultural differences so as to lay the foundation for forming alliances across racial lines.

- Ensure that technical, legal and other important information is useful and accessible to clients and their communities.

- Embrace community based-organizations as partners to help build the leadership capacity of local residents.

- Root all legal strategies in the practical needs of communities.

In El Monte, California, factory owners used locked doors, barbed wire, armed guards and constant threats to contain workers. Like the Triangle Shirtwaist workers, the El Monte workers were mostly women. The El Monte women were also promised a better life, but instead found themselves ruthlessly exploited (left and above).

[1] APALC is the leading organization in southern California dedicated to providing the growing Asian-Pacific American community with multilingual, culturally sensitive legal services, education and civil rights advocacy. The Center provides legal assistance in the areas of worker rights, affirmative action, immigration and citizenship, family law, government benefits, language rights and voting rights. It also operates an innovative, interethnic leadership-training program. It is affiliated with the National Asian Pacific American Legal Consortium.

[2] Julie A. Su, "Making The Invisible Visible: The Garment Industry's Dirty Laundry," 1 J. Gender, Race and Just., 405, 415 (1998) (hereinafter "Invisible").

Overview

In the wake of the discovery of imprisoned garment workers at the El Monte, California, sweatshop, the Asian Pacific American Legal Center of Southern California (APALC)[1] joined with the Korean Immigrant Workers Advocates, the Coalition for Humane Immigrants' Rights of Los Angeles, the Thai Community Development Center, Sweatshop Watch and other organizations to launch a multifaceted campaign. The campaign assisted the El Monte garment workers in their fight for justice and provided momentum for broader industry reform efforts. Each organization brought its own expertise to the work, as the coalition simultaneously sought to obtain justice for the formerly enslaved workers; work with them to gain control of their lives and their advocacy efforts; promote greater racial and gender equity; and forge a multiracial coalition that involved workers from multiple facilities.

A key to this coalition's success was the ability to keep the interests and goals of the individual clients front and center, while also pursuing broader goals. There was an ongoing tension between the immediate needs of the workers and the larger, social-justice ends to which the group committed.[2] As the organization in charge of legal advocacy, APALC never wavered in its commitment first to help the formerly enslaved Thai workers gain control over their lives and their own advocacy efforts. At the same time, APALC formed alliances across racial lines by including Latina workers and attacked the structural inequities within the garment industry.

Early on, APALC made a decision to represent both the formerly enslaved Thai workers from the secret El Monte shop and a group of Latina workers laboring in traditional sweatshops in downtown Los Angeles. The traditional sweatshops served as front shops for the El Monte compound. All of the workers produced garments for the same manufacturers and retailers and were supervised by the same group of people—the captors of the Thai workers. The two groups of workers ultimately built a solid coalition, although the work was painstaking and not without errors along the way.

APALC also employed novel legal strategies. It developed an innovative interpretation of a federal statute to obtain visas for the workers, and it brought a groundbreaking lawsuit against the operators of the sweatshop and the manufacturers and retailers who profited from the labor of those who were enslaved.

In both its litigation and non-litigation work, APALC designed its efforts to involve the workers themselves, so that they became increasingly educated about the process and empowered to make future decisions on their own. The workers attended monthly meetings for more than three years where they both discussed and participated in ongoing litigation and received life-skills training.

APALC's legal advocacy on behalf of the workers was highly successful and is likely to translate into broad-based improvements in the lives of garment workers throughout this troubled industry. APALC's landmark legal claims, in combination with extraordinary media coverage and public pressure, enabled the workers to get legal settlements of more than $4 million in compensation for injuries. Prior to the settlements, APALC also won key motions that established a major new legal precedent. Previously, garment workers had limited redress from the sweatshop operators, many of whom are fly-by-night operators who can quickly close down or in other ways make themselves immune to legal sanctions. By establishing the grounds to hold larger manufacturers and retailers liable for sweatshop abuses, the lawsuit creates incentives for manufacturers and retailers to ensure that their products are manufactured under lawful conditions in the future.

A BILLION DOLLAR PYRAMID

The U.S. garment industry generates billions of dollars each year.[3] The industry is centered around several major cities with large immigrant populations, including San Francisco, Los Angeles and New York. While much of U.S. garment production is located overseas, those retailers and manufacturers that have U.S. operations are able to avoid import quotas and high shipping costs, while still taking advantage of a large pool of easily exploitable labor.[4]

The structure of the garment industry resembles a pyramid, with the manufacturers and retailers at the top, garment-shop operators in the middle, and garment workers at the bottom. The retailer, generally a boutique or major department store, has the highest profit margins in the industry.[5] The manufacturer, ranging from a large company or a well-known fashion designer to smaller companies and little-known labels, designs the particular piece to be produced and dispatches the job to contractors.

Garment shops are often small, transitory operations owned by immigrants. Many such owners are former sweatshop workers who have saved enough money to start their own shops. Start-up costs for a garment shop are modest—rental or purchase of space, sewing-machine rental, and business permit fees. With an abundance of contracting shops, individual operators have little to no bargaining power with the manufacturers, who routinely pit them against each other for the lowest possible prices. In essence, manufacturers set the price and garment shops are forced to agree to survive. The winning operators are often forced to underbid to obtain the work. With their profit margins now radically reduced or eliminated, the shop operators exploit the workers, gouging their salaries to make ends meet.[6]

Garment workers occupy the lowest position in the pyramid. They are typically women immigrants from Latin America and Asia, many of whom have recently arrived in the United States. They are highly vulnerable because they are frequently without English-language skills or employment options other than garment work. Many arrive without the appropriate

[3] See, Leo L. Lam, "Designer Duty: Extending Liability to Manufacturers for Violations of Labor Standards in Garment Industry Sweatshops," 141 U. Pa. L. Rev., 623, 627 (1992) (hereinafter "Designer Duty").

[4] Ibid., at 631-632.

[5] Ibid., at 629-632. The profit per garment to the retailer (typically greater than 100 percent markup to the consumer) usually exceeds twice the profit to the manufacturer, which in turn exceeds twice that to the contractor.

[6] Ibid., at 629-630.

[7] See, also, Fang-Lain Lao, "Illegal Immigrants in Garment Sweatshops: The Universal Declaration of Human Rights and the International Covenant on Civil and Political Rights," 3 SW. J. L. & Trade Am., 487, 496 (1996).

[8] Quotations and other information in this section are from Arianne Callender's interviews with Wan Prachuapsuk, Sunee Shamshukul, Sirilak Rongsak and Maliwan Radomphon, former El Monte workers, in Los Angeles (June 26, 1998) (hereinafter, worker interviews). Their experiences are typical of those of other workers who were imprisoned at El Monte between 1988 and 1995.

visa. Most are unaware of their rights or remain fearful of the consequences should they attempt to assert them. For many, a minimum wage is not even perceived to be a right. This situation is ripe for exploitation.[7]

In the effort to turn a profit, operators may commit egregious labor violations against the workers and threaten them with deportation and blacklisting if they complain. They may deny workers legally required minimum wage and overtime pay. They also encourage employees to take work home, in violation of industrial homework laws, to avoid overtime requirements. In addition to wage violations, the shops are often unsanitary and fraught with fire hazards.

THE EL MONTE EXPERIENCE

Garment workers in Thailand making pennies per day dreamed of immigrating to the United States. One El Monte worker remembered: "I had dreams about the United States since I was a little boy. [But] I thought, I have no education, I'm just garment worker—how can I get to that place?" Another El Monte worker explained: "Everybody has a dream about America, a land of opportunity and freedom. You can make a fortune...if you come." When one of the enslaved workers first heard about a job in a factory in Los Angeles, he mused, "[t]he name of the city—of angels—it must be good!"[8]

The El Monte shop operators had a recruiter in Thailand, who claimed that immigrants would "just work regular 8 to 5, get a lot of pay and do what they did in Thailand." He even showed them a picture of a top-of-the-line factory. The rate of pay promised by the recruiter was so much that a garment worker would have to "work for the whole month in Thailand to make what she would make in a day or two of work in America." After hearing the recruiter's offer, one worker decided to "just get on the plane and go to the United States." Another worker stated: "I never imagined about any danger or that anything might happen...because I heard about the land of freedom and that law and police protect you."

Ready to pursue their dreams, they quit their jobs, packed their bags and said goodbye to their families, promising to send money home as soon as they were settled. The recruiter gave each worker a bracelet and a thin necklace to wear for identification.

But the dream quickly turned sour. Once in America, the workers began to realize that the recruiter had lied to them. Rather than the fancy factory the recruiter had shown them in a photograph, they were taken to an apartment complex that had been converted into a garment factory in El Monte, a town a few miles east of Los Angeles. The workers met the head operator, the mastermind behind the entire operation, a sweet-talking Thai woman who asked everyone to call her Auntie. Auntie instructed the workers: "Don't talk to the people that lived here before you; they will probably lie to you. Don't listen to all those things they put into your mind."

El Monte was grim. All calls were monitored; all mail was censored. High barbed-wire fences surrounded the complex, topped with metal spikes pointed inward. "We couldn't go any-where, we couldn't get through the front gate because of the 24-hour armed guard." The operators constantly made violent threats to frighten workers into submission. They showed them pictures of an injured co-worker brutally beaten for trying to escape. They threatened to beat them, to kill their families and to burn down their homes in Thailand if they ever tried to escape. The operators also told the workers that if they contacted government offi-cials, they would face prosecution for illegal entry into the country. They told the workers lies, such as, "If you get caught, the authorities...will shave your head."

"My hopes and dreams disappeared into thin air," said one worker. "I couldn't believe America had a place like this." Living quarters as well as working quarters were crowded, dirty and infested with rats and roaches. Often, just the act of breathing was difficult because fabric lint from the sewing clogged the air in inadequately ventilated rooms.

When one worker looked for the beds, she was told, "don't even think about [a] bed." The workers had to sew their own mattresses. They slept on the floor, amongst the rats and roaches, sharing a room with up to eight other workers.

The workday was long and treacherous. Workers were at their machines by 7 a.m. and got only two breaks the entire day—15 minutes each for lunch and dinner. The shift ended only when the work order was complete, no matter how long it took. Exhausted workers often found themselves nodding off at the machines and drinking endless cups of coffee in the struggle to stay awake. Often, they didn't finish the job until 2 or 3 o'clock in the morning.

The El Monte operators ran a number of different "front shop" facilities in downtown Los Angeles that, at various times, employed up to 70 Latina workers. These workers were not enslaved, but labored in unsanitary conditions, making clothes for the same operators, manufacturers and retailers. One such sweatshop was an open warehouse with a wall parti-tion in the middle, separating areas where finishing work was done from the area where shipment was made. The facility was crowded and extremely hot. Workers were told that they could not even bring their own fans because it would cost too much in electricity. The bathrooms were filthy, and air quality was poor. The workers were paid below minimum wage and denied overtime compensation.

At the Los Angeles facility, the finishing work—trim-ming, folding, packaging, buttonholes and buttons—was done after the garments had been sewn at the secret El Monte facility. The manufacturers and retailers inspected the front shops regularly, even as

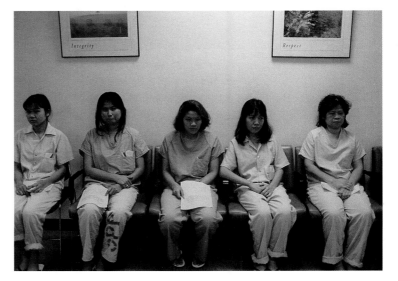

Waiting for an INS ruling: While the workers were detained at the San Pedro Terminal Island federal penitentiary, a coalition of commu-nity groups and lawyers, working with federal authorities, mobilized to win their release and later provided services to help them rebuild their lives.

much as several times a day. The workers claimed in their litigation that the manufacturers and retailers knew or should have known that all of the work was not being performed at the downtown shops.

RESCUED BUT NOT FREED

Several Thai workers risked their lives to escape from the El Monte compound. In 1995, escaped workers took an additional risk to inform law-enforcement officials about the slave shop. Shortly after, a joint task force of federal and state law-enforcement agencies raided the El Monte operation.

That summer, Julie Su, a recent law graduate on a fellowship with APALC, and Chancee Martorell, the director of the Thai Community Development Center, one of APALC's community partners,[9] each received a call from the California Labor Commissioner's office, asking for translation help on a raid. As she sought to understand the sweatshop industry, Su had established relationships with these state officials, accompanying them on other raids and helping with Chinese translation. Martorell arranged to accompany law-enforcement officials on the raid. By agreeing to serve as an interpreter, Martorell was able to make a connection with the El Monte workers and provide inside information from the start of the case. Martorell interpreted the workers' language and, more importantly, their culture. An activist and leader in her own right, she devoted tremendous amounts of time and energy to serving the workers.

The morning of the raid on El Monte, a male worker saw the police begin surrounding the compound. He immediately got scared and went to hide. Another worker, exhausted from work the night before, was sound asleep when a co-worker came to get him up. Everybody was screaming, "Pack! We're gonna go home! Pack!" For a time, some of the workers, in hushed tones, discussed whether to attempt a getaway. But all efforts to hide or escape were in vain. The workers were quickly rounded up and put on a bus bound for an Immigration and Naturalization Service (INS) detention facility.[10]

For most, the bus trip was their first real glimpse of the outside world in the United States. As their relief at being free from El Monte settled in, they marveled at the sight of the passing city. "Oh, this is so beautiful, so light and shiny," thought one. "For once, everybody was happy."[11]

But their happiness ended abruptly. The INS put them in the federal penitentiary at San Pedro Terminal Island, where they were forced to wear prison uniforms.[12] During the daytime, they were taken to an INS holding cell in the basement of the federal building in Los Angeles, transported by bus in shackles. At night they were usually returned to the San Pedro prison, but they spent two nights in the INS holding tank, a concrete room with no beds. When Julie Su first met with the workers at this location, there were 65 women sitting

[9] The Thai Community Development Center is one of a number of "community partners" with which APALC maintains ongoing, working relationships. APALC has been involved in such relationships for many years, providing legal advice and support for citizenship programs and other legal assistance needed by these community groups.

[10] Worker interviews, supra.

[11] Ibid.

[12] "Invisible," supra, at 405, 407.

on the floor, with one toilet in the open along the back wall. To create a modicum of privacy for the toilet, the women had placed a large government trash can in front of it. The heat in the room was unbearable.[13]

The Campaign to Free the Garment Workers

Prior to the El Monte raid, APALC had identified garment-industry exploitation of Asians as a priority issue for its advocacy efforts. Julie Su participated in Sweatshop Watch, a sweatshop monitoring group, and had established relationships with other community groups and legal organizations concerned about sweatshops. Su had also begun to study the structure of the garment industry and to research strategies to address abuses.

The first challenge for APALC was to help the workers remain in the United States despite the INS's plans to deport them immediately. According to APALC's Executive Director Stewart Kwoh, APALC's long-standing relationship with the Thai Community Development Center and with Chancee Martorell was critical. "We were able to get involved immediately. Without that, all the workers would have been deported before any lawyers found out."[14]

Su, Martorell and other young Asian advocates from the Korean Immigrant Workers Advocates and the Coalition for Humane Immigrants Rights of Los Angeles sprang into action as soon as they learned the workers had been arrested. The day after the raid, they went to the INS but were required to provide names and identification numbers for any workers they sought to see. Of course, without access to the workers, they did not know the names and numbers. The next day, Friday afternoon, activists were able to speak to the whole group and to give them a flyer in Thai with phone numbers they could call to get legal representation and help. The Thai Community Development Center received a number of calls the following Saturday. On Sunday, July 24, 1995, Martorell, Su and other colleagues arrived at the San Pedro federal detention center at 6:00 a.m. They waited while, they were told, the workers had breakfast. In fact, the workers were shipped out from under their noses to the INS downtown. The activists spent six hours that day just finding out where the workers were. Martorell recalls that the activists refused to leave.[15] Finally, they were allowed to meet with workers, but only two at a time. The workers were scared and ashamed. It was difficult for the workers to understand that they were not the guilty parties.[16] The members of the coalition assured them that they were not criminals and that coalition members were there to help them.

The activists met with officials from the INS and the U.S. Attorney's office, arguing that detaining the workers would telegraph that those who report abuse and exploitation will be rewarded with imprisonment and deportation.[17] This would only undermine law enforcement, help the sweatshop operators and push those like El Monte further underground. The advocates contended that detaining workers who blew the whistle was essentially the equivalent

[13] P. Hair telephone interview with Julie Su, March 15, 1999 (hereinafter, Su interview, March 1999).

[14] P. Hair interview with Stewart Kwoh, July 24, 1997.

[15] Venu Gupta telephone interview with Chancee Martorell, Dec. 3, 1999 (hereinafter, Martorell interview).

[16] Ibid.

[17] See "Invisible," supra, note 2, at 407.

[18] Ibid.

of conspiring with the exploitative employers. They also argued that if the workers remained in detention, they would become increasingly reluctant to testify against the sweatshop operators and that the cost of keeping the workers imprisoned would prove exorbitant.[18]

Hunkering Down for the Campaign

When the INS was initially unresponsive to these arguments, APALC and the advocacy team prepared for battle by establishing a makeshift office in the basement of the INS facility. Refusing to accept red tape as an excuse, they navigated the INS bureaucracy themselves, following the rules and challenging them at the same time.[19] Much of their strength came from the fact that they were indefatigable and unwilling to abandon the workers at the INS facility. Martorell notes: "It was so tense. We had such a hostile relationship with the INS."[20] At 7 a.m. sharp each morning they assembled, ready to commandeer the pay phones, bang on the INS windows and confront its officials, and they didn't stop until 1 or 2 a.m. the following morning. Most days they held a press conference, enlisting the media to embarrass and keep political pressure on INS officials.

[19] Ibid.

[20] Martorell interview.

The advocates quickly learned that INS officials had considerable discretion in applying the rules. Much could be achieved by talking to the right official or refusing to take no for an answer. Although the incessant battle with the INS bureaucracy was frustrating, it quickly brought the garment workers and the advocates closer together, forging an effective team during the initial week of their relationship. After nine days their collective perseverance succeeded, and the INS officials released the detained workers on bond. It took a massive amount of organizing and advocacy, says Martorell, but INS finally relented.[21]

[21] Ibid.

Without lawyers to intervene immediately in the process, all of the workers would have been deported, and the organizing and other efforts on their behalf would have been moot. Having the workers in this country with legal status helped keep a human face on the issue and was key to maintaining pressure on the clothing companies. APALC actually put up part of the bond for the workers, along with community groups and the UNITE labor union.

A Transactional Campaign on Behalf of the Garment Workers

APALC's lawyers joined with a collaborative of community groups and religious organizations to address all the legal *and* basic needs of the freed Thai workers. An underlying objective was to work with them to become more independent and empowered over time, making them more able to exercise control over the important decisions in their lives. There was never a question of where legal representation ended and the organizing and social work began. From the start, addressing the workers' social and economic concerns outside of the courtroom was considered integral to the legal representation.

Letter from attorney Julie Su to the workers on the second anniversary of their freedom from El Monte: "...you have seen the worst of human actions: greed, violence, cruelty, yet you continue to warm the world with your smiles. I am grateful to you for making me the kind of lawyer I wanted to be and even more than I imagined I could be."

Su explained her expansion of the traditional lawyer-client model, which stresses a dispassionate, professional relationship: "The traditional…lawyers, who are not engaged in the workers' lives, cannot represent them in a lawsuit in a way that is true to the workers. The lawyer-activist has to be an active participant in the litigation to ensure that the workers' lives guide the litigation."[22]

By the time the INS released the workers, a massive outpouring of community resources and support provided temporary housing and food for them in churches and other makeshift shelters. Initially the workers found themselves packed into available shelters, 30 or more to a space. But the coalition envisioned something better for them. "Aside from shelter and food, we wanted medical care and English lessons to develop their self-sufficiency, not just homes, but appliances and phones so they could live regular lives."[23] Ultimately, working together with strong community support, the organizations were able to assist the workers in finding jobs and moving into their own apartments.

Building a Home in a Most Foreign Environment

Speaking no English in a foreign country, in which nothing is familiar beyond the bounds of a prison, was a desperately challenging situation for the workers. They needed new survival and safety skills. English lessons were obviously a crucial part of instilling a sense of self-sufficiency and security. Almost all of the workers learned enough English to communicate successfully regarding their basic, everyday needs. A few became so proficient that they could converse with the media in English. They have served as powerful spokespeople for greater justice in the garment industry.

Advocates organized skills-training sessions for the workers. They covered subjects as diverse as how to manage household finances, use a checking account, safeguard money in public, take a bus and other public transport, shop for groceries and other essentials and seek and land a job. The life-skills training also covered handling advances from strangers, particularly men. As women, the Thai workers were immediately targeted for marriage upon release from their enslavement. Many of the women had been told that their only chance to succeed and remain in the United States was to marry an American. Over time, the women came to understand that their options were not so limited and while a few have married, most remain single.

How Creative Advocacy Won the Workers' Legal Immigration Status

Initially, immigration officials and even some immigrants' advocates insisted that the Thai workers had no hope of obtaining legal immigration status. APALC was persistent in searching for a creative solution that would take into account the unique circumstances under which the Thai workers came to America and were enslaved. At first, they persuaded the INS to grant temporary work permits, a less-desirable option than a visa. When the INS issued six-month work permits, the advocates aggressively pursued a renewal and extension

[22] "Invisible," supra, note 68, at 416, 412.

[23] A. Callender interview with Julie Su, staff attorney, Asian Pacific American Legal Center (interview, June 4, 1998) (hereinafter, Su interview, June 1998).

24 Under an S-visa, a noncitizen may be admitted for up to three years if the U.S. Attorney General's office determines that the applicant possesses critical, reliable information concerning a criminal organization or enterprise and the INS approves the application, 8 U.S.C. 1101(a)(15)(S). If the S-visa holder supplies information which has substantially contributed to the success of an investigation or prosecution, the Attorney General may recommend an upgrade to lawful permanent residence, 8 U.S.C. 245(j).

of the terms. The goal, after all, was to help the workers rebuild their lives *in this* country, and that meant securing their right to remain in the country. Temporary work authorizations, while a fine interim solution, offered no long-term security or stability for the workers.

To support the claim for permanent legal status, Su developed an innovative interpretation of a statutory provision designed to help prisoners who aid law enforcement. The APALC attorneys asserted that the workers, who had been victims of a criminal conspiracy, should be eligible for S-visa status because they were assisting law enforcement officials in bringing the criminals—the sweatshop operators—to justice.[24] The S-visa is designed to ensure that key witnesses are protected and have an incentive to testify. Since some of the enslavers had escaped and fled to Thailand, workers were afraid for their lives if they had to testify and then be deported back to Thailand.

APALC worked in close partnership with the National Asian Pacific American Legal Consortium (NAPALC), whose Executive Director, Karen Narasaki, served as an adviser to this Report. Through this relationship, APALC drew on the low-wage worker organizing and litigation expertise of one of NAPALC's other affiliates, the Asian Law Caucus in San Francisco. Recognized for its national expertise on Asian-Pacific immigration issues, NAPALC worked closely with other immigration policy experts, including the American Bar Association and the American Immigration Lawyers Association. It obtained their support and assistance in advocating for the unique use of the S-visa. Because NAPALC staff had worked on the original legislation for the S-visa, they were able to work behind the scenes to convince key members in Congress and at the INS that its use in the Thai workers' case would not be inconsistent with congressional intent.

The Consortium also met with Attorney General Janet Reno and with senior INS policy officials to push the process forward. Although the Attorney General was very supportive, many officials in Los Angeles and in Washington were less enthusiastic. They tried to use the bureaucracy to their advantage. When the process got stuck, APALC would ask NAPALC to use its contacts to locate the blockages and to alert supportive staff in the Attorney General's office. Knowing that APALC had an independent connection to headquarters at the Department of Justice (DOJ) and the INS made the Los Angeles U.S. Attorney's Office and INS district office less able to stall the visa process.

25 Su interview, June 1998.

26 Ibid.

With NAPALC playing a critical role setting up meetings in Washington, D.C., the legal team presented the case for the workers' visas to Commissioner Doris Meissner of the INS, Deval Patrick, then Assistant Attorney General for Civil Rights, and Janet Reno. Su emphasized the government's direct interest in having the Thai workers testify in what was a criminal case.[25] In addition, she worked to convey "the human side of the argument, trying to tell stories, to make people real, because people sometimes forget that they're dealing with real people instead of abstract policies."[26]

Su seized the opportunity to speak to the Attorney General when she came to Los Angeles to meet with civil rights groups in May 1996. Su found out about the meeting two days in advance and prepared packets about the workers' situation and the arguments in favor of the S-visas. Following the Attorney General's remarks, Su opened the comment period by pointing out that the DOJ needed to provide incentives for victims of enslavement and exploitation to report these crimes. The Attorney General responded: "You have made a very compelling presentation. I'll see what I can do." Su learned that the Attorney General met with government lawyers in Washington, D.C., and said soon thereafter: "Frankly, I don't know why we're not falling all over each other to get this done."[27]

After the meeting with the Attorney General, the government agencies were more cooperative. But the INS still stalled on granting the visas. Su believes that the INS's approach reveals a government preference for enforcement of immigration laws—through detention and deportation—over enforcement of labor and civil rights laws. She argues that such an approach is very problematic for an agency with so much unfettered discretion.[28]

[27] Ibid.

[28] Ibid.

The lawyers continued to offer creative solutions when officials threw up obstacles and claimed that nothing could be done. When the S-visas initially were requested, INS officials said they could not grant the visas, which are normally used in drug cases. The response: There was no strict policy about this; it was nowhere in the law or legislative history. INS officials also claimed that they could not issue S-visas because there were 80 workers in all[29] and the INS was only allowed to grant 100 S-visas each year. As a way around this obstacle, Julie Su suggested a staggered dating of the visas throughout the years since the case had begun. This idea finally broke the logjam, and two years after the workers were freed from the El Monte compound, the INS granted them all S-visas.

[29] This total includes the 71 workers at El Monte when the raid took place, plus nine escaped workers who came forward to testify about the El Monte violations and also were eligible for S-visas.

Pursuing Innovative Legal Claims That Hold Corporations Accountable

Shortly after the Thai workers obtained their freedom, they joined with 22 Latina workers from the downtown facility to file a civil suit against the El Monte operators and their corporate affiliates. The Latina workers had contacted APALC when they heard about the El Monte situation in the media. In the lawsuit, the Latinas charged illegal exploitation, rather than enslavement. Like the Thai workers, the Latina plaintiffs have become strong advocates for reforms to eliminate sweatshops and to protect workers.

The legal team,[30] led by APALC, crafted a litigation strategy that was designed to accomplish two broad goals. The first was to build a cross-racial coalition between the Thai workers from the secret El Monte facility and the Latina workers from the downtown front shops. The advocates and workers reasoned that if a cross-racial, cross-facility coalition of exploited workers could be forged in this case, it would serve as a model for broader, multiracial collaboration among workers in the garment industry in general. The second goal was to crack the wall that has traditionally insulated the garment retailers and

[30] The workers' lawyers included the ACLU of Southern California, Asian Law Caucus, ACLU Immigrants Rights Project, Equal Rights Advocates and several law firms as pro bono co-counsel—Bird, Marella, Boxer & Wolpert; Rothner, Segall, Bahan & Greenstone; and Hadsell & Stormer, Inc.

31 922 F. Supp. 1450 (C.D. Calif. 1996).

manufacturers from legal liability. In combination, these two strategic decisions helped to show that the El Monte operation was not just a shocking aberration within the garment industry but an illustration of a flawed and exploitive industry.

The lawsuit, BUREERONG V. UVAWAS,[31] charged the sweatshop operators with wage and hour violations, involuntary servitude, assault and a host of other civil rights violations. In a landmark challenge to the structure of the sweatshop industry, the workers sued the manufacturers and retailers who profited from the workers' labor. The suit alleged that corporate defendants—Mervyn's, Montgomery Ward, Miller's Outpost, B.U.M., L.F. Sportswear, Tomato,

The National Asian Pacific American Legal Consortium— Restoring Food Stamps to Elderly and Disabled Immigrants

The National Asian Pacific American Legal Consortium was founded by three regionally based Asian-Pacific American (APA) public interest law groups, Asian American Legal Defense and Education Fund in New York, the Asian Law Caucus in San Francisco and the Asian Pacific American Legal Center in Los Angeles. These three organizations maintain significant representation on the Consortium's board and contract with the Consortium as affiliates to jointly accomplish the Consortium's mission.

In addition, the Consortium has created a national network of 74 community partners in 40 cities and 24 states. These nonprofit civic and community service agencies help the Consortium to identify emerging issues, evaluate legislative and agency proposals and monitor local implementation and enforcement of federal laws and regulations. The Consortium provides training, technical assistance and information, as well as an avenue for input into national policies that will affect the network on the local level. APALC is a key partner for NAPALC, and the National Consortium in return played a key role at various pivotal points in APALC's efforts on behalf of the El Monte workers.

NAPALC's relationships with its community partners were particularly important when Congress, in its welfare reform and immigration legislation, stripped legal permanent residents and other immigrants of eligibility for services and benefits. Forty percent of the welfare-reform savings came from making blind, elderly and disabled immigrants ineligible for SSI and food stamps. These provisions had been ignored in the larger debate over welfare reform.

The Consortium and its affiliates developed and translated materials for community-service agencies to explain the complicated new laws. They conducted briefings around the country to help community leaders develop strategies to advocate on the grassroots level for their communities. The Consortium also helped to train community leaders in how to tell their stories to the local media.

The Consortium also took a citizenship program that had been developed by APALC and trained community partners in how to institute similar programs. It realized that citizenship was the only hope for many immigrants facing loss of their only means of survival. It worked to engage and train other APA attorneys to help community-based organizations ensure the accuracy and validity of applications before they went forward.

On a national level, the Consortium worked with many other organizations to advocate for changes to ameliorate the harshest of the provisions. The Consortium's affiliates and community partners helped to set priorities based upon which people were the most vulnerable and whom they would not be able to cover with state and local programs. The Consortium's affiliates and community partners helped to identify and document individual cases. Some of the cases became the foundation of local litigation challenging the constitutionality of the welfare-law provisions. The Consortium worked with other national organizations to plan litigation and with its affiliates to frame the litigation to support ongoing public education and advocacy efforts.

The litigation was not successful in legal terms, but contributed to the success of the larger campaign by serving as an organizing and media vehicle. The national legislative work resulted in significant repeals of the worst of the provisions. The local work also encouraged some state and local programs to help cover the gaps in federal coverage.

Bigin, New Boys, Beniko, Balmara, Ms. Tops and Topson Downs——were joint employers of the workers, and, as such, violated state and federal laws and acted negligently, thus making themselves liable for paying substantial damages to the exploited workers. Plaintiffs also claimed that the corporate defendants were the alter egos of the sweatshop operators. They alleged negligence against the corporate defendants and violation of the "hot-goods" provision of the Fair Labor Standards Act (FLSA).[32] The hot-goods provision prohibits the sale, transport and shipment of goods made in violation of the minimum wage and overtime regulations of the FLSA.

The BUREERONG case survived several motions to dismiss and thus established important new legal precedent. In its first decision, the district court allowed plaintiffs to move forward on claims of joint employer and negligence claims. The court held that with proof of sufficient control by manufacturers and retailers, corporate defendants can be deemed joint employers of workers, notwithstanding formal arrangements to the contrary.[33] In a second opinion, in April 1997, the district court held that the corporate defendants could, upon proof of the allegations against them, be held liable not only for wage violations, but for involuntary servitude and other violations by their so-called contractors.[34]

The court also held the manufacturers and retailers could be held liable under the hot-goods provision of the FLSA.[35] Significantly, the hot-goods prohibition applies whether or not the manufacturers and retailers designed, created, ordered or oversaw the production of the garments. Even if the defendant is a mere retailer, it is still liable if it ships or sells goods made under sweatshop conditions. This case is the first use by sweatshop victims of the hot-goods law, which could develop into a powerful tool for exploited garment workers.[36]

The lawyers' investigation revealed that the manufacturers and retailers had taken minimal steps, if any, to ensure that their clothes were made in legal, humane conditions. Indeed, they seemed to have looked the other way when given indications of abusive conditions. While two defendants declared bankruptcy, several others ultimately agreed to settle out of court for more than $4 million in compensation to the plaintiffs.

BROADENING THE PARADIGM OF SOCIAL JUSTICE

Stewart Kwoh of APALC explains, "we use civil rights broadly defined." He notes that it's no accident that an overwhelming majority of exploited garment-industry workers are both immigrants and women.[37] Sixty-seven of the 71 workers rescued from El Monte were women. Su suggests that the garment workers' situation demands a new legal paradigm of justice. The struggle should not be subdivided into narrow categories of immigrant rights, civil rights or workers rights, according to Su. The Thai workers situation made palpable the many different forms of exploitation and abuse faced by garment workers.[38] The mistreated laborers, in fact, embody many of the characteristics of almost every disaffected group in U.S. society: women of color, the poor, non-English-speaking immigrants and

32 Third Amended Complaint, 1996.

33 922 F. Supp. 1450.

34 959 F. Supp. 1231 (C.D. Calif. 1997).

35 Ibid.

36 Court decisions have held that the hot-goods provision can be used only if the garments have not yet left the factory, making this remedy a valuable, but limited tool. In this case, unshipped goods were seized in the raid.

37 P. Hair interview with Stewart Kwoh, July 24, 1997.

38 "Invisible," at 412.

39 Ibid. (footnote omitted).

40 See, worker interviews, supra.

workers. The case was more than a traditional civil rights enforcement effort. It was nothing less than an effort to enable the workers to regain their humanity and a sense of their place in a just society.[39]

Worker-Guided Representation

One former El Monte worker described the interdependent role of the lawyers and the clients in the case: "It's like a boat. Everybody has to help each other if we are to paddle forward. You can't just sit and have others paddle for you. Everybody has to do the work."[40]

One of APALC's major goals was to ensure that the workers' voice drove the lawsuit. APALC had to teach the workers about the legal system and the garment industry to accomplish this goal. During the first eight months, Su spent long nights in individual workers' homes explaining the basics, such as what it means to bring a lawsuit, what a civil suit is and why so much paperwork is involved. She also explained the structure of the garment industry and took the workers to retail stores so they could see the high prices charged for clothes that they were paid only pennies to make.

Getting to know each other and developing trust was an important outcome of the advocates' visits with workers in their homes. Early on, before the workers could speak English, Su would just come and be there with them. She reports: "Sometimes they would bring me pictures of their children back in Thailand who they had not seen or communicated with in years. They couldn't tell me how much they missed the children, so they just cried and cried."[41]

41 P. Hair interview with Julie Su, May 28, 1999 (hereinafter, Su interview, May 1999).

Education about the law and litigation strategy was woven into the life-skills training. The lawyers even developed games to help the workers understand their rights. In one game, teams of workers raced with each other to answer questions such as: Even if you are paid by the piece, you still have a right to the minimum wage, True or False?

The workers continuously came to court, participated in monthly meetings and considered settlement offers. They also answered the discovery, attended the mediation and played a part in every major decision. The defendants posed pages of questions, or interrogatories, asking almost minute details. The lawyers suspected that the mass of tedious discovery was intended to wear down the workers. Of course, the workers could not remember exact dates and times of events during an imprisonment of several years. Su interviewed the workers individually in preparing responses to these interrogatories. The workers gave answers that were far better than anything the lawyers could have come up with alone. When asked the dates on which she had sewn the defendants' clothes, one worker answered: "I can't remember the exact date. But I will tell you that in my dreams I still see your garments, and I still see your label."[42]

42 Su interview, June 1998.

Lawyers for the garment-industry defendants sometimes suggested that because her clients were poor, Su should accept their settlement offers on the spot. But, Su would tell them, I've got 100 people to consult. She would call a meeting, and within 24 hours the workers would meet and make decisions that were completely their own. While some cynics believed that the workers were just after money, the workers rejected monetary settlement offers. At one meeting they stated, "We don't want to be bought out." They decided that to keep fighting would create publicity and make the garment industry better for others in the future.[43]

[43] Su interview, March 1999.

Although the Latina workers were not enslaved, they suffered other abuses and shared in the financial distribution from the lawsuit settlements. The Thai and Latina workers together designed the formula for dividing the cash settlement among the 102 plaintiffs.[44] Each worker's share is based on the length of time that he or she worked at one of the facilities, as well as their contribution to, and length of time involved in, the case.

[44] The plaintiffs consist of 71 Thai workers from the raid, nine who had escaped and 22 Latina workers.

Su spoke to the workers as peers. She didn't refer to them as clients, feeling that the word depersonalized them and placed them in a dependent relationship: "As clients, the relationship is defined by my education and skills as their lawyer. Instead, by referring to them as workers, their experiences defined our work together," she says. "For many people, when language is framed as law, I have seen an immediate shift in their willingness to engage in the dialogue; many people think the discussion is suddenly taking place in a language they do not and cannot understand. What workers do understand is a language of human dignity....Human dignity must be the measure of what we recognize as legal rights."[45]

Su stresses the need to let people speak for themselves. "The workers will often ask me to tell their story for them," she says, "both because I can tell it in English and because they believe my knowledge of the law instills in me instant efficacy as a spokesperson. However, they are wrong. When I listen to them tell their stories in their own language, listen to them describe their suffering, their pain, their hope through the long, dark days, they become poetic and strong. We, as lawyers and advocates, must always encourage those who have lived the experiences to tell them, in whatever language they speak."[46]

[45] "Invisible," at 412.

[46] Ibid.

The lawyers structured the representation so that the workers would benefit from their active participation in the process, regardless of the ultimate outcome. One of the positive outcomes is the workers' willingness to continue to fight for garment-industry reform even after the case was over. The workers experienced personal and interpersonal changes, but also the building of an activist consciousness so important for social-change work. Su explains: "If you're a client in a case and you sit and wait for a result, you'll never achieve that kind of transformation."[47]

[47] Su interview, May 1999.

Su points out that the criminal justice system is not structured to facilitate the interests of the victims of crimes such as the El Monte enslavement. Because the workers were key witnesses in the criminal case, the prosecutors at the U.S. Attorney's Office warned them not to speak out about the abuses they had endured. While such a restriction may make sense in the context of a criminal prosecution, it served to silence—in fact, make invisible again—the exploited Thai workers at a time when their own voices needed to be heard.

The criminal law's narrow focus on a court proceeding to punish the operators who mistreated the workers conflicted with the larger objective of giving subjugated laborers greater control over their own lives.[48]

Su's relationship with the workers shatters traditional notions of professional and personal boundaries. Su and the workers are friends in the deepest sense. The workers even took charge of Su's wedding on August 2, 1998, the third anniversary of their release from El Monte. They chose her dress, served as her attendants, and incorporated Thai and Chinese cultural traditions into the occasion. Su comments: "So many people said you can't get that close and still be a strong advocate. I've been as strong as I have *because* of that closeness."[49]

BUILDING AN EFFECTIVE COALITION

The El Monte case offered a unique opportunity to build a strong coalition between Asians and Latinos, the two major ethnic groups that have been exploited in the garment industry. There were undeniable obstacles in the process. The structure of the industry itself creates division between groups at the bottom of the pyramid. The Asian and Latina women tend to have little understanding of each other's cultural backgrounds. Oftentimes the operators, who are exploitative and abusive, are Asian, and thus many Latina workers view Asians not just as strangers but as enemies and the source of endless subjugation.[50] Su explained: "Asians and Latinos suffer similar exploitation in the underworld of American garment-industry sweatshops. They often labor side by side, where their inability to talk to each other, given their language differences and the daily indignities they suffer, make them shy away from contact, at best, and hate each other, at worst."[51]

Occasionally, racial tensions led to misplaced anger. Su recalls that after a particularly difficult meeting, one Latina worker finally admitted that shouting at Su and the Thai workers was just like yelling at her supervisor. Su says, "I told her she needed to just get over that; that if she had problems with me or something I was doing, I needed to hear it, but if she wanted me to answer for all the pain and indignities she suffered from Asian faces, I would not be her punching bag."[52]

[48] "Invisible," at 408-409.

[49] Su interview, May 1999.

[50] Su interview, June 1998.

[51] Ibid.

[52] Ibid.

Signing a consent decree (above): The El Monte workers participated in every aspect of the lawsuit against the garment manufacturers—responding to discovery, fashioning a settlement and talking to the media. A group of Latina garment workers from the manufacturers' downtown sweatshops heard about the lawsuit through the media and joined as plaintiffs.

Su readily admits that she made mistakes while learning to relate to the workers. Once, when she used a Spanish-language dictionary to try to speak to the workers, a Latina worker commented, "Oh, that's just like what our *patrones* do." Then and there, Su recalls, she discarded the dictionary and if she couldn't think of the appropriate Spanish words, she would gesture, use 50 words, even make a drawing of what she was trying to describe, anything but use that dictionary.[53]

Outside forces also exacerbated the tensions between the workers. Some government agencies, Su believes, were seeking credit and good publicity for helping enslaved Thai workers, and thus excluded Latina workers from any of their services.[54] The media often ignored the Latina workers completely. Su notes: "In one instance, a major Spanish-language paper ran a front-page article about the case and failed to mention the Latina workers at all, even though I had spoken to the reporter for about 40 minutes emphasizing the importance of the cross-racial alliance. The morning that article came out, there was no mistaking the 10 angry faces of Latina workers in my office who blamed me for the oversight."[55]

[53] Ibid.

[54] Ibid.

[55] Ibid.

In spite of setbacks, the Asian and Latina workers managed to create a strong and effective partnership over time. The workers came together often in advocacy projects, to plan presentations, pass out leaflets and speak to other garment workers and the general public about their experiences. Often the meetings felt interminable because every word had to be translated into Thai, English and Spanish. Ultimately, they realized that by working together they had far more power to demand corporate accountability, to expect just treatment and to affect change than if they worked separately.

[56] "Invisible," at 411.

Su described a transformative moment in the relationship between the Asian and Latina workers: "A Thai worker says in Thai, 'We are so grateful finally to be free so we can stand alongside you and to struggle with you, to make better lives for us all,' and her words are translated from Thai into English, then from English into Spanish. At the moment when comprehension washed over the faces of the Latina workers, a light of understanding went on in their eyes, and they began to nod their heads slowly in agreement, and you could feel the depth of that connection."[56]

Beating the odds: The lawsuit established new rules for manufacturers who subcontract work, prompted passage of stronger state protections for low-wage workers and immigrants, and spurred enactment of the federal Trafficking Victims Protection Act of 2000, an effort to combat modern-day slavery. Attorney Julie Su (pictured right, above) with workers.

MEDIA STRATEGIES

Given the sensational nature of the El Monte story, it grabbed the media's attention from the start. The coalition took advantage of this and did its best to keep the media on the story in order to keep pressure on government officials and the corporate actors.

The coalition also used the El Monte case as a way of discussing the overall problems in the garment industry. The media subsequently began breaking other major stories, including ones on the sweatshop that produced clothing with Kathy Lee's label and the Disney sweatshop in Haiti.

The advocates attempted, with only partial success, to influence the way the media covered the story. "Reporters tended to focus on isolated 'heroes' and nameless 'victims'," says Su, "obscuring the fact that these are real human beings engaged in making change and winning control of their lives. When the workers were first discovered, the news media referred to them as Thai nationals or illegal immigrants. We insisted on calling them workers, thus shifting the focus from their immigration status to their experiences in the United States in the garment industry."[57]

The media also were reluctant to report on the broad coalition that had been established to support the workers or on the role of the Latina workers. "While racial discord between communities of color is newsworthy, particularly in Los Angeles, interracial solidarity is not," laments Su. The Latina workers have thus remained largely invisible to the public.[58]

Epilogue—The Anti-Sweatshop Movement Continues

The anti-sweatshop movement has been built gradually through the painstaking investment of time and resources by many workers and activists, including labor unions, religious organizations and human-rights entities. El Monte stands out because the exploitation was a particularly egregious form to occur within the United States, and the lawyers and the workers made courageous decisions that maximized the impact of El Monte as a catalyst for change. "Many people see El Monte as freeing slaves. It's really about pushing for institutional change," says Su.[59]

BROADER IMPLICATIONS

The El Monte precedent, holding corporations liable for violations of the law committed by their so-called "independent contractors," could have much wider significance. Corporations increasingly cut costs by using independent contractors for work that formerly would have been performed by employees. In this way they avoid the responsibility and costs associated with providing benefits, such as health insurance, as well as the coverage of labor and civil rights laws triggered by employee status. The BUREERONG precedent suggests that with the appropriate factual showing, the corporate veil may be pierced in other exploitative circumstances, resulting in great improvement in the condition of workers.[60] Recent litigation against the tobacco industry and gun manufacturers is another variation on the theme of

[57] Ibid., at 416.

[58] Ibid., at 414.

[59] Su interview, June 1999.

[60] For example, Microsoft has been held liable for improperly treating long-term temporary employees as independent contractors. See, Richard Carelli, **Associated Press**, Jan. 10, 2000.

holding the entities that reap huge profits liable for a larger share of the negative consequences their businesses produce.

[61] Interview with Julie Su, Dec. 3, 1999.

The legal precedent and the decision of the El Monte workers to speak out have provided
momentum to an ongoing international movement to eliminate the use of sweatshop labor. In
response to El Monte, the DOJ improved its enforcement efforts and formed an anti-enslave-
ment task force that has dealt with other similar situations that have come to light. Media
coverage also has improved. Su reports: "Now when corporations are linked to sweatshop
labor practices, it makes the news. Five years ago that would never have happened."[61]

An example of the growing strength of the movement is the mobilization of students across
the country who have demonstrated, boycotted and taken over campus buildings to force
universities to be accountable for the labor practices of the manufacturers that provide col-
lege-label clothing. The University of California and other universities have adopted new
policies on monitoring their apparel suppliers, and many companies are now agreeing to
disclose their factory locations. Multinational companies increasingly are adopting codes of
conduct to avoid a negative public image.

[62] Ibid.

The activists and workers involved in the El Monte case have continued their advocacy. In
1999, one of the former El Monte prisoners testified before a California Assembly committee in favor of a bill that would require manufacturers and retailers to guarantee the wages
of garment workers. Su met with legislators, industry representatives and elected officials to
discuss the need for such legislation. Her role in El Monte
enhanced her credibility. The bill was enacted, although it
provides for enforcement of wage guarantees through
administrative proceedings rather than a lawsuit.

Julie Su sums up: "Those involved in El Monte have given
other [exploited] workers the courage to step forward and
activists the consciousness to rise up."[62]

*Advocates created games to teach life skills that helped the workers function in an urban environment. They also learned
about workers' rights and other issues to help them avoid exploitative situations in the future.*

Chapter

3

Siezing a Voice in Democracy

In the 1950s, blacks in Mississippi faced certain intimidation and violence for trying to register to vote. As a result, the state with the largest black population had the fewest registered black voters. In 1963, the Council of Federated Organizations (COFO) held a mock "freedom election" in which 93,000 blacks cast practice ballots. The following year, over 80,000 people registered to vote during Freedom Summer (right).

In the Mississippi Delta, over the past 10 years African-American community groups, with the help of Southern Echo, a grassroots group whose organizers have decades of experience, waged a quiet revolution. Building on indefatigable community organizing, a true partnership of grassroots activists and community-focused lawyers mounted a highly successful redistricting campaign on the local, state and congressional level. It resulted in the election of record numbers of African-Americans to office and a greater level of accountability by elected officials. Their success has inspired the black community and is the catalyst for new efforts by African-Americans to use the democratic process to address pressing problems in education, housing and quality of life.

Chapter 3
Seizing a Voice in Democracy:
The Mississippi Redistricting Campaign

Key Lessons Learned

- Support client groups' opportunities to make their own decisions, participate in policymaking, and work interactively with lawyers and experts, as well as governmental officials.

- Build communities' understanding of the legal process as a means of increasing capacity and confidence among politically marginalized people.

- Improve policy outcomes by joining community-based knowledge or "lived experience" with legal expertise.

- Devise strategies to sustain the community's energy and participation during a prolonged litigation process.

In the 1990s, fear of reprisals continued to suppress black political participation in Mississippi. Southern Echo's redistricting education workshops (left) helped local residents address their fear and explore how voting and better political representation could help them further their policy goals.

To actively participate in the redistricting process, community activists educated themselves about the politics and history of redistricting, and learned how to analyze data and draw district lines (above). Residents worked with attorneys to propose state legislative-redistricting plans based on a detailed knowledge of local communities. The coherence of the majority African-American districts ultimately helped Mississippi avoid federal legal challenges.

Overview

In 1955, Emmett Till, a 16-year-old African-American visiting Tallahatchie County, Mississippi, from Chicago, was kidnapped and lynched by whites, his body thrown in the Tallahachie River. His only crime: glancing at a white woman. An all-white jury acquitted Till's murderers.

Improvements in the culture of racism have come very, very slowly in the Mississippi Delta. In 1992, 37 years after Till's murder, meaningful democratic participation remained an elusive dream for Tallahatchie's African-American citizens, who comprised 59 percent of its population. No African-American had ever been elected to the powerful Board of Supervisors or to any other countywide office.

Such lack of representation hit home for the county's low-income residents, who rank among the poorest in the country. The white plantation owners who controlled the Board of Supervisors seemed content to keep out the kind of economic growth that creates jobs and might draw African-Americans out of the cotton fields and catfish factories, the main source of employment in the area. Because the all-white Board of Supervisors had consistently refused to approve the county's participation in federal programs to build low-income housing in the community, poor residents continued to live in rundown shacks and grossly overcrowded apartments. In fact, Tallahatchie had experienced little development of any kind for decades.

But by 1998, the racial barriers in Tallahatchie County had diminished a bit and were being challenged in many other parts of the Delta. In just six years, since the Board of Supervisors ceased blocking federal low-income housing initiatives, Tallahatchie Housing has built 230 units of badly needed housing in Mississippi Delta. Vice President Gore and other dignitaries have streamed into Tallahatchie County to study the extraordinary work of Tallahatchie Housing, the county's first nonprofit housing organization—created and led by African-Americans. Among those presiding at the November 1998 dedication of a modern, federally funded housing complex with 33 ranch-style single-story homes in the heavily African-American western part of the county, was Jerome Little, Tallahatchie's first African-American supervisor.

In a very real sense, the Tallahatchie County housing development is a result of the African-American community's success in gaining the vote and holding its elected represen-tatives accountable. Tallahatchie County is an example of a successful statewide campaign to use redistricting and the Voting Rights Act as the centerpiece of a long-term effort to enable African-Americans to participate meaningfully in democratic governance. Under the leadership of Southern Echo, a civil rights organization created in 1989 by three veteran Mississippi organizers, African-Americans across the Delta have overcome fear and gained the knowledge and skills needed to exercise their democratic muscle.

Litigation to enforce the Voting Rights Act was an essential element of this campaign. But the role of lawyers was broader than handling court cases. A group of local attorneys served as integral partners with African-American residents, participating in community organizing, developing training materials and advising during negotiations. The effort produced extraordinary success at the polls. In 1993, after settlement of a Voting Rights Act lawsuit, two African-Americans took seats for the first time on the five-member Board of Supervisors.

THE MISSISSIPPI DELTA: A CULTURE OF DEEP POVERTY ROOTED IN RACISM

The Deep South remains America's poorest region, and the Mississippi Delta is the poorest part of that region. According to the 1990 census, three Delta counties—Tallahatchie, Tunica and Holmes—are among the 10 poorest counties in the United States. Poor people still live on plantations and the Delta is an area where racism is deeply institutionalized and continues to permeate virtually every aspect of life.

African-Americans represent 37 percent of the residents of Mississippi, the highest proportion of any state in the union. Yet currently, the governor and both U.S. senators are white, as are four of the five members of the House of Representatives. The only African-American member of U.S. Congress from Mississippi is Bennie Thompson, whose district includes most of the Delta region.

The Voting Rights Act of 1965 brought a substantial increase in the number of African-Americans registered to vote and routinely voting. But, in response, the white political structure created a variety of barriers to keep black Mississippians from effectively exercising their franchise, including gerrymandering, runoff primaries, and outright fraud and intimidation. There were myriad ways to discourage, even waylay, a voter. For instance, when it looked like an African-American might have a real chance of winning an election, the owners of one local catfish farm reportedly put their predominantly African-American workers on overtime. The fear of retaliation if they left the workplace discouraged most of the employees from heading to the polls.

SOUTHERN ECHO: A SUSTAINABLE MODEL FOR COMMUNITY ORGANIZING

Southern Echo has been a principal catalyst in the African-American community's successful effort to assert its democratic voice. Echo was founded to help Mississippi communities make the political, economic, environmental and educational systems accountable to the needs and interests of African-Americans. Founding members Hollis Watkins, Leroy Johnson and Michael Sayer are all longtime activists and community organizers in Mississippi. Sayer is also an attorney. Watkins and Johnson are African-American; Sayer is white.

Echo's leaders are determined to build on their experiences in the civil rights movement of the 1960s, while not limiting themselves to past strategies. Watkins notes that many of the students who came during "Freedom Summer" were young and energetic, with a natural tendency to get things done, but too often they did the work for the community, with the result that they left nothing sustainable behind. Echo's goal is to give community members the tools they need to do the work themselves, thus achieving sustainability in local organizing and in the initiatives such organizing creates.

Southern Echo also believes that the civil rights movement dissipated energy and creativity by fracturing people along age lines with separate programs and initiatives for youth and for old folks. In its own organizing efforts, Southern Echo draws no age distinctions. Young people, only 11 and 12 years of age, participate fully, and some even sit on Echo's Board of Directors.

The Mississippi Delta is a stretch of heavily African-American counties, in central and western Mississippi, bordered by the Mississippi River on the west.

The journal entries below set out the observations and information gathered by the author of this Report upon her first visit.

Penda Hair's Mississippi Journal,

Some folks call the Mississippi Delta "the land the civil rights movement passed over." Actually, the Delta was one of the epicenters of the civil rights movement. The movement didn't pass over the Delta; the entrenched opposition was just stronger.

Drew Municipal School District in Sunflower County, one of the strongholds of voting activism in the 1960s: A student at Hunter Middle School in Drew, Mississippi, who needs to go to the bathroom first has to stop by the principal's office to ask for toilet paper. Sometimes the keeper of the toilet paper will give a student only one tiny square. When a 12-year-old girl recently asked for toilet paper, the response was, "What are you going to do with it?" A joking retort would have earned the young woman a multiday suspension, if not expulsion. Parents complain that the children are suffering from trying to hold their water to avoid the humiliating experience of going to the restroom.

Talking is prohibited in the middle-school cafeteria during lunch. Violating this rule can earn a student "five licks," the common punishment for "insubordination" or "defiance of authority." This is not a gentle paddling; parents and community leaders report that the children are being "beaten." Teachers place notches in their paddles to commemorate the beatings. Students are continuously disciplined for "defiance of authority," which covers conduct as innocent as asking questions in class.

Kindergartners at the E. W. James Elementary School down the street often are given only five minutes to eat lunch. Parents who barely scrape together the 75 cents lunch money watch in horror as food their children didn't have time to eat is scraped into the trash.

The parents who get to watch are fortunate. Most parents are never able to observe the lunch hour or any other aspect of their children's educational experience. The public schools in Drew require that a parent receive permission 24 hours in advance to visit to the child's school. Parents without advance permission are stopped at the principal's office.

Last February, Black History Month, one history teacher in Drew put up a picture of Hitler in the middle of the bulletin board outside her room. Everyone passing through the school walked by it.

No teacher at Drew teaches black history as part of the regular curriculum. Some teachers allow students to do research projects on black history for extra credit. The teacher with the Hitler bulletin board will not give the students credit for anything on black history. Her response is that all she cares about is "American history."

Echo's staff members reside all over the Delta. The organization endures this administrative inconvenience in order to keep leaders rooted in local communities. Echo believes that the 1960s civil rights movement took too many leaders and talented organizers—such as Fannie Lou Hammer of Sunflower County—away from their home base. This ultimately undermined long-term sustainability.

October 1998

On the highway—Holmes, Sunflower, Tallahatchie Counties: This is cotton country. The big farms are called "plantations" by everyone, black and white. Cotton fields line both sides of the road, dotted by the occasional cotton gin (usually in one of a rusted collection of buildings close to the road) and clusters of plantation cabins, called shotgun houses, for farm workers. Each plantation seems to have six or so identical shotgun houses for workers, standing in a row in the middle of cotton fields. Occasionally the "big house" of the plantation owner is visible. Those are usually white clapboard or brick, spacious and comfortable and very distinct from the tiny, ramshackle cabins for farm workers.

The terrain is flat. We drive past miles and miles of flat farmland, the vastness of it overwhelming, spreading in all directions. All this land, still owned by white people. And still worked by black people. About the only traditional word that isn't spoken in the Delta anymore is "slave." African-Americans in the Delta are not called slaves anymore, but they are surely not free.

They closed all the public parks in this part of Mississippi in the 1960s, rather than desegregate them. They opened private parks for the white residents. Today, in most counties in the Mississippi Delta, there are no parks or recreational facilities for African-Americans, who comprise about 65 percent of the area's residents. No ball fields for middle-school students. No swing sets, monkey bars or sandboxes for the smaller children. In the summer when the public schools close their playgrounds, the children have nowhere to play.

Tunica County (one county northwest of Tallahatchie): All up and down the Mississippi River each county has its private school—"segregation academies" for whites only. In Tunica County, a local church raises money for scholarships, so poor white students can attend the local academy, Tunica Institute for Learning. The Tunica County public schools are 98 percent African-American.

Tunica County has a population of around 8,000, of whom about 76 percent are African-Americans. Until the casinos came in 1992, Tunica was the second poorest county in the United States. When we drive through the blacktop driveway leading to Tunica High School our guide tells us that it is homecoming weekend. African-American teenagers are outside, working intently on floats for the parade. Colorful paper and streamers combine with the sunny day to create a festive atmosphere.

Inside the limits of Tunica City (the only incorporated town in Tunica County) is the white area. We turn off the main highway into "white sub," the commonly-used name by everyone, black and white, for the small subdivision where the white

MISSISSIPPI'S VOTING-RIGHTS PROGRESS AND POTENTIAL

Despite enactment of the Voting Rights Act in 1965, Mississippi fought African-American political participation every step of the way, with hostile courts, official defiance, and widespread violence and intimidation. Many were murdered simply for attempting to register and vote or for encouraging others to do so; bombings, fires and cross-burnings all were common. There was virtually no black representation in the Mississippi Legislature (or in other offices) until breakthrough victories in the 1979 elections—15 years after the Voting Rights Act. That year the U.S. Supreme Court finally forced a hostile local three-judge district court

Mississippi Journal, (cont.)

folks live. White sub is a pleasant, shady contrast to the relentless cotton fields. White sub has wide tree-lined streets with neat lawns and sidewalks. At the end of one street, closest to the elementary school, are some smaller houses. The main street dissecting white sub is called "School Road," ending at the elementary school. This used to be the white elementary school, but now it is 99 percent black. A couple of blocks before you reach the elementary school, School Road is bisected by "Academy Road," which leads to TIL (Tunica Institute for Learning). Noticing that the word "Academy" doesn't appear in the name of TIL, I wonder why they just didn't name the street "Segregation Academy Road." The academy is housed in a neat brick building, surrounded by a football/soccer field in front and a baseball field and playground in the rear.

A large bell sits on a pedestal a few feet in front of the entrance to TIL. "That's a plantation bell," our guide notes. "They rang these bells on the plantations to tell the slaves when to start working and when they could stop, to eat, for example. Now, the academy rings it in the opening ceremony at the beginning of each school year."

The "black sub" is just over the city line. The city line is most ingenuously drawn to include all the white residences and none of the black residences. The city limits have been stretched out to incorporate the airport, via a narrow tentacle running down the middle of a street, but excluding the residences alongside the street. Black sub is a collection of ramshackle houses sitting in the middle of a field, crisscrossed by a few narrow, treeless streets.

The "growth" industries in this part of Mississippi are casinos and prisons. In Tallahatchie County they have landed a new private prison.

Tallahatchie County—a ray of progress: The small housing development sits beside the main highway, a monotonous road lined on both sides by miles and miles of cottonfields. The Old South seems incarnate in the few wisps of white fluff still floating around the rows of barren plants this late in the fall. But at this complex, which Jerome Little calls his "jewel," everything looks new, even the churned-up mud from the just-completed construction. These apartments would seem ordinary to most Americans. Clean, bright and safe, but not grand or luxurious. But in this part of Mississippi, these stacks of bricks and mortar, of picture windows overlooking flower-lined walkways, represent more than just decent, affordable housing for the elderly. Rising out of the flat, unending cotton fields like an oasis, they provide a glimmer of what Mississippi

to adopt a legislative redistricting plan with black-majority districts.[1] There was no black congressional representation in Mississippi until 1986. Again, the creation of the first black-majority district came about only after the Supreme Court invalidated the Legislature's 1980 redistricting plan.

Persistent enforcement and litigation by national civil rights groups in partnership with local practitioners, as well as the Department of Justice, brought a significant increase in local African-American office-holding during 1980. Several additional African-Americans won seats in the Legislature, as well. But the momentum of community organizers began to slow under the false belief that sustained citizen involvement was no longer needed once a number of African-Americans were in office. By the late 1980s, even with a considerable number of African-Americans in office in Mississippi, the African-American community was still without a strong voice. There were not enough black elected officials to exercise real power. In addition, some African-American elected officials were not accountable to the needs and interests of the black community.[2]

In light of these problems, Southern Echo identified redistricting as the organizing focus to generate the broad grassroots participation sparked by segregation earlier in the century. Every 10 years, after the U.S. Census, voting districts at the local, state and congressional levels are redrawn ("redistricted") to reflect population shifts and to comply with the constitutional requirement of "one person, one vote." The issue could inspire large numbers of black Mississippians, Echo thought, since it might enable them to gain political power to address inequitable access to housing, jobs and education.

Redistricting in the 1990s

The challenges of organizing in the Mississippi Delta were daunting. Southern Echo's Executive Director, Leroy Johnson, says "fear is the first and the deepest obstacle."[3] White plantation owners still ruled with an iron fist, even dominating local school boards where the students were 100 percent black. African-Americans participating in organized political activity could lose their jobs, have bank loans suddenly called in and be evicted from their housing. Johnson says the climate of fear among African-Americans was oppressive. "It held them back from working against injustice even when they could succeed. The fear was so heavy, you could feel it, grab it, hold onto it."[4]

At the beginning of the redistricting campaign, Southern Echo staff spent considerable time analyzing this fear. They concluded that the first tangible step in overcoming it would be for African-Americans to come together across county lines. Stemming from the history of slavery, when leaving the plantation could result in immediate death, African-Americans in the Delta feared traveling away from home. Johnson says that "community leaders needed to break out of the culture of county lines."[5] Echo also recognized that they would have to organize across county lines to participate effectively in redistricting of the state Legislature.

[1] Connor v. Finch, 431 U.S. 407(1977). For example, the three-judge federal court presiding over the litigation addressing the 1970-1980 round of redistricting included Fifth Circuit Judge J. P. Coleman, who had served as governor of Mississippi from 1956-1960 after running as a strong segregationist and promising to oppose all federal intervention in Mississippi, as well as District Judge Harold Cox, well-known for his anti-civil-rights rulings. See, Frank R. Parker, Black Votes Count (University of North Carolina Press, 1990), at 83-85.

[2] See, Madeline Adamson, "Drawing the Lines," in Politics Unusual, a report from the Applied Research Center (1996), at 42.

[3] P. Hair interview with Leroy Johnson, Oct. 18, 1998.

[4] Ibid.

[5] Ibid.

Southern Echo began its redistricting education effort in 1990 with a series of community meetings. The meetings led to a large black turnout at the first public hearings held by the Joint Standing Committee on Legislative and Congressional Reapportionment. Also in 1990, a coalition of attorneys who had been active in redistricting work in the past formed the Mississippi Redistricting Coalition (MRC) as a vehicle "to change the way redistricting work was done" in Mississippi.[6] Southern Echo, Mississippi Legal Services, the Center for Constitutional Rights and other organizations became involved in MRC. Two lawyers, Echo's Mike Sayer and Carroll Rhodes, a private practitioner based in Jackson, played key leadership roles in MRC, working side by side with community residents, historian and demographer Henry Kirksey, and Echo's Hollis Watkins. Under their leadership, the MRC involved communities in the redistricting process, mobilizing hundreds of concerned citizens to attend meetings of the Legislature's Joint Committee on Legislative Reapportionment beginning in the fall of 1990. The momentum continued in 1991 with a series of 12 workshops, covering 25 counties, jointly convened by Southern Echo, MRC, Rural Organizing and Culture Center (Holmes County), and Mississippi Action for Community Education (MACE). The workshops brought in residents from other counties, but sites were selected so that no one had to travel for more than an hour.

An initial task was helping community members to see redistricting and voting as a pathway toward their substantive goals—better housing, jobs and education. Community members did their own analysis, thinking through the reasons why past reform had failed. When the residents concluded that "the Board of Supervisors would not approve low-income housing construction" or "the Board would not pursue economic development," the linkage had been made.

Echo also devoted effort at the outset to conflict resolution between persons and organizations in local communities. Tallahatchie County presented a particularly difficult challenge. Turf tensions among local organizations made the leaders pessimistic that the cooperation needed for successful redistricting efforts would be attainable. Echo interpreted it as a manifestation of "a culture of powerlessness." "Whatever little turf a group may have becomes overwhelmingly important to them."[7]

ACCOUNTABILITY: PUTTING COMMUNITY INTEREST OVER SELF-INTEREST

Echo hammered away at the concept of accountability, which it defined as putting the community's interest over self-interest. This simple, but demanding, principle took hold and helped overcome the resistance to collaboration. Echo also suggested the novel idea of creating a temporary organization for the redistricting campaign, which removed the necessity of identifying a single existing organization and prevented the infighting over credit for successes. All three of Tallahatchie's rival organizations agreed to participate in the newly formed Tallahatchie County Redistricting Committee.

AFRICAN-AMERICANS ENGAGED IN THE REDISTRICTING PROCESS

In workshops throughout the state, community residents learned about the politics and history of redistricting, as well as the tactics that have been used to prevent African-Americans from obtaining real representation. They also gained practical skills like data analysis and how to draw district lines. Considerable attention was paid to understanding legal standards and requirements of the Voting Rights Act. Their lawyers helped prepare the training materials and participated in the workshops. Traditionally, the redistricting process had been considered the domain of the county supervisors, state legislators and the lawyers who did battle with them. Now, African-American communities at the grassroots level were getting involved, learning the laws and regulations and beginning to participate in the redistricting process.

Whites in Mississippi, as well as many other places in the United States, tend not to vote for African-American candidates. This "racial-bloc voting" can operate to allow a white majority to cancel out all political power of a racial minority. To address this problem, the Voting Rights Act can require that districts be created in which racially marginalized groups have a fair chance to elect representatives of their choice. Mississippi's African-American voting population is poorer, less well-educated and subject to intimidation in voting—all factors that tend to suppress voting numbers. In these circumstances, voting-rights districts typically have required an African-American population in the vicinity of 65 percent to be "electable." The Mississippi Redistricting Coalition (MRC) adopted the goal of creating as many "electable" districts as possible, given the population and demographics of the state.

REDISTRICTING THE STATE LEGISLATURE

In the MRC, African-Americans from many counties came together around five demands made to the Joint Committee. Under intense pressure from the communities, the Joint Committee agreed that: 1) the state was obligated under the Voting Rights Act to create electable African-American districts where possible; 2) the Committee would appoint an African-American to serve as one of its attorneys (resulting in the appointment of Reuban Anderson, who had served as the first African-American on the State Supreme Court); and 3) the public would have access to the Committee's computers and databases, enabling community members to use the sophisticated mapping technology and census information to propose districts and analyze proposals made by others.[8] The Joint Committee's acceptance of three of the five demands gave the MRC legitimacy, recognizing for the first time in the state's history African-Americans' right to active involvement in the districting process.

The mobilization of large numbers of their constituents also served as a wake-up call to African-American legislators. While incumbents often focus their energies during redistricting on preserving their own seats, African-American residents of the Delta demanded that the members of the Legislative Black Caucus support three crucial MRC principles:

[8] The Joint Committee rejected demands that the Committee size be increased to permit the addition of African-American members, and that the Committee hire African-American demographers with experience in working with African-American communities.

- Legislative seats belong to the people, not the officeholders;

- African-American legislators have all African-Americans in Mississippi as their constituents, not just those within their district lines; and

- The goal of redistricting is to create the maximum number of electable African-American districts.

Even with highly mobilized communities and a strongly supportive Legislative Black Caucus, MRC's efforts in the Joint Committee were not initially successful. The Committee rejected several MRC proposals and, in the spring of 1991, adopted a plan that offered minimal change and few new African-American seats. Because of Mississippi's history of discrimination against African-American political participation, the state was required to obtain approval (preclearance) of its plan by the U.S. Department of Justice (DOJ). Assisted by attorneys Rhodes and Sayer, Southern Echo and the MRC opposed preclearance and submitted evidence to DOJ. DOJ denied preclearance, finding that the 1991 Plan had been adopted with a discriminatory purpose.[9]

DOJ's denial of preclearance left the state with no districting plan for the 1991 elections. MRC had shown considerable political strength, but now it had to wage a legal fight. Soon after the Legislature adopted its 1991 plan, Hollis Watkins and a group of MRC members filed suit in federal court challenging the new plan, as well as the existing one which had been approved in 1982.[10] While the lawyers sparred in the courts,[11] efforts to convince the Legislature to adopt a plan that complied with the Voting Rights Act continued into 1992. When a heated battle over the selection of the speaker of the House arose in 1992, the Legislative Black Caucus held the balance of power between two Democratic contenders, one considered "progressive" and the other "conservative." The Legislative Black Caucus normally would have supported the candidate labeled as progressive. The MRC eschewed labels, however, and staked out a thoroughly pragmatic position. MRC supported the "conservative" candidate for speaker because he supported a districting plan that doubled the number of electable black districts. At the urging of the MRC, the Legislative Black Caucus used its "swing vote" leverage to elect the conservative speaker. The novel alliance, and political debts that came out of the vote for speaker, eventually led in 1992 to passage of a districting plan that created even *more* majority-black districts than a court would have ordered.[12] The court subsequently upheld the plan, and it was used for the first time in court-ordered 1992 special elections.[13]

After the Legislature adopted the plan, Rep. James Simpson, one of the deans of the Legislature and the author of the 1982 plan, sought out Watkins and Sayer to say: "I know when we started out this process, I didn't show you much respect. I, too, have learned a lot. Anytime you're down on the coast, you're welcome in my house."[14]

[9] Under Voting Rights Act standards at the time, preclearance would be denied if the voting change is either intentionally discriminatory or, regardless of intent, it worsens the position of a protected minority group ("retrogression").

[10] See, WATKINS V. MABUS, 771 F. Supp. 789 (S.D. Miss. 1991), aff'd. in part and vacated in part as moot, 502 U.S. 954 (1991).

[11] The court refused to enjoin the fall 1991 election and instead ordered the election to be held under the existing, 1982 districting plan. Ibid.

[12] See, WATKINS V. FORDICE, 807 F. Supp. 406, 411 (S.D. Miss. 1992).

[13] See, WATKINS V. FORDICE, 791 F. Supp. 646 (S.D. Miss. 1992), describing procedures for special elections.

[14] P. Hair interview with M. Sayer, Oct. 18, 1998.

REDISTRICTING AT THE CONGRESSIONAL LEVEL

In the 1980s, Mike Espy, an African-American, had been elected to represent Congressional District 2, encompassing a large part of the Mississippi Delta. When District 2 was to be redrawn, MRC sought an African-American voting-age population of 60 percent in order to solidify it as a district to advance African-American voters' preferences. The national Democratic Party and the AFL-CIO campaigned for a much lower African-American presence in this district—52 percent. They contended that spreading out black voters into other districts would increase the chance of electing Democrats from those districts.[15]

The districting process became a partisan issue. In Mississippi, like the rest of the United States, African-Americans are the Democratic Party's most loyal voters: 90 percent routinely vote for the Democratic candidate. Yet, the Democratic Party has often opposed African-American efforts to create districts from which their candidate has a good shot of getting elected. In the 1990s, Republicans, who sought to minimize Democratic voting strength, sometimes were more willing to support such districts than white Democrats.

African-Americans in the Mississippi Delta took the position that their interests were best served by the creation of districts in which they could elect representatives accountable to them, even if this resulted in fewer Democrats overall. The experience in Mississippi was that white legislators did not see their African-American constituents as people to whom they had to be accountable, even in districts with large percentages of black voters. For the MRC, the issue was not Democratic or Republican, or black versus white, but accountability. Because of the culture of white domination, white officeholders who sided with the African-American community on any significant or controversial issue would be ostracized in their own communities—at the Rotary Club, in church and even dining out in restaurants.

The MRC took the position that if the African-American population in District 2 were only 52 percent, it would be impossible to elect an accountable African-American candidate. This would leave the African-American community in Mississippi without any representation at all. The MRC took the position that districts should not be created with the expectation of any particular candidate running for office. So, even though Espy, as an incumbent, might be able to win an election in a district with a lower African-American population, the MRC opposed drawing a district to Espy's specifications—particularly as rumors were already flying that Espy would be appointed Secretary of Agriculture.

The MRC needed to present its own alternative congressional districting plan to the Legislative Joint Committee at its final hearing in early 1992. All of the political insiders and experts were certain that it was impossible to produce a district with at least 60 percent African-American voting-age population. The night before the hearing, the demographers from Atlanta with whom MRC had been working for months unexpectedly became unavailable. Deprived of sophisticated, computer-assisted districting techniques, the MRC fell back

[15] The analysis behind this contention is complex and political scientists disagree about what conclusions to draw from it.

SOUTHERN ECHO, INC

EMPOWERMENT
ACCOUNTABILITY
TRUTHTELLING
FIGHTING RACISM
TRAINING
ASSISTANCE

A thousand spider webs linked together can catch and hold the king of beasts!

Southern Echo, Inc.
P.O. Box 10433
Jackson, MS 39289
Phone: 601-352-1500
Fax: 601-352-2266

Mississippi Education Working Group

Working Together to Develop Accountable Grassroots Organizations that Empower Our Communities to Build Quality Public Education Systems and Erect Bridges to Justice and Opportunity for African-American Families in Mississippi

FOR MORE INFORMATION, PLEASE CONTACT:
SOUTHERN ECHO, INC.
P.O. Box 10433, JACKSON, MS
PHONE: 601-352-1500
FAX: 601-352-2266

To encourage greater understanding of the redistricting process, community activists prepared education materials (above) on the history and politics of redistricting.

on its local knowledge and old-fashioned technology. Armed with an antique adding machine, a big map of the state and colored markers, Watkins and Sayer stayed up all night. The next morning they had a plan with hand-colored districts backed by many yards of adding machine tape. They presented the manually produced plan, which included a 62 percent black population in District 2, to the Joint Committee.

As described by Sayer: "The plan, taped to a marble column for all the redistricting committee and the assembled community to see, seemed almost radiant, the colors iridescent under the bright fluorescent lights of the hearing room in the Old Supreme Court Chamber. It was the only plan to be presented in five distinct colors so that you could clearly see from a distance the delineation of each of the districts."[16]

Two hundred African-American community members packed the small hearing room. The MRC analysis and strong support of community groups proved effective. The Joint Committee immediately asked MRC to work with its demographers to produce a plan with at least 60 percent African-Americans. The Joint Committee rejected the arguments of some white Democrats and their supporters, who sought to break up the Delta's African-American population.

After the House of Representatives and the Senate adopted different plans, MRC was asked whether it would accept a 58 percent African-American district. Viewing 58 percent as a victory, the community accepted the compromise. Congressman Bennie Thompson was elected to represent District 2 after Mike Espy was named Secretary of Agriculture. Thompson is viewed by African-Americans in the Delta as a responsive and accountable representative.

REDISTRICTING ON THE LOCAL LEVEL

With political power in Mississippi highly concentrated at the local level, it was critical to create districts in which accountable African-Americans could be elected to county boards, city councils and school boards. The redistricting process at the local level was controlled by white elected officials who had little interest in sharing power with African-Americans.

The experience in Tallahatchie County typifies the local redistricting process that occurred in communities across the Delta in the early 1990s. Southern Echo conducted a redistricting workshop with community groups in Tallahatchie County in January 1991. These groups formed the Tallahatchie County Redistricting Committee, which appeared before the County Board of Supervisors in February 1991, to request that the Board seats be redistricted. The Board initially refused outright, in direct contravention of legal requirements.

Three local attorneys—Sayer of Southern Echo, Margaret Carey of the Center for Constitutional Rights, and Victor McTeer, a private attorney based in Greenville—assisted the Tallahatchie County Redistricting Committee, along with demographers from the Southern Regional Council in Atlanta. They developed several plans and submitted them to the County Board of Supervisors. In the face of considerable community pressure, the Board quickly

[16] M. Sayer e-mail to P. Hair, Jan. 23, 2000.

abandoned its recalcitrant position and began drawing its own plan for redistricting. After a six-month campaign in which African-Americans packed the Board meetings and kept the community pressure on, the Board of Supervisors agreed to negotiate with the Tallahatchie Redistricting Committee over new district lines. This was unprecedented—the first time the all-white Board ever agreed to negotiate with an African-American organization.

Community members were well-prepared for the negotiations, having attended Echo-run workshops where they trained and engaged in role-playing. Just the act of pretending to be members of the Board of Supervisors was empowering for the black community in a county where no African-American had ever served as a member of the Board of Supervisors. In one training session, Jerome Little, a local African-American community leader, represented the black community, while other African-American county residents played the white members of the Board of Supervisors. The community members gave Little a very hard time, "doing to Jerome just what the Board does to the community." This process "broke the tension" and helped the community understand its own power.[17] Through such play-acting, community members realized the strength of their own knowledge and the flimsiness of the arguments typically made by white officials.

The negotiations were held in the Sumner Courthouse, in the very same room where the whites who lynched Emmett Till were tried and acquitted. Even going into the courthouse was an intimidating experience for African-American Tallahatchie residents. Over a four-month period in the spring of 1991, the Tallahatchie County Redistricting Committee participated in more than a dozen publicly held negotiating sessions with the Tallahatchie Board of Supervisors. A large contingent of community members were at each meeting, demonstrating the resolve of the black community. Initially, the supervisors would not even speak to the African-American representatives, leaving the verbal sparring to their lawyer and demographer. Gradually, however, the supervisors came to respect the expertise and outright persistence of the Tallahatchie County Redistricting Committee members. The supervisors "were blown away" by seemingly small things, such as the fact that the community had notebooks and access to the same information about the process that the supervisors had.[18]

At one point in the sessions, Little took a very strong position. Sayer recounts: "Here we are sitting in this room and Jerome throws an enormous tantrum in front of everybody. The supervisors were stunned. They could not imagine an African-American standing up like that." When the community members went out of the room to caucus among themselves, Little whispered to Sayer, "that was just like in the workshops."[19]

The community and the all-white Board eventually agreed on a plan that would create three majority-black districts out of five. But this hard-won victory unraveled when white farmers who had boycotted the negotiations demanded that the supervisors withdraw from the plan.

[17] Sayer interview, supra.

[18] Ibid.

[19] Ibid.

The supervisors caved in to intimidating pressure from the powerful plantation owners and adopted a plan that was essentially the same as the existing one, under which no African-American had ever been elected.

As with the state Legislative districts, the U.S. Department of Justice refused to preclear the Tallahatchie Board's redistricting plan. Members of the MRC, represented by McTeer, a highly respected and experienced civil rights attorney from a nearby county, then filed a lawsuit under the Voting Rights Act and the Constitution, seeking the adoption of an alternative plan that did not dilute black voting strength.[20] For more than a year, the battle languished in the courts. Unfortunately, much of the community organizing languished right along with it. Litigation is inevitably slow, and often lawyers can do little to speed up the process. But in this case, the community members were *afraid* to confront their own attorneys about how the slow pace of the litigation was dissipating much of the organizing energy. Because the community members and the lawyers never squarely faced this tension they did not explore whether a better solution was possible. As a result of this experience, Southern Echo and local residents are determined to address this issue directly in any future litigation and to seek creative approaches to better harmonize litigation work and organizing efforts.

Despite these problems, litigation proved to be an indispensable tool. Without this lawsuit, the Tallahatchie Supervisors' plan would have prevailed. Fortunately, the negative effects of the slow legal process were short-lived. The community organizing effort revived when the federal court finally ordered a new interim plan for Tallahatchie Supervisor districts and scheduled a special election for November 1992. The plan created three majority-black districts. Local leaders asked Southern Echo to conduct a series of workshops to train the community members about the voting process. In the election, African-American candidates ended up winning two of the five supervisor seats. The third African-American candidate lost by only 19 votes. Candidates strongly supported by the African-American community also won a majority of seats on the County Election Commission and one of two County Justice Court seats.

Results from the Redistricting Campaign

The 1992 elections were a watershed. Southern Echo believes that these elections brought the largest black turnout in the Mississippi Delta in the history of the state. The number of African-American members of the state Legislature doubled from 21 to 42, giving African-Americans a substantial voting bloc in the state Senate and House. Several powerful white incumbents were defeated, including a longtime opponent of the interests of African-Americans in the Delta, Sen. Ollie Mohamed, the chairman pro tem of the Senate. These results shocked the white-controlled power structure. Robert Crook, an unresponsive Sunflower County senator with a 29-year tenure, also was turned out of office. He was

[20] See, Gardner v. Tallahatchie County, MS, 1997 WL 170322 (N.D. Miss. 1997).

defeated by Willie Simmons, the first black state senator to represent Sunflower County, where in 1954 the architects of massive resistance to court-mandated school desegregation formed the Citizens' Councils.

The 1995 elections brought another three African-American members to the state Legislature, raising the total to 45. During the 1990s, the election of African-American mayors, county supervisors, city aldermen and other local officials also increased substantially as a result of the community organizing and participation in the districting process. The 1995 elections resulted in African-Americans representing 30 percent of the county supervisors statewide. A statewide referendum followed, which proposed to reduce the number of supervisors per county from five to three. Such a move would have forced the creation of larger districts, making it more difficult to create electable black districts. The referendum was defeated with a strong education and mobilization effort in the black community.

When oddly shaped districts were created in other states, even though they were constructed using sophisticated computer-mapping technology and data, they proved contentious. Several were invalidated under the new "wrongful districting" Equal Protection claim created by the U.S. Supreme Court in the 1993 decision, SHAW V. RENO.[21] However, Mississippi's congressional and state legislative voting-rights districts were not challenged under the SHAW standard.[22]

Southern Echo credits community involvement for the successful creation of voting-rights districts across Mississippi. Sayer states that "the community is the expert." In one county redistricting, officials drew a district which it claimed was majority black. An African-American resident disputed this, claiming that there were 45 more registered whites than blacks.

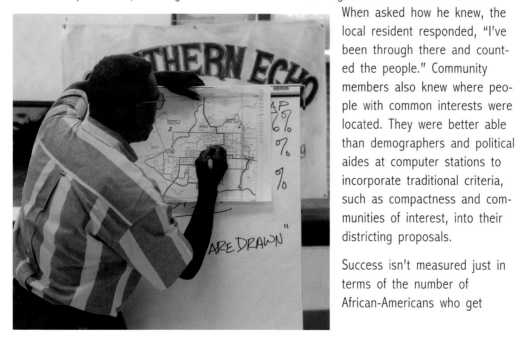

When asked how he knew, the local resident responded, "I've been through there and counted the people." Community members also knew where people with common interests were located. They were better able than demographers and political aides at computer stations to incorporate traditional criteria, such as compactness and communities of interest, into their districting proposals.

Success isn't measured just in terms of the number of African-Americans who get

Southern Echo's creed: "Legislative seats belong to the people, not the officeholders."

[21] The U.S. Supreme Court is deeply divided over the SHAW doctrine, which has provoked sharply worded dissents. See, e.g., BUSH V. VERA, 517 U.S. 952 (1996) (J. Stevens dissenting). Voting-rights scholars and advocates strongly criticize the SHAW V. RENO decision. See, e.g., Frank R. Parker, "The Constitutionality of Racial Redistricting: A Critique of SHAW V. RENO," 3 D.C. L. Rev. 1 (1995); Jamin B. Raskin, "The Supreme Court's Racial Double Standard in Redistricting: Unequal Protection in Politics and the Scholarship That Defends It," 14 J. L. & Pol. 591 (1998); Samuel Issacharoff and Pamela S. Karlan, "Standing and Misunderstanding in Voting Rights Law," 111 Harv. L. Rev. 2276 (1998); Brenda Wright, "Reflections and Projections," in Redistricting and Minority Representation (David Bositis, ed., Joint Center on Political and Economic Studies, 1998); A. Leon Higginbotham Jr., Gregory A. Clarick and Marcella David, "SHAW V. RENO: A Mirage of Good Intentions With Devastating Consequences," 62 Fordham L. Rev. 1593 (1994).

[22] There have been a few SHAW challenges to local districts in Mississippi counties where Southern Echo was not involved.

elected to office. For several years, African-American communities across the Delta had been using Southern Echo's definition of accountability—putting the community's interest over self-interest. Since they had come to expect this type of accountability from each other, it was a natural conclusion to expect it from elected representatives. Most of the newly elected representatives came out of the community redistricting process and have themselves committed to Echo's concept of accountability.

Once African-American representatives obtained seats on governing bodies, they were able to create alliances with white officials. In Tallahatchie County, for example, the African-American community was bitterly disappointed at failing to win a third seat on the Board of Supervisors. However, on joining the Board, the two African-American supervisors discovered an ally in a white supervisor who represented a large number of fixed income, elderly constituents. With the white supervisor as the third vote, the Board adopted a resolution establishing an ambulance service which the previous, all-white Board had rejected. The white supervisor realized that forming an alliance with the newly elected African-Americans could save lives in his district.[23]

Even opponents have been known to temper their feelings once actually working with African-American officeholders. Robert Grayson was elected as the first African-American mayor of Tutwiler, a city in Tallahatchie County, in 1996. Prior to his election, one of the town's citizens, "an admitted racist," told Grayson that he could not support the election of African-Americans. "Y'all come in here to stir up trouble," he complained. A few months after Grayson was in office, this same man complimented him: "I can see some things happening around here," he said. "I really appreciate the hard work you're doing. Seems like you're trying to bring this town back. If there's anything I can do to help, let me know."[24]

The enlarged contingent of African-Americans in the state Legislature also has made it possible to form coalitions with members of the white majority on certain issues. In 1997, they were able to obtain a $650 million appropriation for education spending over five years. This huge increase in the education budget was the direct result of efforts by the bigger and more powerful Legislative Black Caucus. When legislation was vetoed by the governor, many white legislators wanted to compromise and bring the appropriation down to $380 million. The Legislative Black Caucus took the lead and demanded no compromise and attempted to override the veto. It succeeded. The veto was overridden in the Senate by one vote and in the House by three votes. That was not the only success: in 1995, 130 years after the Civil War, the Mississippi Legislature finally ratified the 13th Amendment to the Constitution, which prohibits slavery.

[23] P. Hair interview of J. Little, supra.

[24] P. Hair interview with Robert Grayson, Oct. 19, 1998.

The Role of Lawyers and Legal Claims

Strong legal protections provided by the federal Constitution and Voting Rights Act were pivotal to the Mississippi redistricting successes. Organizing by itself would not have brought the white-controlled state Legislature, the supervisors of Tallahatchie County and other white officials across the state for negotiations with the African-American community. The Department of Justice preclearance process and strategic lawsuits were critical.

The 1990s redistricting success was possible in part because of the legal and political infrastructure built by intense voting-rights enforcement efforts in Mississippi over 30 years. Partnering with the few Mississippi attorneys willing to handle such cases, the Lawyers' Committee for Civil Rights Under Law (LCCRUL) and the NAACP Legal Defense & Educational Fund, Inc. (LDF), litigated scores of voting-rights cases in Mississippi. Among the key cases was Allen v. State Board of Elections,[25] which ruled that the Voting Rights Act should be given "the broadest scope possible" and that Mississippi jurisdictions switching from single-member districts to at-large elections were subject to federal review under Section 5 of the Voting Rights Act. The Supreme Court's decision in Allen marked a turning point in efforts of black Mississippians to overcome the state's "massive resistance" to the civil rights of its black citizens.[26] Connor v. Johnson, requiring single-member districts in court-ordered reapportionment plans, eventually meant the end of the state Legislature's reliance on mul-timember districting as way of diluting black voting power in legislative elections. In 1987, LCCRUL and LDF filed a suit alleging racially discriminatory statutes such as a "dual regis-tration" requirement continued to act as barriers to voter registration in Mississippi. The court victory was the first successful challenge to statewide voter registration procedures for restrictions on time and place of registration.[27]

President Ronald Reagan called the 1982 amendments to the Voting Rights Act the "crown jewel" of American democracy. They were the catalyst for the creation of scores of elec-table voting-rights districts across the United States. Lawyers with the Leadership Conference on Civil Rights (LCCR), LDF, LCCRUL, MALDEF and other organizations played a vital role in convincing Congress to strengthen the Voting Rights Act, laying the foundation for the success in Mississippi.

The availability of lawyers to assist community members during the Mississippi districting process also was an essential ingredient. The community's relationship with these lawyers illustrates effective transactional lawyering. Carroll Rhodes, a local African-American lawyer, prepared a legal memorandum at the beginning of the community-organizing process, laying out the requirements of the Voting Rights Act and the procedures for redistricting. Rhodes and Sayer worked together to translate the legal jargon into training materials for communi-ty members. Rhodes also participated in workshops for community members, teaching them about the law, the process and how to draw plans.

[25] 393 U.S. 544 (1969).

[26] See, generally, Parker, Black Votes Count, supra.

[27] See, Connor v. Johnson, 402 US 690 (1971); See also Mississippi State Chapter, Operation PUSH v. Allain, 717 F. Supp. 1189 (N.D. Miss., 1989), affirmed 932 F. 2d 400 (5th Cir. Miss., 1991).

Even though the lawyers charged no fees, they played very much the same role as private attorneys with paying clients. They helped to advise the shaping of claims and helped to keep tabs on the other side's lawyer. The community groups were the decision makers guiding the process. Echo is proud that it told its attorneys: "We don't care that you are unpaid; if you don't follow the instructions of your clients, you will be fired." Indeed, MRC initially explored whether out-of-state legal organizations would handle the Mississippi redistricting litigation but ultimately settled on in-state practitioners.

Lawyers and community members worked as teams in the districting negotiations. Southern Echo felt strongly that community members should have a working knowledge of legal requirements and be integrally involved in the entire legal process. If community members went into a negotiation without an attorney, the lawyer on the other side might take over, denouncing the community's proposal as not legal. But with an attorney accompanying the community, more often than not, both lawyers would end up sitting quietly while the real stakeholders—the community members and the county representatives—negotiated. In fact, at times, the community members knew more law than the County's attorney.

At one point in the Legislative districting case, the attorneys for the MRC plaintiffs did not want to take an appeal to the U.S. Supreme Court, though they felt that there was a sufficient legal claim, because they were not confident it could be won. But the community felt that appealing was an important tactical signal to the other side. The lawyers took the appeal. According to Echo's Johnson, "it was an absolutely integral evolutionary development in the process." While the Supreme Court appeal did not succeed on the merits, "it told the white community they can't wear us down."[28]

Carroll Rhodes reports that this was the first time black residents were able to participate in the districting process on a mass scale. For the lawyers, it was more work to do it this way, but it was also more rewarding and produced greater results. "Lawyers learned how to listen to actual concerns of people in the community, rather than fashion a remedy which the lawyers thought was in the people's best interest."[29]

Epilogue
Demanding more accountable government through the successful redistricting campaign was only the first step in community participation in policymaking. Echo and the community groups are now using their new-found grassroots strength to address difficult quality-of-life issues. Tallahatchie County has chosen to focus on housing. For many other counties, the main issue they have selected is improving the quality of education in the principally black schools.

When Southern Echo held its first series of community meetings to hear the concerns of African-Americans in the Delta, no one spoke about education—even though Mississippi consistently ranked 50th among the states. In time, Echo staff members discovered within

[28] L. Johnson interview, supra.

[29] Lincoln Mitchell telephone interview with Carroll Rhodes, March 4, 1999.

the African-American community a degree of anger and disillusionment over the quality of their children's education that residents were intimidated from even verbalizing. According to Johnson, "sometimes the things you don't hear are as important as what is said." The common consensus was that the Mississippi education system for African-American students excelled in only one area—disciplining youngsters and making them submissive to the white power structure.

Already African-American community groups with the help of Southern Echo are taking their first steps in what will be a long campaign to stop physical and emotional abuse of school children, unnecessary and unjust disciplinary action and school location decisions that threaten to perpetuate and reinforce segregation in schools. The ultimate goal is a high-quality, challenging curriculum and learning experience for every Mississippi schoolchild.

BROADER IMPLICATIONS

Much work remains to be done to improve the quality of life of African-Americans in the Mississippi Delta. But the redistricting effort was a success at putting together the mechanism for greater representation and more government accountability on the local, state and congressional levels. It has created an approach that can be adapted to a variety of circumstances in which communities are seeking to give real meaning to the protections and promises of the Voting Rights Act. The result could be creation of a potent dynamic in the struggle against the last vestiges of racism that continue to affect black communities and black lives.

Chapter

Rerouting the Revenue

In the 1950s, segregated public buses were an omnipresent feature of the Jim Crow South. After paying their fare at the front of the bus, African-American riders, often the most frequent bus users, had to exit the front and reboard the black section in the back. In addition, bus service in black neighborhoods was inadequate. In Montgomery, Alabama, the Women's Political Council began organizing against segregated buses in 1946. In 1955 the Council called a one-day boycott to protest the arrest of seamstress Rosa Parks, who refused to give her seat to a white man. The boycott lasted 13 months and became one of the most important campaigns of the civil rights movement. For a time after the laws were changed, people continued to sit in segregated patterns (right).

For decades, working-class and low-income residents in Los Angeles endured poor and unsafe bus service. So when the Metropolitan Transportation Authority (MTA) announced that it was cutting service and raising fares while simultaneously shifting the lion's share of the budget to new rail services targeted principally for wealthy suburbanites, city residents cried foul. Then they got organized and mounted a campaign of smart legal tactics, backed by compelling research, which, combined with continuous protest and educational outreach, galvanized public support for their cause. The result was a settlement with the city that brings up to $1 billion in improvements in bus service—a victory for every Los Angeles resident.

Chapter 4
Rerouting the Revenue:
Los Angeles Community Residents Take on the Transit Authority to Get Bus Service That Meets Their Needs

Key Lessons Learned

- Utilize the strengths of public-interest attorneys to ensure effective government enforcement of legal protections where government agencies lack the resources, will or community connections to produce adequate enforcement.

- Use Title VI's prohibition against discrimination by recipients of federal funding to expand the reach of civil rights enforcement to a broad range of unfair policies and practices.

- Where possible, exhaustively research, analyze and document claims prior to filing suit rather than depending on discovery to produce key evidence.

- Where possible, leverage the value of a whistle-blower or knowledgeable insider to bring offending institutions to the bargaining table and to build leverage in the litigation process.

- Translate legal victories into lasting, practical benefits by encouraging broad-based, sustained community participation in monitoring and enforcement of legal remedies.

As in Montgomery in the 1950s, for many Latino, African-American and low-income people in Los Angeles, the bus is the only means of access to life's necessities—day care, shopping, work, health care and more (left).

Second-class citizens: Despite continuing poor service for the most frequent bus users, new investment went to rail lines for the suburbs rather than to improvement of service within the city. Such inequities have also led to safety concerns for women and late-night bus riders (above).

Overview

In the largely poor, minority neighborhoods of Los Angeles, a high percentage of residents rely on MTA buses for their transportation needs. For years, buses often were overcrowded and, once filled to capacity, the drivers skipped the remaining stops altogether. Residents sometimes waited an hour or more until a bus came by with room enough for them. More than a few workers lost their jobs because poor bus service made them chronically late. A large number of bus stops were without shelters, and many were unsafe. So when the MTA met in July 1994 to raise fares, eliminate bus passes and reduce service, city bus riders already fed up with the existing service that was unreliable, inadequate and unsafe, said, "Enough!"

The frustration of Los Angeles bus riders was compounded by long-term disinvestment in their neighborhoods. As inner-city industries have relocated to locations farther from the city's center, a job drain occurred in South Central and other Los Angeles neighborhoods. The area's residents were forced to look farther afield—including the distant suburbs—for employment opportunities, medical care and other essential services. But the MTA has been slow to develop new routes that can effectively get these residents to and from the suburbs.

Poor MTA service is not a new phenomenon in Los Angeles. In 1965, a commission established to study the causes of the Los Angeles riots found the city's inadequate and costly transportation service to be one of the reasons for the sense of isolation and frustration among the city's black residents. The commission's report noted the dependency of residents, particularly in South Central, on public transportation and condemned the bus system's practice of responding to increases in operating costs by imposing fare increases and service cuts. The commission urged MTA to improve service and to reduce its "prohibitively expensive" fare, which, in today's terms, would have been about $1.14.[1]

The MTA never implemented the recommendations. Fares continued to rise, prompting significant drops in ridership as poor residents of the inner city became unable to pay the costs of transit.[2] Service was reduced and remained uncoordinated and ill-suited to the transit needs of those who depended on it.

Almost 30 years later, the MTA's own 1993, "Inner-City Transit Needs Assessment Study," reached many of the same conclusions as the 1965 commission. The study noted the complete absence of major transportation investments in the inner city, contrasting this with significant investments in commuter rail, rail transit, exclusive transit/HOV lanes on freeways and shared-ride taxis for people who didn't live in the inner city. The study recommended that service be expanded to relieve overcrowding and provide faster connections, that the security and cleanliness of buses and bus stops be improved, and that transit be made more affordable.[3] Once again, the MTA failed to implement the recommended changes.

[1] McCone Commission Report, Dec. 2, 1965, 950484, 950559-60.

[2] Bus ridership dropped from a peak of 497 million passengers in 1985 to 375 million in 1994, a drop largely attributed to the more than doubling of the fare during that period from 50 cents to $1.10.

[3] Inner-City Transit Needs Assessment Study, July 1, 1993.

The MTA Board ignited a storm of protest (right) when it voted to terminate bus passes and raise fares without assessing the impact of its actions on transit-dependent poor people.

4 Mike Davis, "L.A.'s Transit Apartheid: Runaway Train Crushes Buses," **The Nation**, Sept. 18, 1995.

Instead, the MTA embarked on an ambitious and extraordinarily expensive effort to develop a system of rail lines to serve the suburbs and the downtown business district. The 400-mile network, planned in 1980, was originally estimated to cost over $180 billion during the 30 years it would take to build it. By the early 1990s, the combined cost of the rail projects was consuming 70 percent of the MTA's nearly $3 billion annual budget. The MTA's rail projects constituted the largest public-works project in the United States and were receiving almost one quarter of the federal government's rail-transit construction budget.[4]

Serious doubts began to surface about such huge expenditures, the wisdom of the design itself and the ability of the MTA to carry it out effectively. Much of the criticism focused on the Red Line subway project, which, at $5.8 billion, was the most expensive subway in history. The project was plagued with cost overruns and, in 1994, remained only half finished. More generally, the MTA was seen as an agency increasingly out of control. Although responsible for an annual budget exceeding $2 billion, the board entrusted with MTA's oversight did little to restrain its rail-at-any-cost strategy. Instead, the MTA became an opportunity for political leaders to obtain lucrative contracts for local entrepreneurs in the classic pork-barrel politics tradition.[5]

5 Ibid.

NURTURING GRASSROOTS ADVOCACY

Sporadic protests about inadequate bus service and the shifting of expenditures to rail projects had occurred over the years. But in the summer of 1993, opposition to the MTA gained a new degree of organization when the Labor/Community Strategy Center, headed by Director Eric Mann, formed the Bus Rider's Union (BRU).

The catalyst for the creation of BRU was the MTA's decision to allocate $60 million in discretionary funds to a Pasadena light rail extension (the Blue Line). Given past experience, BRU was sure that if the MTA made such a commitment to the Blue Line, it would face a budgetary shortfall the following year—a shortfall that would almost certainly trigger cuts in bus service, a rise in fares or a combination of both.

On the day the MTA was to vote on the Blue Line extension, Mann and others testified against it. They decried the huge subsidies to develop new rail systems while the existing, heavily traveled bus system received less than a third of MTA appropriations. They painted a damning picture of the MTA's priorities: for every new suburban commuter added, the MTA was losing six bus riders because of service cutbacks and fare increases. The MTA ultimately approved the money for the Blue Line project, but bus riders began actively lobbying for a dramatic shift in MTA priorities to benefit the inner city. They named their campaign, "Billions for Buses."

BRU soon enlisted a committed, organized, dues-paying membership that would play an activist role in determining the organization's goals and tactics. By mid-1994, BRU estimated that more than 20,000 identified themselves as supporters of the union.

BRU members began appearing at all the MTA public meetings, staging demonstrations, distributing literature and enlisting the support of passengers on buses throughout the city. BRU succeeded in getting the attention of the media, especially after the MTA began to float plans for increasing fares and reducing service in the first half of 1994. At that time, in light of a $126 million operating deficit, the MTA proposed raising fares 36 percent, from $1.10 to $1.50. BRU fought the fare increase, citing how dependent many poor residents were on MTA transit and the dramatic impact the fare increase would have on such riders. The proposal was swiftly retracted at the MTA's April 1994 meeting, after a storm of BRU-inspired protest was covered extensively in the media.

BRU Joins Forces With LDF

While BRU and other grassroots organizations were becoming organized against the MTA initiatives, the Western Regional Office of the NAACP Legal Defense and Educational Fund, Inc. (LDF) also began to focus its attention on the MTA. Two years before the suit was filed against the MTA, LDF began identifying the most pressing issues in the area on which it might provide assistance. Concern about the MTA ranked high, particularly frustration that so much of the MTA's revenue and subsidies were being directed to developments outside the city's most transit-dependent neighborhoods. Contance Rice and Bill Lann Lee, then LDF co-directors, were impressed with the organized strength of the bus riders but at that point could not see a compelling enough legal hook to confront transit inequity successfully in the courts. Still, they recognized the importance of BRU's work, and the two groups began to join forces.

The MTA Votes to Raise Bus Fares and the Lawsuit Begins

When the MTA met on July 14, 1994, to debate fare increases and service reductions, it was the catalyst needed to fire a political movement and a legal challenge that ultimately brought a change in MTA transit policies. The testimony of riders, and the indifferent response of the MTA Board at the hearing, revealed how disconnected MTA policies were from the real needs of the communities it purported to serve.

The public testimony was by turns angry and frightened. Speakers highlighted the heavy toll the proposal would place on already frustrated inner-city residents. Riders were particularly upset at the proposal to eliminate monthly passes, which allowed unlimited use of the buses for a monthly fee of $42. Without such passes, transit costs for some poor residents would more than double to over $100 a month—an amount equal to 25 percent of their monthly income.

The dramatic testimony was put into even sharper relief by the shabby treatment the MTA Board members gave to witnesses. Board members were distracted, laughing with each other and eating—often taking little notice of the testimony being delivered before them.

6 P. Hair interview with Constance Rice, July 1997. Rice is an adviser to this Report.

7 Bill Boyarsky, "MTA's Rude Behavior Shows it Is Out of Touch With its Riders," **Los Angeles Times**, July 17, 1994, B1.

8 42 U.S.C. 2000d (1994).

9 See, 49 C.F.R. 21.9 (1997). Although the adverse-impact standard of the regulations was originally viewed as applicable only to administrative complaints filed with the federal agency, courts have subsequently held that plaintiffs can also bring suits directly against recipients of federal funds. See, e.g., COALITION OF CONCERNED CITIZENS AGAINST I-670 V. DAMIEN, 608 F. Supp. 110 (1984).

10 Despite the availability of the adverse-impact standard, Title VI claims are viewed as difficult to win. In large part this is because of restrictive rulings in the 1980s that tended to narrow the availability of Title VI, and to raise the burden of proof that plaintiffs had to meet. For a fuller discussion of the restrictions on access to Title VI imposed by courts in the 1980s, see, Michael Fisher, "Environmental Racism Claims Brought under Title VI of the Civil Rights Act," 25 Envtl. L. 285, 316 (1995).

Rice points out the startling contrast in the room: people were in tears at the mike. Blind bus riders were begging the Board not to impose a fare for them. But there were the mayor and other politicians telling jokes and giving high fives.[6]

At the end of the hearing, the Board swiftly voted to end the bus pass, to increase the fares from $1.10 to $1.50, and to fund a $60 million planning project for the Pasadena Blue Line. The next day, the **Los Angeles Times** concluded, "the Board's conduct while pushing through a fare increase…was so outrageous that it's hard to single out its most offensive act."[7]

With that vote, says, Rice, the Board had taken a specific action resulting in an enormous impact on the transit-dependent poor without even assessing what that impact was going to be. She and her LDF colleagues knew immediately that the Board had given the bus riders a clear legal issue on which to bring a lawsuit. They felt sure that, at the very least, a strong procedural claim existed obligating the MTA to analyze the effect of the proposal before adopting it. They also realized that the Board's action—raising almost the entire amount of the Blue Line investment on the backs of those least able to pay—put the inequity of the decision in the clearest light.

MAKING THE LEGAL ARGUMENT

Three seasoned advocates—Lee, Rice and LDF staff attorney Robert Garcia—sprang into action with only a few weeks before the effective date of the fair hike. The ACLU of Southern California and a private law firm also joined the legal team. Working day and night, side by side with members of BRU, they developed a lawsuit filed in federal court on August 31, 1994.

The complaint alleged that in implementing the fare increase and pass elimination, MTA had violated the Equal Protection Clause of the 14th Amendment and Title VI of the Civil Rights Act of 1964.[8] In addition to forbidding intentional discrimination, since the 1970s, federal grantmaking agencies—including the Department of Transportation (DOT), a major source of funds for the MTA—have adopted Title VI "implementing regulations" that prohibit recipients from operating programs in a way that has an adverse impact on protected groups.[9]

The complaint against the MTA included both adverse-impact[10] and intentional-discrimination claims. First, plaintiffs alleged that the MTA's bus-fare increase and pass elimination, with no comparable increases on the largely white rail lines, would produce an adverse impact on minorities, in violation of DOT's Title VI implementing regulations. In addition, they asserted that the MTA's history of indifference to minority concerns suggested purposeful discrimination in violation of the Constitution, as well as Title VI. The suit was brought as a class action, on behalf of all poor minority and other riders of MTA buses who are denied equal opportunity to receive transportation services because of the MTA's operation of discriminatory mass-transportation system. BRU was representative of the class, along with the

Labor/Community Strategy Center, the Southern Christian Leadership Conference and Korean Immigrant Workers Advocates. The class was not explicitly limited to minority riders; rather, the pleadings included all city residents impeded by the unfair discrimination. Both BRU and LDF considered it strategically important that the case was brought on behalf of almost 20 percent of city bus riders who are white, some of whom were also members of BRU. The inclusion of white bus riders was never challenged by the defendants.

The complaint included impressive supporting material—nearly 1,000 pages documenting the disparities in MTA funding practices and the severe impact its most recent decisions would have on poor and minority riders. The information about MTA funding practices was strengthened considerably by the contributions of a former MTA financial analyst,[11] who offered an insider's perspective and a wealth of documentary evidence. One important aspect of the plaintiffs' submission was its extensive statistical analysis of where MTA money was going. It showed that the bus system, although it carried 94 percent of the MTA's passengers (80 percent of whom were minority), received only 30 percent of its capital and operating budget.[12] These numbers were broken down further to show the operating and capital subsidies of the bus and rail on a per-rider and per-rider-mile basis.[13] For example, the per-rider subsidy for the Metrolink commuter line, at just over $21.00, was 18 times higher than the $1.17 subsidy for each bus rider.

Plaintiffs also showed that the MTA customarily tolerated overcrowding levels of 140 percent of capacity on its buses. In contrast, there was no overcrowding of riders on Metrolink- and MTA-operated rail lines. The MTA's own figures showed huge disparities in spending for the personal security of its riders. While only 3 cents was spent for the

[11] This analyst, Tom Rubin, had written a memo to the entire MTA Board shortly before the vote, which broke down the impact of fare increase by income levels and demonstrated the impact it would have on inner-city riders.

[12] Plaintiffs' Revised Statement of Contentions of Fact and Law, 60-61, filed with Plaintiff's Memorandum in Support of Proposed Consent Decree on October 24, 1996, available at www.ldflaframest.htm and www.edf.org/ej.

[13] This data is from the Court's Findings of Fact and Conclusions of Law Re: Preliminary Injunction (Sept. 21, 1994)(hereinafter, Findings of Fact).

Poor service and old buses prone to breakdowns meant that riders often were left stranded.

14 Plaintiffs' Revised Statement of Contentions of Fact and Law, supra.

security of each bus passenger in fiscal year 1993, 43 times as much was spent for the security of each passenger of Metrolink and the MTA Blue Line, and 19 times as much for each passenger on the MTA Red Line subway.[14]

The documentation also showed the effect that the combined elimination of the monthly pass and raising of the bus fares would have on low-income riders. More than 60 percent of bus riders earned less than $15,000 a year, yet even a minimal user, who rode the bus to work and back, would face an effective fare increase of almost 30 percent. For the transit-dependent, who relied on the bus for shopping, child care and other needs, the increase would be as high as 150 percent or more. These levels of increase would result in many transit-dependent riders spending a quarter or more of their income on bus fares alone. By contrast, the average Metrolink riders, who enjoyed the largest level of subsidy, had an income of $65,000 and owned two cars. The documentation also included internal reports, memoranda and minutes of meetings demonstrating that the MTA had been made aware of these facts repeatedly, by its staff and consultants, but nonetheless ignored them.[15]

15 Ibid.

On September 1, 1994—the day the bus fares were set to go up—the plaintiffs appeared in federal court, seeking a temporary restraining order (TRO) to block the implementation of the fare increase. To obtain a TRO, the plaintiffs were required to show that they were likely to prevail on the merits of the case and that the bus riders would suffer irreparable harm if the fare hike and pass elimination went into effect.

Although the attorneys for the bus riders felt that the case was strong, they were also aware that the court would be extremely reluctant to grant the TRO, as the changes had already been implemented that morning. Using information from the former MTA analyst who had contributed to the complaint, the lawyers were able to demonstrate to the judge that at minimal cost, it would be possible quickly to rescind the increase and issue new passes. The judge granted the TRO.

While the MTA expressed shock at the decision, others were less surprised. The **Los Angeles Times** quoted John Pucher, professor of urban policy at Rutgers University, who said, "It surprises me that it's taken this long for a case to be brought in Los Angeles, given the extensive history of disproportionate funding for suburban transportation."[16]

16 Henry Chu, "Are Bus and Rail Fares Separate and Unequal?" **Los Angeles Times**, Sept. 3, 1994, B1.

Eleven days later the court held a second hearing where more extensive evidence could be presented on whether the fare hike should be barred until trial. Plaintiffs were allowed to present written witness statements, including compelling stories that brought home the reality of what the MTA decision would mean to poor, transit-dependent Los Angeles residents. One was the story of Blanca Vasquez, a $666-a-month dressmaker, who stated that she would be hard-pressed to pay the bus fare to and from work if her pass were eliminated.

The MTA's lawyers argued that the fare hike was prompted by business necessity. Without an increase, service would have had to be cut even more dramatically if the MTA's budget were to be balanced.[17] Rice countered on behalf of the plaintiffs that the $60 million appropriation for the Blue Line was evidence in itself that there were less discriminatory alternatives available.

At this second proceeding to consider a more long-term preliminary injunction, the court found that the plaintiffs had presented "more than sufficient evidence" to make an initial showing that MTA's actions disproportionately affected minorities, were not adequately justified and were taken despite the availability of less discriminatory alternatives. The court also found that the plaintiffs had raised "serious questions" concerning the charge of intentional discrimination. From the "findings of fact" accompanying the decision, it is clear that the court was particularly influenced by the callous indifference evident in the events leading up to the fare increase.[18]

Court hearings continued through the rest of 1994 as the MTA pursued two motions in the 9th U.S. Circuit Court of Appeals, seeking to have the preliminary injunction lifted. In January 1995, after a round of negotiations, the court approved an agreement reached by the parties to raise the bus fare to $1.35 and the price of a pass from $42 to $49, pending the outcome of the trial. Although it was not an unequivocal victory for the bus riders, the agreement at least allowed them to continue using the monthly passes.[19] And in the interim, BRU continued to apply "moral pressure" on the MTA with a series of protests in front of its headquarters.

The case moved forward slowly. In the fall of 1995, the MTA filed a motion for summary judgment, which the court denied in December of that year. In 1996, the parties began settlement discussions with a court-appointed mediator, Donald Bliss, a Washington, D.C., attorney who had previously served as Acting General Counsel of the Department of Transportation.

THE CAMPAIGN TO FORCE A SETTLEMENT: ELEMENTS OF SUCCESS

While pleased with their initial success, BRU and the lawyers recognized that real victory lay in their ability to force the MTA to settle on terms favorable to the bus riders. Throughout the 20 months of mediation, they kept up the protests and the "moral pressure," and they also mounted a highly effective and well-organized media campaign. They stuck to a simple, compelling message—ordinary people, poor inner-city residents, were fighting for a fair deal. And they backed it with extraordinary research.

The campaign's organizers also drove home repeatedly the wastefulness and fiscal imprudence of the MTA—a theme designed to appeal to taxpayers who might not otherwise identify with the interests of inner-city riders. The excessive cost of the rail projects was brought to life in vivid detail with charts and graphs.

[17] MTA also challenged the evidence of disproportionate funding for rail development, arguing that Metrolink, one of the three major rail systems, should not be included in the calculations because it was, in fact, run by another city agency.

[18] Findings of Fact, supra.

[19] Richard Simon, "MTA to Proceed with Adjusted Bus Fare Hike," **Los Angeles Times**, Jan. 26, 1995, B1.

[20] The MTA was also coming under increasing severe criticism for its mismanagement of the projects, and for unscrupulous and outright illegal practices in the awarding of bids. Many prime MTA contracts for rail construction eventually cost taxpayers more than three times the original amount of the bid. In 1993, contractors bored into an underground river, stopping construction for six months. A year later, the same contractors weakened supports under Hollywood Boulevard so severely that buildings began to sink, bursting pipes and forcing the evacuation of nearby residents. See, Davis, supra.

[21] Ibid. In the wake of these and other disasters, the Justice Department intensified an investigation into fraud and corruption at all levels of the MTA, which had already found evidence of rigged bidding procedures, shredding of documents and influence peddling. The first arrest, an MTA official involved in a kickback scheme with insurers, occurred in 1995.

[22] See, "Think Tank Report Challenges MTA Plan: $72 Million Gambled in Los Angeles Metrorail Boondoggle," **Business Wire**, June 25, 1996.

[23] Rice statement, adviser meeting, July 30, 1997.

[24] See, Jane Gross, "Getting There the Hard Way: For L.A.'s Car-Less Poor, Dependence on Buses Means a Life of Grinding Inconvenience," **Los Angeles Times**, July 16, 1995, Metro Desk Section, A1.

[25] Adviser Mark Soler uses a similar strategy, noting that making the issue "real" works with both the media and the judge or magistrate. "We get a judge inside a jail, lock the door and walk away. For the first 60 seconds, there's no sound. The second 60 seconds, there's one of these things [KNOCKS], and then two minutes it's let me out of here." Adviser Meeting, July 30, 1997.

The plaintiffs were able to build effectively on growing public skepticism about MTA's management in the wake of continuing revelations about questionable bidding practices and several highly visible building disasters.[20] One of the most dramatic occurred in 1996, when a subway tunnel collapsed and produced a hole 70 feet deep and a half block long in the middle of Hollywood Boulevard.[21]

Key elements of the successful strategy were:

RESEARCH EXPERTISE: Tapping the expertise of respected research specialists in transit and urban planning from nearby universities and throughout the country strengthened the caliber of the litigation and of efforts to sway public opinion. The researchers all concurred that the MTA's actions simply did not make sense as a matter of transportation policy. The drumbeat of criticism came from across the political spectrum. For example, the Reason Foundation, a Libertarian/Conservative institution, released a 1996 report aptly titled, "Why Rail Will Fail," which concluded that the MTA's ambitious 20-year plan for rail improvements should be scrapped in favor of expanded bus service.[22]

PUBLIC PRESSURE: Effectively bringing pressure to bear on the MTA was a key component of the overall settlement strategy. LDF's Rice had a relationship with Mayor Richard Riordan dating from the time he appointed her to the Department of Water and Power. The Department of Water and Power is an important public agency in a city with a perpetual water shortage. Rice felt that the mayor could be convinced of the political necessity of settlement. Rice enlisted the support of respected religious leaders. She told these top officials in the Los Angeles Archdiocese that their worshipers might not be able to get to mass if the buses weren't running. The leaders then informed the mayor that MTA's fare increases and service reductions were insupportable.[23]

After the initial court victories, the federal Department of Transportation put the MTA under closer oversight.

MEDIA COVERAGE: The press coverage was extensive and almost uniformly favorable to the bus riders. Many stories painted in stark terms the difficulties inner-city riders were having with the bus system and castigated the MTA for doing little to improve service. A **Los Angeles Times** reporter even traveled with two plaintiffs, Latina mothers, on city buses from 4 in the morning until 10 at night. The story ran with photographs of the women, arms weighed down with groceries and babies, struggling home.[24] Rice and BRU also took the mediator onto the buses, seeking to give him a taste of the reality poor riders were experiencing.[25]

WINNING MTA'S AGREEMENT TO INVEST BILLIONS IN BUSES
On October 28, 1996, a little more than two years after the initial suit was filed, the court approved a negotiated settlement as more than 100 supporters of the bus riders packed

As lawyers investigated their legal claims, Bus Riders' Union members staged protests throughout the city to call attention to the MTA's planned fare increases and service cuts to pay for suburban rail lines (right).

26 **Los Angeles Times**, Sept. 26, 1996, A1.

the courtroom and cheered. The settlement was described in the press as a "sweeping plan to make bus travel safer, cheaper and more convenient."[26]

Under the Consent Decree, the MTA agreed to return the fee for the monthly bus pass to its pre-suit cost of $42.00; to reduce the price of a biweekly pass from $26.50 to $21.00; and to create a new, unlimited-use, weekly pass for $11.00. The MTA agreed to purchase 102 buses to increase service and reduce crowding on the busiest lines; to add as many more buses as needed to reduce the average number of standees at peak times from more than 20 to eight; and to purchase 50 new buses for a pilot project of "reverse commuting"

Follow the Money—Title VI of the 1964 Civil Rights Act

Title VI is a powerful force in advocacy efforts to hold public institutions accountable for equitable use of public resources. Title VI prohibits discrimination on the basis of race, color or national origin in any program or activity receiving federal assistance. A similar statute, Title IX, prohibits gender discrimination in education programs receiving federal financial assistance. Federal funding generally is spread throughout the major activities of state and local governments that affect communities, including public education (at the primary, secondary and postsecondary levels), low- and moderate-income housing, transportation, municipal services such as sidewalks and street lamps, and the siting of environmental hazards. Thus, Title VI potentially has broad reach.

Title VI originally was used to challenge segregated schools in the South. The nature of the claim was *intentional* discrimination, such as excluding black children. As incidents of blatant intentional discrimination have become less common and actors have become more sophisticated in covering up intentional discrimination, the real force of Title VI today is in its prohibition on actions that have an *adverse impact* on protected groups. The adverse-impact standard for proving discrimination recognizes that proving discriminatory motive is very difficult, even when it likely exists. It prohibits use of practices that produce a disproportionate adverse impact on protected racial groups unless they are justified by a strong "necessity." This standard also recognizes the unfairness of practices that, regardless of motive, pile disadvantages on groups that already suffer from a history of exclusion.

Because there are no hard-and-fast rules about when a practice is necessary enough to justify a harsh racial impact, Title VI cases need to be well researched, and surrounded by out-of-court advocacy, including mobilization, public education and strong communication about the goals of the lawsuit and the reasonableness of the plaintiffs' position. The MTA case demonstrates a particularly effective combination of litigation and out-of-court policy advocacy that put pressure on the governmental actors to settle.

service to suburban job centers. The MTA also agreed to post security personnel on a number of lines; to create a special MTA unit focusing on the security of women; and to improve bus shelters throughout the city. The total cost of implementing the provisions of the settlement was at least $610 million and could be as high as $1 billion. The entire agreement was to be implemented jointly by a working group of plaintiff and MTA representatives, under the continuing jurisdiction of the special master, Donald Bliss, and the court.

While the monetary aspects of the settlement were significant, the creation of the working group was perhaps the most innovative aspect of the agreement. It was, as Rice noted, the beginning of a partnership that would ensure bus-rider involvement in, and consent to, any future change to bus fares or service. "We built in a process...so that the grassroots groups are the primary negotiators over how the decree gets implemented."[27]

[27] Adviser meeting, July 30, 1997.

[28] Ibid.

Race and Class Dynamics of the Case

While the cause of action in the suit was discrimination against people of color, it was also a case fought on behalf of poor white bus riders, who constituted almost 20 percent of the ridership. White bus riders were involved in all public-education efforts. Rice says this was a case where class and race were intertwined: "We were representing poor Latinos...people who just got here, and poor blacks; the poorest of the Asian immigrants, Cambodian, Thai, Mong...and...poor whites, overwhelmingly female."[28]

While minority plaintiffs stood to benefit from the suit, the defendants included their share of minorities, as well. A number of prominent African-Americans hold important positions in the MTA, and others were contractors on its rail projects.

The fact that prominent blacks held positions of power at the MTA had not, in the end, done much to help the truly poor of all races who depended on its services. Nor, surprisingly, had many minority politicians in Los Angeles taken a stand on the issue, despite the fact that it was their constituents who stood to lose the most.

The Role of Lawyers and Litigation in a Social Movement

Occasional tensions could be found between the grassroots advocates and the legal advocates in a relationship that was for the most part, amiable and productive. From the perspective of BRU organizers, the campaign was *theirs*, and thus the LDF attorneys were *their* lawyers. But for LDF, the client was *all* bus riders, and court rules governing class actions dictated that the legal strategies be designed in the best interest of the entire class.

Rice describes the decision-making process for the MTA advocacy:

> We had agreed from the outset to share power over final decisions—that all would listen very carefully to each set of arguments and, where possible, resolve disagreements through consensus negotiation. The lawyers agreed that in all arenas outside of the courtroom (and there were many), the advocates had final say,

[29] Rice e-mail to P. Hair, Dec. 15, 1999.

unless action taken in outside arenas would adversely affect what needed to happen in court. Eric Mann and the bus riders' leadership agreed that on decisions substantially impacting legal strategy or what happened in the courtroom, the advocates would defer to the lawyers. Even then, there were several times when lawyers deferred to the clients' decisions. For example, lawyers counseled against, but deferred to, BRU fare-strike campaigns and efforts to disrupt MTA Board meetings, which resulted in arrests. And in those instances, the clients agreed to do damage control, permitting only advocates who were not in the settlement negotiations to get arrested and asking lawyers to negotiate with the police ahead of time to choreograph the arrests.[29]

[30] See, Eric Mann, "Confronting Transportation Racism in Los Angeles," in Just Transportation (Robert D. Bullard and Glenn S. Johnson, eds., 1997), at 68.

One conflict arose over the relative merits of moving for settlement versus taking the case to trial. Eager that the courtroom provide a platform for voicing their concerns, the grassroots activists were anxious to have the case go to trial. But the lawyers felt that the remedy under the proposed settlement was at least as good or better than plaintiffs and the class could obtain at trial. A trial would take weeks, and the inevitable appeals would consume months or years. Ultimately, BRU leaders came to agree with the lawyers that a settlement was in the best interests of all bus riders.[30]

[31] See, Transcript of Fairness Hearing, Oct. 28, 1996, at 7-19.

Another conflict arose in the final weeks of the settlement process. The MTA was researching a proposal to reserve lower-priced passes exclusively for poor riders. BRU's Mann feared that such a pass would stigmatize low-income bus riders and deter undocumented riders from seeking the pass. He also feared it would not be available to enough riders. LDF believed that these concerns were speculative because a low-income pass was not administratively feasible and therefore MTA would never implement it, and that, in any event, the Joint Working Group, LDF, the special master and the court could remedy any problems if MTA ever did attempt to adopt a low-income pass. After considerable internal debate, it was decided that LDF would continue to represent the class and the plaintiff Southern Christian Leadership Conference in support of the settlement. BRU and the other named plaintiffs would obtain separate representation for the sole purpose of questioning the low-income pass. At the fairness hearing, the MTA and the court confirmed that the low-income pass would be subject to review by the Joint Working Group. Once this issue was resolved, the court signed the settlement, and LDF once again represented the class and all the named plaintiffs.[31]

Reflecting on the coalition of lawyers, activists and community organizers who came together during this process, Mann states: "It has been a very unique relationship. It has been a difficult relationship. Sometimes we had to make [the lawyers] understand that the movement is not like a faucet...if there is an abuse we have to respond." Consequently, the lawyers and organizers sometimes had disagreements about the timing of demonstrations. Mann emphasizes, however: "In general, our lawyers have been very supportive of the movement and some of the complications which existed [between us] two to three years ago have evolved radically. It has gotten better over time." Rice similarly believes: "While the dynamic between the lawyers and clients is today very healthy, it took a lot of angry give and take, many mistakes and skillful balancing of the different obligations to get here."[32]

In the end, Rice and Mann agree that the combination of community mobilization and effective lawyering produces the most transformative and sustainable results. Without the court case the social movement could not have succeeded in the way that it has, and the legal battles would not have been as successful without the social movement.

Epilogue

As is frequently the case in litigation seeking structural reform, the settlement did not mark the end of the story. Implementation of the settlement has been slow, delayed in part by an MTA Board that remains committed to an increasingly expensive and controversial subway and rail system.

Almost three years after the agreement was struck, MTA admitted that it had violated the provisions of the settlement requiring MTA to reduce overcrowding by specified levels and specified dates. The special master issued an order directing MTA to buy more buses to remedy the overcrowding violations.[33] MTA refused to comply with the decision and appealed to the District Court, which ordered MTA to buy 248 more buses to remedy the overcrowding violations.[34] MTA filed an appeal with the 9th Circuit Court of Appeals in December 1999, challenging the remedy and the authority of the court to impose any remedy.[35] Plaintiffs and the class filed their responsive brief in January 2000. A broad-based, multicultural coalition of environmental, environmental-justice, civil rights and grassroots advocates—the Environmental Defense Fund, Natural Resources Defense Counsel, the American Civil Liberties Union of Southern California, Asian Pacific American Legal Center of Southern California and Communities for a Better Environment—submitted a friend of the court brief in support of plaintiffs and the class. The case is pending.

Mann and the BRU believe that finally achieving transportation equity requires a long-term campaign: "We have a social movement...fare boycotts and sit-ins...and our movement is growing."[36]

BROADER IMPLICATIONS

The Los Angeles MTA advocacy is a recent manifestation of a long line of civil rights efforts focused on transportation justice. Segregated railroad cars led to the infamous separate-but-equal doctrine put forth by the Supreme Court in its 1896 PLESSY V. FERGUSON ruling. Segregated buses sparked Rosa Parks' refusal to relinquish her seat in Montgomery, Alabama, in 1955, launching not only the Montgomery Bus Boycott but the modern civil

[32] Rice e-mail to P. Hair, Dec. 15, 1999.

[33] Special Master's Memorandum Decision and Order, May 14, 1999, at 29.

[34] LABOR/COMMUNITY STRATEGY CENTER, ET. AL., V. LOS ANGELES COUNTY METROPOLITAN TRANSPORTATION AUTHORITY, ET. AL., Memorandum Opinion and Order, CV 94-5936 TJH (C.D. Ca 1999).

[35] The 9th Circuit granted the MTA a stay pending appeal, which had the effect of relieving MTA of the duty to implement the District Court's rulings until the Court of Appeals has concluded its review. Order, LABOR/COMMUNITY STRATEGY CENTER, ET. AL., V. LOS ANGELES COUNTY METROPOLITAN TRANSPORTATION AUTHORITY, ET. AL., No. 99-56581 (9th Cir. Nov. 19, 1999).

[36] Venu Gupta, telephone interview with Eric Mann, Dec. 15, 1999.

rights movement in the South. In the 1960s, young Freedom Riders tested the Supreme Court's decision prohibiting discrimination in interstate travel by traveling by bus through the Deep South.

Dr. Martin Luther King Jr. captured the structural element of modern transportation policies in terms that continue to resonate today:

> Urban transit systems in most American cities…have become a genuine civil rights issue and a valid one because the layout of rapid-transit systems determines the accessibility of jobs.…If transportation systems in American cities could be laid out

The Lawyers Committee for Civil Rights Under Law and Environmental Justice

The environmental-justice movement is a grassroots effort to address community health and environmental issues through multidisciplinary mechanisms. Many communities have realized that entities responsible for the toxic pollutants harming their neighborhoods are regulated by local, state and federal agencies, each with their own political and regulatory process. Communities of color have organized to stop the inequity of siting environmental hazards in their communities. While many of these communities have fought for environmental equality without the help of outside entities, others have been forced to address these issues by utilizing the law as a resource. National environmental groups have been slow to take on environmental matters in people-of-color communities, however, grassroots groups had success utilizing civil rights networks as a means to reach and organize support and legal assistance for their struggle. The problems in Portsmouth, Virginia, are unfortunately a typical example of the struggle and determination necessary to achieve victory in environmental-justice struggles.

The Washington Park Lead Committee (WPLC) has been involved in environmental-justice work for over 10 years. WPLC is a grassroots organization that represents the African-American community residing at the Washington Park Housing Project, a 160 unit public housing project in Portsmouth, Virginia, designated by the federal government as "negro housing" over 35 years ago. It was constructed on highly lead-contaminated waste sand and within 50 feet of an operating lead foundry. Recently, the Environmental Protection Agency (EPA) designated the area, particularly the former foundry and the adjacent public housing project, as a Superfund Site. It requested that residents be relocated as part of the cleanup to escape the contamination. EPA, however, approved a cleanup plan that relocated private property owners only. Adjacent to industrial levels of lead and without an adequate buffer, residents have continued to be exposed to lead, which easily migrates off-site through the air, soil and water. The WPLC turned to the Lawyers' Committee for Civil Rights Under Law (LCCRUL).

After its discussions with the EPA were unsuccessful, the Lawyers' Committee filed a lawsuit on behalf of the WPLC and residents of Washington Park to compel the relocation of the residents.

A federal district court ruled that the Washington Park plaintiffs could pursue a constitutional claim against the cleanup plan. Until this ruling, the law had been interpreted to prohibit challenges to Superfund cleanup plans until the cleanup had been completed and its impacts were known. The court prohibited the EPA from using Superfund money in any way that would perpetuate existing segregation. While the LCCRUL and the Washington Park residents are seeking to compel EPA to relocate them in order to improve their health and economic well-being, and provide integrated housing opportunities, they also are advancing environmental-justice law by changing the precedent barring Superfund challenges prior to completion of cleanup processes. They have also helped to establish the EPA's constitutional obligation to dismantle federally established segregated housing as part of a Superfund remedy. The Lawyers' Committee is now negotiating relocation as part of a proposed settlement.

so as to provide an opportunity for poor people to get meaningful employment, then they could begin to move into the mainstream of American life. A good example of this problem is my home city of Atlanta, where the rapid-transit system has been laid out for the convenience of the white upper-middle-class suburbanites who commute to their jobs downtown. The system has virtually no consideration for connecting the poor people with their jobs. There is only one possible explanation for this situation, and that is the racist blindness of city planners.[37]

The MTA case spotlights inequities in the allocation of transportation resources and burdens. These inequities remain a major national civil rights concern. While buses and railcars were being desegregated, huge expenditures of public funds to build highways to the suburbs contributed directly to the continued residential segregation of the United States. Today, segregation between the front and the back of the bus has been replaced by entire systems that are effectively segregated, with wealthy areas getting rail lines and highways for their automobiles, and the poor suffering on dilapidated buses and deteriorating subways.

Across the country, transportation funding and benefits accrue to the wealthy at many times the rate that they do for the poor, with the overwhelming mass of transportation dollars going to roads and automobiles. As two commentators put it: "Having a seven-lane freeway next door is not a benefit to someone who does not even own a car."[38] This reality was underscored by a recent tragic death in Buffalo, New York, when a black teenager, Cynthia Wiggins, was killed crossing a seven-lane highway to get to her job at an upscale suburban shopping mall because the mall would not allow the city bus, which mainly served poor, minority neighborhoods, to stop on its property. Communities populated by the poor and people of color suffer disproportionately from the burdens of transportation. Their neighborhoods frequently are divided and destroyed by interstate highways and their health affected by the siting of bus depots and the dumping of hazardous waste produced by the transportation industry.

The success of the MTA effort and other recent transportation-justice campaigns holds out promise for a broader national strategy. Advocates are extending the lessons of the MTA case to cases in Atlanta, Milwaukee and other cities.[39] LDF and the Environmental Defense Fund are working with the DOT to implement a transportation-equity agenda across the nation.

[37] "A Testament of Hope," reprinted in A Testament of Hope, the Essential Writings and Speeches of Martin Luther King Jr. (James M. Washington, ed., 1986) (essay published posthumously).

[38] Robert D. Bullard and Glenn S. Johnson, "Introduction," in Just Transportation, Dismantling Race and Class Barriers to Mobility (Bullard and Johnson, eds., 1997), at 1.

[39] See, Robert Garcia, "Mean Streets: Transportation Equity at the Crossroads of Race, Poverty and the Environment," 15 Forum for Applied Research and Public Policy (2000) (forthcoming). V. Gupta, telephone interview with Eric Mann, supra.

5

Prayer and Protest

Chapter

On February 1, 1960, four North Carolina A&T University freshmen sat down at the "whites-only" Woolworth's lunch counter in Greensboro, North Carolina, and refused to leave until they were served. Their protests inspired African-Americans to do the same at segregated lunch counters across the South. The lunch counter sit-ins led to the integration of the Woolworth and Kress chains, two fixtures of Southern downtown shopping districts. The sit-in movement gave birth to the Student Non-Violent Coordinating Committee (SNCC), of which many of the founding members were ministers (right).

At the huge Kmart distribution center in Greensboro, North Carolina, the principally African-American work force was harassed and insulted by management, and paid far less than white Kmart workers doing the very same tasks in its other facilities throughout the country. The workers saw it as outright discrimination of a kind that is rooted in the Southern legacy of racism and Jim Crow. When they declared their intention to unionize, the workers locked horns with a Kmart management that was determined to keep the workers intimidated and wages at rock bottom. The cause of the workers proved so compelling, it inspired the African-American community in Greensboro first to prayer vigils and public protest and then to begin an educational effort and a dialogue with the Chamber of Commerce and the business community at large. The result was a union contract guaranteeing more equitable terms for Kmart workers. Greensboro developed a new sense of self—one that demands greater accountability from the giant corporations that choose to locate facilities there, and one with a more compassionate and clearheaded vision for community sustainability and for the rights of its workers of all races, who contribute so much to the region's economic and social vitality.

Chapter 5
Prayer and Protest:
Bringing a Community Vision of Justice to a Labor Dispute

Key Lessons Learned

- Keep focused on the broader interests of whole communities; while simultaneously addressing the racial dimensions of the problem.

- Use legal skills to revitalize public institutions, make them more responsive to communities and more capable of addressing local economic dislocation wrought by globalization.

- Draw on the power of past civil rights efforts to strengthen current struggles.

- Strategically employ adversarial techniques including time-tested protest strategies to challenge intransigence and gain access to decision-making processes.

- Structure representation and litigation to voice, and build support for, community claims.

Ministers and Kmart: The involvement of ministers transformed the Kmart struggle from a labor-management dispute into an issue of sustaining community living standards and defining responsible corporate citizenship (above and left).

OVERVIEW

Greensboro, North Carolina, is home to a deeply rooted civil rights movement and years of union organizing at major local manufacturers. In the 1960s, Greensboro gave birth to the civil rights sit-in movement. Students from North Carolina A&T University sat in to demand service at the local Woolworth's lunch counter. In the 1970s, a union effort to organize black and white workers in the textile industry had picked up steam. Union organizers report that some in the industry encouraged the Ku Klux Klan to disrupt the cross-racial coalition and undermine the union's fledgling movement. At a peaceful demonstration by civil rights and union organizers in 1979, Klansmen and Nazis gunned down 13 participants, killing five of them in the infamous "Greensboro Massacre."

The Kmart Corporation, a $35 billion international retail chain with 200,000 employees nationwide, opened a distribution center in Greensboro in April 1992. The Greensboro facility supplies hard-goods stock for all Kmart stores in five states—North Carolina, South Carolina, Virginia, West Virginia and Tennessee. The distribution center is massive. Located on 37 acres, it is the size of 35 football fields. The entire facility is surrounded by barbed wire; a guard house stands at the entrance. Thousands of tractor trailers line up row after row in the huge parking area around the warehouse. It is one of 13 such Kmart distribution centers in the United States.

Greensboro was attractive to Kmart because of its centrality as a regional transportation center and because North Carolina is an anti-union state where wages are low. Kmart negotiated more than $1 million in concessions from the local and state governments, including construction of roads and provision of public water to the site.

Kmart hired 550 workers for the Greensboro location, approximately 65 percent African-American and 35 percent white. The work is relatively low-skilled, involving a lot of moving, lifting and transporting. For the first few years, the managers were all white.

The plant opened in the spring before construction was complete. The weather was very hot, and workers complained that temperatures in this huge, unventilated warehouse often would soar above 100 degrees. Port-O-Johns were the only restroom facilities. Workers and management were not allowed to use the same bathrooms, managers insulted workers frequently and sexual harassment and racial slurs were common and tolerated. Complaints about injuries or sickness were ignored.[1]

According to the Rev. Nelson Johnson, the level of injuries, back injuries in particular, was "horrendous." More than 200 injuries to workers occurred at the facility during the first year of operation. In one case, when a worker injured her back, she was referred to a company doctor who told her to go back to work. Upon following the doctor's orders, she reinjured her back, causing permanent damage. Another worker fell and hurt his leg. His co-workers carried him to the company nurse, who gave him some ice and told him to

[1] The Rev. Nelson Johnson, statement at the Rockefeller Foundation convening on Normative Lawyering, May 31, 1996 (hereinafter, Normative Lawyering Session).

Workers and ministers believed that low wages and poor working conditions at Kmart were placing an undue strain on families. Workers couldn't spend time with their families because they needed to work overtime in order to make ends meet.

2 The Story of the Greensboro Kmart Workers: Moving Toward Authentic Community, Friends of the Poor People's Organization, Aug. 1996. The worker was Mike Thompson.

3 For example, a lengthy national boycott of J. P. Stevens resulted from that company's tactics in opposing unionization of its work force.

4 The Amalgamated Clothing and Textile Workers Union in 1995 merged with the International Ladies Garment Workers Union (ILGWU) to form the Union of Needletrades, Industrial and Textile Employees (UNITE). For convenience, we consistently refer to the union by its current name, UNITE.

5 Lincoln Mitchell interview with Phil Cohen, April 28, 1998.

6 Normative Lawyering Session, supra.

7 A second set of NLRB charges was settled on similar terms in the spring of 1996.

8 Normative Lawyering Session, supra.

return to work. When the injury worsened, the worker's private doctor prescribed surgery. That worker reports: "I will have to wear a brace the rest of my life, and the doctor said I should be on permanent light duty. But the first day back I was assigned to loading trucks."[2]

NEGOTIATION AND PROTEST

North Carolina is a "right-to-work" state with a well-publicized history of vehement, sometimes violent, corporate opposition to union organizing in the state's textile and other industries.[3] Despite the anti-union tradition of the region, Kmart workers decided they needed to form a labor union to combat the worker mistreatment. The workers had no organizing or union experience. After several unions turned them down, the Amalgamated Clothing and Textile Workers Union, which later merged to form UNITE, agreed to represent them.[4]

The union supporters began very cautiously in the spring of 1993 by passing around a toll-free number to workers who seemed supportive. Union organizers met with interested workers on the weekends at their homes. Secrecy was closely guarded. Nonetheless, Kmart management soon found out and began fighting the unionizing efforts, portraying the labor representatives as outsiders, coming from the North to stir up trouble. Over Kmart's vigorous opposition, the union won the certification vote by a 2–1 margin in September 1993.

The real battle began after certification. Phil Cohen, the UNITE business agent for the Greensboro local, says, "[t]he real challenge was negotiating the first contract."[5] The company hired an aggressive law firm, known throughout the community as a "union-busting" firm.[6]

Contract negotiations proceeded sporadically, a few hours here and there, with Kmart management putting them off for weeks in between. No union had ever organized a Kmart distribution facility and won a collective-bargaining agreement. Union leaders believed that the company had no intention of reaching agreement on a contract.

After the union certification vote, workers who were thought to support the union reported harassment on the job. The union's lawyers filed scores of claims with the National Labor Relations Board (NLRB), charging Kmart with illegal firings and unfair labor practices. After conducting its own investigations, the NLRB issued at least four separate complaints against Kmart, charging it with more than 100 unfair labor practices from 1994 to mid-1996. Kmart settled the first set of NLRB charges against it in late 1994, agreeing to reinstate and pay back wages to workers who had been fired allegedly because of their pro-union activities.[7] This victory reinvigorated the workers, at least temporarily. Nonetheless, the workers sensed that real help from the NLRB was unlikely because its remedies amounted to no more than a slap on the wrist for Kmart. To the Reverend Johnson it was "amazingly clear" that Kmart was not trying to work out the terms of a contract but was "simply trying to wear out these young men and women."[8]

The workers identified Kmart's impact on the entire community in quite specific ways. "Workers lived in the community. If they could not provide for their families and contribute to the community, it would pull the community down. Parents who can barely make enough to pay the bills have no money left for activities which can enrich the family."[9]

[9] Lincoln Mitchell interview with Sullivan Hamlet, April 29, 1998.

Deborah Compton-Holt, an African-American and Kmart's housekeeping supervisor who later sued Kmart, claims that the damage to the community as a whole included: hard-working people who could not afford to pay the rent, buy groceries and obtain health care and were under so much stress that they abused substances and took out anger on their families.

Compton-Holt was one of the workers who enlisted the help of the Pulpit Forum, an alliance of black Greensboro ministers founded in the 1960s, that had been actively supporting the workers' struggle, distributing leaflets to their congregations, meeting with local leaders and even initiating a national boycott of the Kmart chain. The Pulpit Forum took out an ad in the local African-American newspaper expressing support for the workers. The clergy also wrote to the Kmart corporate officials and a company vice president who came from Troy, Michigan, to meet with a group of the ministers.[10]

[10] Normative Lawyering Session, supra.

When, in 1994, Kmart became the lead corporate sponsor of the Greater Greensboro Open, an annual golf tournament with prominent professional golfers and national television coverage, the workers wrote letters to the sponsors explaining Kmart's mistreatment of its employees. As the tournament approached, the union and some workers indicated that they might use the tournament as an opportunity to draw some attention to their dispute with Kmart and to demonstrate that Kmart was not working very well with the community of Greensboro.[11]

[11] Ibid.
[12] Ibid.
[13] Ibid.

According to the Reverend Johnson, the Open that year was like "a huge party...and out on the green it was beautiful."[12] During the tournament, "64 workers went out and sat in the middle and were arrested."[13] This incident provided a brief stage for the protesters but drew a mixed reaction from the media and the Greensboro community. Many in the media were critical of the demonstrators for disrupting an event that they felt had nothing to do with Kmart's labor strife and was meant to make everybody feel good about the community. However, the workers viewed the golf tournament as a turning point in the development of their movement. The experience of planning and carrying out this mission solidified their bonds with each other and strengthened their resolve.

The effort to negotiate a new contract had been going on for more than a year when the union discovered that workers in Greensboro were earning about $5.00 less per hour than Kmart workers doing the same tasks in other sites, including areas with a lower cost of living than Greensboro. The Greensboro workers also accumulated personal leave time at a lower rate than employees at other distribution centers and were provided fewer benefits. The work force at most of Kmart's other hard-goods distribution facilities had a white majority.[14]

[14] Kmart claimed that one other distribution center had a work force that had no white majority. However, according to the union's research this facility, in Ontario, California, had a lower percentage of both nonwhite and African-American workers than the Greensboro distribution center.

Greensboro activists carefully built a cross-racial coalition to support the Kmart workers.

DON'T SHOP at K

Protest activity escalated during 1994 and 1995. The Pulpit Forum started its own newsletter—The Faith Forum—as a way to continuously update the community about the situation at Kmart. On Thanksgiving Day, 1995, the ministers, workers and their supporters held a press conference at the historic Greensboro Woolworth building, where the 1960s sit-in movement began, to announce a local consumer boycott of Kmart, targeted to the Christmas shopping season. On December 2, 1995, 1,700 people held a rally at a local black high school, followed by a demonstration at the Super Kmart.

Despite continuous efforts and escalating protest activity, the union and Kmart remained very far apart on the terms of a contract. The Pulpit Forum felt that Kmart's response was combative, and the larger community seemed unsympathetic, the general feeling being that union people had invaded and taken over the city according to the ministers; elected officials seemed to believe that the dispute was a matter of labor and management, and they had no business getting involved in it. The Pulpit Forum strenuously disagreed with this "structure of fragmentation of the community's interests." It unsuccessfully pleaded with the Chamber of Commerce and elected officials, calling on these political and business leaders to put pressure on Kmart in the interests of the entire Greensboro community.[15]

Finally, during the Christmas season of 1995, the Pulpit Forum determined to raise its involvement to a new level, putting ministers themselves on the front lines. The workers were tired and deeply dispirited, particularly when their scant pay could not support holiday celebrations or the purchase of gifts. Several workers planned to sit down en masse at the local Kmart store until they were arrested. After talking and praying together, eight pastors decided that they should take the workers' place and risk getting arrested and sent to jail. By doing this, they would send a clear message that the plight of the low-paid, mistreated Kmart laborers was not a "special interest" but a matter of communitywide concern. The Rev. William W. Wright explained that the workers' claims needed to have a spiritual connection to "the biblical mandate for justice and righteousness" and that the clergy was the group best suited to make this connection.[16]

It was Sunday morning, December 17, 1995, and a Christmas tree topped by a black angel stood in the entryway of the Faith Community Church. The African-American congregation sang "Joy to the World." But as their pastor, the Rev. Nelson Johnson, gave his sermon, the congregation quickly realized that this was not a routine Sunday. Several Kmart workers, including members of Faith Community Church, had decided to protest in the parking lot of the local Super Kmart store until they were arrested. The Reverend Johnson had been up most of the night. He understood that an arrest record could ruin the workers' lives. They might lose their jobs and go to prison. The ministers feared that Greensboro police might brutalize and injure the workers.

[15] Normative Lawyering Session, supra.

[16] Lincoln Mitchell interview with the Rev. William F. Wright, African-American member of the Pulpit Forum, April 28, 1998.

The Reverend Johnson's sermon that morning reminded the congregation of the gospel message to assist "the least and the lame and those who have to struggle." He explained his decision to stand in the place of the Kmart workers and concluded by asking the members of the congregation to join him at the Super Kmart, to bear witness and support them.

Thus, instead of the Kmart workers, eight pastors were arrested as they prayed in the Kmart parking lot that day along with three others—the president of the local Poor People's Organization, a state representative and an aide to the governor, who happened to be in town and felt moved to join in the protest.

The ministers' protest did not bring an immediate resolution to the dispute. But, for the first time, the mayor and the president of the Chamber of Commerce "got in touch and said we really need to talk this matter through because this is really not good for business." These leaders began efforts to broker a resolution of the workers' claims. Michael Zucker, the director of Corporate and Financial Affairs for UNITE, felt that the ministers' decision was critical. "Once the ministers got arrested, Kmart had no chance of winning, because the ministers had tremendous moral authority in the community."[17]

[17] Lincoln Mitchell telephone interview with Michael Zucker.

The pastors' arrests increased community understanding and concern about the situation. The arrests changed the newspaper coverage of the Kmart dispute, raising it "from the business page to the community page." As the Reverend Johnson relates: "Up until this point, we [had] not been able to have any meaningful conversation with the majority community." The arrests "turned our city into a discussion. You couldn't go anywhere without having to discuss this now. And when people started talking, no matter where they started, there were some possibilities." When the ministers' arrests caught the attention of the mayor and the city council, the Pulpit Forum started conversations with the white business community resolved "to lead this city towards itself."[18]

[18] Normative Lawyering Session, supra.

The ministers selected Martin Luther King Jr. Day, January 15, 1996, as the appropriate occasion for another mass demonstration and civil disobedience. They concluded that "the only way we could celebrate the King holiday is to invite others to join us in jail."[19] The Pulpit Forum conducted training sessions on "the spiritual basis for, and proper conduct during, nonviolent civil disobedience."[20] The ministers invoked the history and imagery of the civil rights movement, tying the Kmart struggle to Dr. King's campaign for economic justice and his last effort with the garbage workers of Memphis, Tennessee. At the same time, the Pulpit Forum emphasized the growing participation in the demonstrations by white members of the Greensboro community, particularly the Friends of Poor People Organization. The Pulpit Forum's newsletter stressed: "Race has historically been used to divide blacks and whites, and thereby to drive down the wages of both races. It is important that black and white workers in the plant join together. It is also important that the

[19] Ibid.

[20] The Faith Forum, Sunday, Jan. 14, 1996, p. 1.

white community challenge the policies of race discrimination." A large demonstration at the Super Kmart, with arrests of 39 ministers, workers and community members, marked the 1996 King holiday in Greensboro.[21]

[21] Ibid., p. 4.

Further demonstrations were held on many of the following Sundays. Gradually, the workers from the plant joined in. Students (mostly white) from Guillford College, led by Professor Joe Groves, as well as from other local colleges, filled the ranks of those arrested, which numbered dozens each Sunday. Over time, the weekly demonstrations came to include a diverse array of community members: white and black workers and ministers, representatives of the local business community, politicians, university professors and students. Even children joined the picket lines.

In the spring of 1996, as protesters continued to return to the site regularly, the media and public pressure grew. The boycott of Kmart retail stores, initially limited to Greensboro, expanded throughout the country. UNITE members in other communities mobilized to support the Greensboro workers, and the Pulpit Forum used its network of African-American clergy throughout the South to spread the word about the protests and boycott. In March 1996, marches and rallies to publicize the boycott were held in numerous cities, including Atlanta, Chicago, Cleveland, Norfolk, Memphis and Houston.

THE SEARCH FOR HEALTHY COMMUNITY

The large-scale arrests helped recast the Kmart struggle—which had been perceived by most city residents as simply a labor-management dispute—as a moral challenge to decide the future of Greensboro as a community. The Beloved Community Center, a multiracial organization founded by two white ministers and the Reverend Johnson, took the lead in developing a dialogue with business leaders. While agreeing with the Chamber of Commerce that the community needed economic growth, the Pulpit Forum and the Beloved Community Center asserted: "It just can't be any kind of economic growth....We need environmentally safe, good economic growth." They framed the issue as "how to bring this...corporate citizen...under the discipline of citizens in this community."[22]

[22] Normative Lawyering Session, supra.

Under the auspices of the Beloved Community Center, the ministers went to work with the Chamber of Commerce and the business community to address the larger issue of creating a healthy, sustainable community. The political and business leaders initially requested that

The workers' first contract with Kmart ultimately included a $2.50 per hour pay raise, access to arbitration and stronger safety laws.

the protests end before a dialogue could begin. But the movement's leadership refused, believing that a two-part strategy of protest and negotiation would be most effective.

23 Ibid.

The Reverend Johnson emphasizes that the ministers' goal was to make the workers' plight a public issue: "We made a deliberate effort to not let the issue be defined as a labor-management or racial-discrimination issue, but rather as a community issue with labor and race as central concerns."[23] Beloved Community Center highlighted Kmart's status as a large, corporate outsider that might not have operated so unfairly if it were a local company with roots in the community. It emphasized that the problem with such international companies is that their management is elsewhere. The ministers framed Kmart's refusal to pay a living wage as both an economic injustice to its employees and a financial insult to Greensboro itself, saying that it undermined efforts to create a "sustainable community" where workers could afford to fully pay their way in the city's economy.

24 Ibid.

In the discussions with business leaders, the Reverend Johnson reports: "it first was a struggle just to have a [common] language because we were coming from such different places."[24] However, the group overcame its differences, and diverse members of the community were able to agree on a five-point plan for achieving a healthy community: 1) admitting that racial discrimination in the workplace exists and must be actively addressed; 2) raising wages in the city to a sustainable level; 3) preparing the work force for the jobs of the future; 4) seeking environmentally safe, good economic growth; and

5) developing a way that "citizens can begin to hold corporate citizens accountable for their behavior."[25]

25 Ibid.

COMMUNITY-FOCUSED LAWYERING

UNITE's lawyers played several critical roles in the Kmart campaign. The filing of NLRB claims, the NLRB's issuance of complaints after its own investigations and the settlement of two sets of complaints gave independent proof to the community that Kmart was violating workers' rights. The union's lawyers also prevented efforts to decertify the union, thus preserving the workers' vehicle for gaining Kmart's agreement to a contract. In addition, UNITE's Southern regional counsel, David Prouty, participated in the contract negotiations with Kmart. Finally, when Kmart sued the workers,

UNITE hired James Ferguson from the firm of Ferguson, Stein, Wallace, Adkins, Greshan & Sumpter, and helped to coordinate the defense.

Ferguson, Stein, was among the original interracial law firms established through a Ford Foundation program that aimed to build legal capacity on a local and regional level. Several of these firms became part of a network of skilled cooperating attorneys who served as community-based partners for NAACP Legal Defense Fund (LDF) litigation. Ferguson, Stein, for example, has been responsible for many major civil rights precedents in the U.S. Supreme Court.

26 Ibid.

After another mass arrest in March 1996, Kmart sued several of the Greensboro pastors and workers, as well as the union, seeking an injunction prohibiting them from entering Kmart property. The Reverend Johnson recounts: "[Kmart] said that we had irreparably damaged their business...such good news we had not recently heard." The activists immediately incorporated Kmart's lawsuit against their group into their communications strategy. "[W]e felt honored to have been sued by Kmart, and we immediately went to the state Baptist Convention and announced it, and we wrote Kmart and told them that we were going to all of the national conventions and announce [it]. We want[ed] to tell the world about it."[26]

27 Robert J. Warren, "Protesters Hire Noted Attorney to Battle Kmart," **High Point Enterprise**, April 19, 1996.

28 Ibid.

Attorney James Ferguson ("Fergie"), is a giant of civil rights litigation nationally. Simply obtaining his agreement to represent the defendants was itself a victory that sent a strong message to Kmart and the public that Kmart's conduct was a civil rights issue. Fergie understood the movement's strong interest in handling the lawsuit in a manner that served the broader goals of keeping pressure on Kmart and consolidating community support for the protesters. The activists seized the public stage to announce their choice of counsel. Fergie's first official appearance on behalf of the Kmart protesters was not in court but at a press conference, during which he read aloud from customer complaints filed by Kmart, noting that customers said they were afraid during the demonstrations because of the large police presence. Fergie suggested: "Maybe they're (Kmart) suing the wrong party."[27] Also during that press conference, Robyn Estes, one of the four workers sued by Kmart, commented: "The CEO of Kmart makes $20 million a year; I make less than $20,000."[28] UNITE representative Ben Hensler stated: "Many people...have stopped shopping at Kmart....But that is in response to our moral blockade, not a physical blockade."[29]

29 Ibid.

According to Ben Hensler, Kmart's suit had positive results. Kmart sued only black workers and pastors though whites participated in protests too, reinforcing a sense that the company's policies were motivated by race. In addition, the lawsuit was an admission that the boycott was having an effect. Finally, the fact that Kmart sued the pastors showed that the issue had been embraced by the community and was no longer simply a labor issue.

In May 1996, when Kmart argued for a preliminary injunction, the courtroom "was just full of people" supporting the workers. The Reverend Johnson describes the scene. "An old black woman stood up and started singing in this judge's court. 'Ain't gonna let nobody turn me around' and he [the judge] left the court. He came outside and asked us to ask her to stop, and she did, *but not until she finished the song*. Then someone prayed."[30]

[30] Normative Lawyering Session, supra.

In traditional terms, Fergie and his clients "lost" that round of legal battles. The court entered an injunction against further civil disobedience. But, in broader terms, Fergie's clients "won" by insisting on telling their stories to the public both inside and outside the courtroom.

Mobilizing Demand and Consumer Purchasing Power

It is impossible to sort out precisely which of the multifaceted activities on behalf of the Kmart workers finally brought the company to the bargaining table. But, it seems clear that Kmart was particularly influenced by the negative publicity and the actual or potential impact of the growing consumer boycott. When the company finally went to court against the activists, it was to seek an injunction prohibiting them from demonstrating on any Kmart property, worldwide. In the highly competitive retail environment, a company's image and its brand name carry enormous value, making adverse publicity particularly potent.

Boycotts can help energize community activists, as well as put pressure on an entity or even an entire state. For example, the NAACP's ongoing boycott over the display of the Confederate battle flag at the South Carolina Capitol reportedly has cost the state's businesses millions of dollars in lost revenues. Taking youth on buses to demonstrate in South Carolina also has been an effective way to pass on the lessons of the civil rights movement to the younger generation.

Organizing consumer demand can be a powerful tool in community efforts to hold corporations accountable for the way they conduct their business. Particularly in this era of globalization and intense competition, communities may find use of their purchasing power to be an effective way to make businesses accountable to local values. If the facts are known, many consumers will choose not to purchase from companies that treat their workers badly, pay below a living wage, pollute the environment, produce their clothing in sweatshops or otherwise harm communities. This approach puts a value, not just on consumer goods, but on social goods. Communities can also assert the value of social goods by mobilizing themselves to patronize good corporate citizens. Taking advantage of deregulation of a former monopoly, some communities are organizing cooperatives to purchase power from environmentally conscious utility companies, often getting a lower price in the bargain. And, businesses themselves are seeking to attract customers by touting their social values.

Consumer boycotts are constitutionally protected First Amendment activity, as long as they do not use coercive tactics to cause third parties to comply with the boycott. Communities seeking to organize consumer demand need access to lawyers with problem-solving skills to help them navigate the legal shoals involved in boycotts, defend themselves in litigation if necessary, and structure buying cooperatives or other vehicles. Communities also may need access to research to help them distinguish good corporate citizens from bad ones. Finally, organizing demand often involves communication strategies, such as the successful efforts of anti-sweatshop activists to inform the American public about alleged abuses by Nike and Disney.

Winning a Contract and Continuing the Struggle

In 1996, after years of foot-dragging, Kmart finally came to the bargaining table for serious negotiations with the workers' union. That year, the union reached its first contract with Kmart, which included a $2.50 per hour pay raise. The agreement also included a number of protections for workers, such as access to arbitration and stronger safety laws.

In the years since the first contract was won, conditions have improved somewhat for workers. Although Kmart failed in its repeated efforts to have the union decertified, problems still exist. The company has unilaterally made decisions about overtime pay and had several claims of worker mistreatment sent to arbitration. The union, the workers and the clergy continue to educate the larger community about the issues at stake in the Kmart situation and their connections to worker struggles and anti-racism efforts throughout the globe.[31]

Race, Economics and Community—Lessons from the Kmart Struggle

Race infuses the Kmart story in layered and cross-cutting ways. At one level, old-fashioned racial and gender discrimination resulted in the low wages and mistreatment of workers. While all workers at the Greensboro facility were treated badly, minority and female employees were treated worse. Both white and black workers felt that Kmart attempted to sow seeds of racial divisiveness among them as part of its anti-union strategy. Workers who were divided on racial grounds would have difficulty bonding together to address their common problems with Kmart. A wage differential of $5.00 an hour for identical work between Greensboro, where the workers were 65 percent nonwhite, and the 12 other Kmart distribution centers also stands as stark evidence that racial discrimination played a part in the mistreatment of the Kmart workers.

At another level, race influences the economic structure in a way that is more difficult for the public to understand as "discrimination." Like slavery, many racial-justice issues are deeply intertwined with economic issues. Without an understanding of the history and the structural role of race, the prevailing low wage rate in Greensboro might not be perceived as racially based but simply as flowing from economic factors in the region. Businesses that claim to have no conscious, or invidious, racial intent see themselves as just taking advantage of the "economic" factor of the prevailing wage rate, which tends to be lower in the South because of a history of racial oppression.

The highly competitive global economy, with its own racial component, also plays a strong role. Political leaders and corporate interests are locked into fierce global competition. Cities compete with each other for industrial sites, while corporations search the globe for low-cost labor, business-friendly environments, and tax and financial concessions. The rules of *this* game encourage the mayor, the City Council, even the community of Greensboro, to ignore social-justice factors and to focus their efforts on granting tax breaks to attract new corporate ventures.

[31] In 1999, UNITE won a second contract with Kmart, which brought the salary and benefits of Greensboro workers up to full parity with workers at Kmart's other facilities.

Race also played a very positive role in the Kmart dispute—African-Americans were in the lead, organizing and educating the entire community, including whites. One white worker, David Bloom, reports that "whites learned from African-Americans about the power of sticking together."[32] Another white worker, Gail Simon, similarly recounted that the Kmart struggle helped bring African-Americans and whites together.[33]

[32] Lincoln Mitchell interview with David Bloom, April 30, 1998.

[33] Lincoln Mitchell interview with Gail Simon, April 30, 1998.

African-American preachers taught the white mayor and members of the Chamber of Commerce about the importance of the black church as a valued institution that is rooted in the culture and traditions of the black community *and* that can exercise leadership for the entire community. Black preachers showed the mayor and Chamber the value of moderating and re-evaluating their zeal for market-driven economic development where social harms may result. The results can be seen in their joint dialogue and the fruit it bore—the five-point plan for a healthy community. That plan explicitly takes into consideration the issue of racial discrimination, setting goals of improved education, employment and corporate responsibility to ensure all are lifted up and no one is left behind. And with the plan, the white community acknowledges that racial discrimination handicaps the entire community, not just its minority members.

The African-American community brought knowledge, experience and perseverance to the fight for justice. Members of the community identified collectively with a shared history of overcoming great obstacles and enduring great pain. They drew together internally in a crisis, providing support and comfort to each other. This type of identity seems negative to many whites—a refusal to submerge into the "melting pot," a perpetual self-victimization or, even worse, a hostile separatism. But to African-Americans, it is not about separatism or cultural isolation; it is about having a safe space of love and comfort in the midst of a hostile world.

Adviser Lani Guinier, in writing about the Kmart campaign, notes the dilemma of trying to address race with both white and African-American communities:

> Reverend Johnson concluded that "race and racism was the major factor in the assumption that you could set up this distribution center in a right-to-work state, hire a lot of black people and pay them essentially nothing." Reverend Johnson recognized, however, that if they framed the issue as one of race, many white people would hear it and say, "That does not concern me, or even worse, I disagree." But if they framed the issue without discussing race, many blacks would hear it and say, "That is not responsive to my concerns."[34]

[34] Lani Guinier, Lift Every Voice: Turning a Civil Rights Setback Into a New Vision of Social Justice (Simon & Schuster, 1998).

In many situations involving similar issues of race, public discussion are engulfed in conflict, and racially distinct communities do battle. This story is different because it shows, after years of isolation and conflict, a coming together of diverse communities to work for the common good. It demonstrates that there are ways to open up all Americans' ability to

35 Lincoln Mitchell interview with Dwight Davidson, April 30, 1998.

more fully understand the harms caused by racial discrimination. By putting a community-based framework on the struggle, the Greensboro activists found a way to make race "visible" to whites. White workers learned that *their* wages were depressed because of racial discrimination directed at blacks, but affecting all. One white Greensboro businessman who participated in the Pulpit/Business Forum's efforts to mediate the contract negotiations came to realize that "nobody ever put obstacles in my way, like they did to the African-American workers at Kmart."[35]

Once the issue caught hold as a community struggle, whites did participate and played an important role in the Kmart campaign. White clergy got involved in advocacy and protests, as did many white college students. By the end of the long period of contract negotiations, white workers were so aligned with their African-American counterparts that when individual African-American workers were sued, the white workers protested because they had not also been sued though they had engaged in the same boycott and protest activities.

There are also growing numbers of Latinos, Asian-Americans and other racial and ethnic groups living in Greensboro and working at Kmart. In a country that has barely started to address the black/white paradigm of race, these "other minorities" do not fit neatly into any historically defined lines. Black and white workers report that Kmart began hiring immigrants as "temporary" or contract workers in what has been perceived as another effort to divide and conquer. Vulnerable immigrants were initially particularly susceptible to Kmart's tactics of intimidation. But the union and the clergy reached out to the immigrants, many of whom became active in challenging Kmart.

UNITE played a critical role in organizing the workers and fighting for a contract. Union leaders report that it would not have been possible to represent the workers without their strong participation and leadership. The workers were on the front lines against Kmart and provided strength that made it possible for the whole community to persevere.

Epilogue

In 1994, two white Presbyterian ministers joined with the Rev. Nelson Johnson to form the Beloved Community Center. Named in honor of Dr. Martin Luther King's vision of a "beloved community," it seeks to build a society in which the social and economic structures affirm the equality and worth of every person. The center has developed into a continuing institutional base for multifaceted work toward the vision of a healthy Greensboro. The Beloved Community Center has a solid, multiracial membership and is making progress in tackling other tough, and previously intractable, issues faced by the Greensboro region, including consolidation of the predominantly minority city school system with the predominantly white suburban system, the plight of the homeless, and the soaring levels of incarceration of African-Americans for nonviolent offenses.

Broader Implications

The Reverend Johnson elaborates on the broader structural issues that the Beloved Community Center is starting to address:

> We are building nonsustainable places of pain and hurt and sickness, where people don't feel affirmed, and are kicked around and treated any way. Then we set up a network of social-services programs, a colonial apparatus, to lay on top of them when what they need is work. A decent job, so that they can take care of their families and send their children to school, and that's the issue that we've lifted up Sunday after Sunday in our churches, and we lifted it up so that the city and everybody else can see that there is a way out of this.[36]

The Kmart struggle has thus revived an activist movement in Greensboro that has deep roots in earlier civil rights efforts, but which had been demoralized by the trauma of the Greensboro killings and related events. In the words of the Reverend Johnson: "We have tried to say to the workers at Kmart that you are our gift. That God sent you as a gift because you stirred a stumbling, bumbling people just enough to stand up and try to discover what it means to be human, what it means to call a community into being a community."[37]

[36] Normative Lawyering Session, supra.

[37] Ibid.

chapter 6

Reflections on Community Lawyering

Chinese immigrants fleeing growing nativism on the West Coast settled in the area of Boston that would come to be known as Chinatown. By the 1920s, Chinatown was well settled with a thriving business sector and an active civic and community life (right).

When a major research university obtained city approval to turn one of the remaining parcels of open space in Boston's Chinatown into a multistory parking lot, residents sprang into action. Years of hostile land-use decisions by city officials had already blighted the neighborhood with numerous highway arteries and a red-light district. Hazards included poor air quality, inadequate housing and one of Boston's highest concentrations of parking lots per acre in a neighborhood where 70 percent of residents do not own cars. Using creative legal strategies supplemented by protests, media campaigns, neighborhood coalition building and strategic alliances with powerful environmental groups, a disenfranchised immigrant community with limited English was able to stop the parking-lot project and win back use of the space. A community complex will soon be constructed on the site.

Chapter 6
Reflections on Community Lawyering:
The Struggle for Parcel C

Excerpted from the article of Zenobia Lai, Andrew Leong and Chi Chi Wu, 6 UCLA Asian Pacific American Law Journal 1, at 1.

Key Lessons Learned

- Document the history of policy decisions that have created racial barriers in order to help community members understand structural exclusion and to build the record for possible litigation.

- Recognize the tension between raising community members' awareness of their legal rights and acknowledging the limits of legal strategies.

- Elicit the community's own voice, creativity and judgment on all matters including legal strategy and advocacy.

- Mobilize young people in outreach efforts.

- Work with lawyers who speak the language of the community and share its culture.

- Carefully monitor translators to ensure accurate communication with clients and community groups. Remain connected to the community to build trust. Shared ethnicity and/or language alone are insufficient.

"Chinatowns" are among the most vibrant ethnic neighborhoods in America's urban landscape (left). Boston's Chinatown has had a rich tradition of commerce, restaurants and community life, as well as a history of protest against unfair local policies.

Boston's Chinatown has not been well served by urban renewal (above). Through the 1950s and '60s, substantial portions of Chinatown's land and housing were taken for major highway construction and the expansion of the Tufts–New England Medical Center. In 1974, the city moved an adult-entertainment district to Chinatown to make way for the construction of the new government center.

Overview

Chinatowns are among the most vibrant ethnic neighborhoods in America's landscape. Home to recent immigrants and old-timers alike, a city's Chinatown is the heart of many urban Asian-American communities. Chinatowns are often found in city centers, in crowded and polluted environments. Boston's Chinatown, the fourth largest in the United States, is no exception.

Since the 1950s, urban planning has given Boston's Chinatown two massive highways, land-hungry medical institutions and a red-light district. Decades of such harmful policies came to a head in 1993, when the city of Boston tried to sell open land in the heart of Chinatown to build a mammoth parking garage. The proposed sale of this land, known as "Parcel C," sparked protest and galvanized resistance.

The Parcel C struggle combined grassroots community organizing and community lawyering. This case study explores what "community lawyering" means in practice, especially when the community is disenfranchised, immigrant and not fluent in English. It also addresses how to go beyond the limitations of traditional lawyering, which often focuses narrowly on legal remedies granted by a court of law. The struggle succeeded only because legal strategies were supplemented with political protests, media campaigns, neighborhood coalition building and alliances with powerful environmental groups.

THE LEGACY OF URBAN PLANNING

Boston's Chinatown is a small but densely populated community encompassing 46 acres in the downtown. For many, Chinatown is a pleasant stop on weekend excursions, a purely commercial district of "exotic" shops, markets and restaurants. But it is also a residential community and home to more than 5,000 people.

During the 1880s, Chinese immigrants fled the rising nativism of the West Coast and arrived in Boston to develop the area known today as Chinatown. The Chinese community was well-settled and growing during the early and mid-20th century. After World War II, the business sector—especially restaurants—flourished, bringing economic prosperity as well as new civic and community associations.

Starting in the 1950s, Chinatown became a victim of "urban renewal."[1] Cities such as Boston adopted strategies specifically to attract businesses and industries back into downtown, to refurbish its tax base, and to entice urban residents to remain. Unfortunately, all communities did not equally share in the burdens and benefits of urban renewal.[2] In the 1950s and 1960s, Boston's Chinatown lost one half of its land and one third of its housing to two new highways: the Central Artery and the Massachusetts Turnpike Extension. Built between 1953 and 1959, the Central Artery destroyed more than 50 housing structures as well as half of the celebrated On Leong Merchant Association building. In 1963,

[1] Urban renewal, refers to the federal program heralded by the Housing Act of 1949 and its subsequent amendments. PL 81-171, 42 U.S.C. § 1441, et seq. (1949).

[2] The destructive legacy of urban renewal in numerous cities is well documented. See, John Stainton, Urban Renewal and Planning in Boston—A Review of the Past and Look at the Future, a Consultative Study, at 19 (Nov. 1972, BRA) (hereinafter, Stainton). See, also, Martin Anderson, The Federal Bulldozer: A Critical Analysis of Urban Renewal, 1949-1962 (MIT Press, Cambridge, Mass., 1964); Jewell Bellush and Murray Hausknecht, Urban Renewal: People, Politics and Planning (Anchor Books, New York, N.Y., 1967).

the Massachusetts Turnpike Extension destroyed 60 more housing structures. Cutting off potential routes of expansion, these highways eliminated much affordable housing, reduced the number of commercial venues and added enormous traffic congestion, noise and pollution.[3]

Federal urban-renewal policy started to restructure Chinatown when the city of Boston adopted the 1965 South Cove Urban Renewal Plan (the Plan) that slated Chinatown for "slum clearance." The Boston Redevelopment Authority (BRA), the city agency in charge of urban renewal, took land from Chinatown residents and sold it to Tufts–New England Medical Center (T–NEMC). This exchange of land enabled T–NEMC to triple in size in the 1970s and 1980s.[4]

As a tax-exempt entity, T–NEMC received federal funds to acquire and demolish Chinatown properties in order to develop its own buildings.[5] In its role as landlord of the newly acquired properties, T–NEMC refused to renew leases for both residential and commercial tenants, which meant the loss of both jobs and affordable housing for the Chinatown community.[6]

Having a modern hospital in the heart of Chinatown might have been expected to soften those blows. Unfortunately, T–NEMC has given little back to the community in which it is housed. Most Chinatown residents have not and do not today receive medical care at T–NEMC. Instead, they go to the South Cove Community Health Center in Chinatown, founded in 1976. Before that time, residents traveled about 1.5 miles to Boston City Hospital for medical services because T–NEMC declined to provide outpatient facilities. Even after T–NEMC began operating some outpatient facilities in the 1970s, few Chinatown residents used its services because it did not provide interpreter services, provided less free health care, and was less culturally sensitive to the Chinese population's dietary preferences, Eastern medicine and work schedules.[7] Indeed, when South Cove was first formed, its doctors were not allowed patient-admitting privileges to T–NEMC, although only half a block separated the two facilities and such referrals would have greatly benefited patients.

Urban renewal also moved a red-light district into Chinatown. Before urban renewal, adult-entertainment shops were located in Scollay Square, about 1.2 miles away from Chinatown. When the Square was demolished to make way for the new Government Center, these establishments scattered across the city, with a few relocating to lower Washington Street beside Chinatown. In 1974, the city of Boston took an unprecedented action by creating a safe haven for adult-entertainment businesses. The idea was to contain these businesses, prevent their spread into other neighborhoods and make them easier to police. The city chose to create this "Combat Zone" beside Chinatown, rather than next to Back Bay or Beacon Hill, which are predominantly white and wealthier neighborhoods.[8] Throughout the

3 Chinese Economic Development Council, Economic Development for Boston's Chinese Community, Phase II, the Acquisition of Title VII-D Community Development Corporation on Planning Grant Proposal (Dec. 1, 1975), at 12-13.

4 See, e.g., New England Medical Center, Master Plan 1990-2000, at 6-13 (Boston, March 1990).

5. See, Section 112 of the Housing Act of 1961, Pub. L. 87-70. 75 Stat. 149 (June 30, 1961); Julian H. Levi, Municipal and Institutional Relations with Boston: The Benefits of Section 112 of the Federal Housing Act of 1961 (Chicago, University of Chicago Press, 1964), at 2, 12-14.

6 See, **Singtao Daily News** (April 27, 1981). See, also, Joan Axlerod, "Rent Hikes Force Needle Trades to Look Elsewhere: Tufts Puts Squeeze on Chinatown," **Boston Ledger**, July 31, 1981, p. 3, col. 1.

7 See, Sullivan and Hatch, The Chinese in Boston, 1970, at 66. Action for Boston Community Development, p. 20 (Boston, 1970). See, also, Boston Redevelopment Authority, Chinatown-South Cove District Profile and Proposed 1978-1980 Neighborhood Improvement Program, p. 19 (Boston, Summer 1977).

8 See, e.g., Robert A. Jordan, "In the Zone: It will Be Business as Usual, says Boston Counsel," **Boston Sunday Globe**, July 22, 1973, p. 27, col. 1; Robert Jordan, "Board OKs Zone for Hub's Adult Shows," **Boston Evening Globe**, Nov. 14, 1974, p. 1, col. 4; Edward Burke amd Peter Mancusi, "Combat Zone is Alive, Well...and Still Hard Core," **Boston Globe**, Aug. 28, 1974, p. 1, col. 1.

1970s and '80s, Chinatown endured the Combat Zone, with its peep shows, striptease clubs, adult bookstores and X-rated movie theaters. Today, due to high real-estate prices in Boston, much of the Combat Zone has disappeared.

THE ENVIRONMENTAL IMPACT

For Chinatown, urban renewal produced one of the worst urban environments in Boston. A housing crisis resulted from this process. While the population in Boston Chinatown almost doubled between 1975 and 1985, the housing stock had no room to grow. Institutional expansion by T–NEMC throughout the 1970s and 1980s drove up real-estate prices, making Chinatown's housing unaffordable.[9] In addition to losing housing stock by eminent domain, Chinatown also lost units when landlords eagerly evicted their tenants and sold their properties to Tufts or T–NEMC. The limited housing in Chinatown led to severe overcrowding. Recent immigrants seeking to live in Chinatown for both community and employment have been forced to reside in overcrowded dwellings or to settle elsewhere. Chinatown is the most densely populated neighborhood in Boston, with a ratio of 111 residents per acre, compared to 26 residents per acre in the nearby neighborhood of South End.

Lack of open space is another result of urban renewal. Chinatown has only 2.9 acres of open space—a mere 0.6-acre per 1,000 residents—the least amount per resident in the city.

[9] See, e.g., Chinatown-South Cove District Profile and Proposed 1979-1981 Neighborhood Improvement Plan 1979, at 3, 9, 20 (1979 BRA Neighborhood Planning Program) (hereinafter, 1979 Chinatown/South Cove Profile); 1978 Chinatown/South Cove Profile, at 7.

The Chinatown community is surrounded by parking lots and high rises. Residential Chinatown consists of four housing projects and several blocks of modest row houses and triple-deckers. T–NEMC expansion has inserted 8-, 11- and 15-story buildings into the landscape. Thus, most Chinatown residents live either in one of the huge gray slabs of housing development or in the shadows of T–NEMC concrete. T–NEMC expansion has also produced in Chinatown one of the highest concentrations of parking lots in Boston, with 34 spaces per acre. By comparison, South End has 4.6 parking spaces per acre, and the city of Boston, as a whole, has 1.7 per acre. In 1990, Chinatown had 1,573 off-street parking spaces, taking up 9 acres of land. Most of these parking lots or garages are used by the medical institutions for employees, clients and patients and not by Chinatown residents, since 70 percent of them do not own cars.

Finally, traffic and pollution plague the area. A study performed for the Massachusetts Turnpike Authority Associates concluded that Chinatown streets are overloaded,[10] producing extremely high rates of pedestrian accidents and fatalities.[11] Even the BRA has conceded that Chinatown suffers from "chronic traffic congestion [and that] pedestrian safety in the heavily concentrated residential areas has been threatened."[12] Bounded by the massive Central Artery and the Massachusetts Turnpike, Chinatown also suffers from air quality that violates national carbon monoxide safety standards.

[10] See, Massachusetts Turnpike Authority, Air Rights Study (1993), at 52 (hereinafter, Mass. Turnpike Study).

[11] Boston Transportation Department, Pedestrian Safety Task Force, Report on Pedestrian Safety (Spring, 1992), at 2 (hereinafter, Pedestrian Safety Report).

[12] Pedestrian Safety Report, at 18. Between 1992 and 1995, one child and two senior citizens were fatally struck by vehicles in the vicinity of Parcel C.

As a result of urban renewal efforts, Chinatown has more than its share of parking lots, traffic congestion, pollution and housing shortages. Open space is in very short supply.

[13] Master Highway Plan for the Boston Metropolitan Area, prepared for the Joint Board for the Metropolitan Master Highway Plan (1948).

[14] See, e.g., "Council Opposes Artery Route in Chinatown," **Boston Daily Globe**, Oct. 19, 1953, p. 1, col. 3 ; "Garment Area Issue Taken to Herter's Home," **Boston Daily Globe**, Oct. 27, 1953, p. 1, col. 6.

[15] See, Real Estate Research Corp., Urban Renewal Land Disposition Study (Washington, D.C., Dec. 1973). Walter L. Smart, Diagnostic report of residents to be relocated, South Cove Urban Renewal Project, at 6-10 (Boston Redevelopment Authority, Oct. 1967) (hereinafter, Diagnostic Report of Residents).

THE SACRIFICE OF CHINATOWN

The Central Artery was not originally planned to run through Chinatown.[13] Instead, it was supposed to trace the waterfront, bisecting the Leather District to the east of Chinatown before it snaked along the eastern edge of Chinatown, south of the commercial core. The original plan kept the commercial core of Chinatown undisturbed, taking housing on only two streets. However, vehement protests from powerful leather and garment industries adjacent to Chinatown prompted the Boston City Council to change the route.[14]

While the South Cove Urban Renewal Plan shifted land from Chinatown to T—NEMC, no part of the adjacent Bay Village was taken by eminent domain for T—NEMC's benefit. To prevent T—NEMC from expanding into the Bay Village, the BRA allowed T—NEMC three acres of land for their expansion within the Chinatown portion of the Plan, displacing approximately 585 households.[15] In fact, the BRA specifically prohibited T—NEMC from expanding into Bay

NAACP LDF Division of Legal Information and Community Service

Among the most important legacies for innovative lawyers is the Division of Legal Information and Community Service of the NAACP Legal Defense and Educational Fund (LDF) ("the Division"), founded with a Rockefeller grant in 1965 by veteran civil rights activist, Jean Fairfax. Over the subsequent 20 years the Division developed a multitiered strategy of enforcement, monitoring, study, evaluation, reporting and mobilization around civil rights issues. Its objectives:

- Exposing government failures to guarantee and enforce civil rights;

- Identifying and seeking to rectify structural impediments to effective civil rights implementation by civil rights administrators;

- Strengthening the capacity of organized minority citizens to work for their own liberation; and

- Initiating cooperative ventures with public agencies and minority citizens to fashion and test innovative approaches to civil rights enforcement and programs.

The Division provided LDF tactical flexibility when litigation had limited effectiveness. It developed long-standing relationships of trust with the permanent staff of federal agencies. It worked with a range of government actors from cabinet secretaries to local officials. Division staff worked simultaneously on the local, state and regional levels, with constituents gathering information and engaging in action projects.

Strong relationships with community leaders around the country, and a well-credentialed field staff listening on the ground, enabled the Division to gather information and to make assessments of African-American priorities on issues. It helped LDF legal staff to shape litigation programs, select issues, identify plaintiffs, prepare for hearings, shape remedies, monitor compliance and organize citizens. The Division used flexible problem-solving approaches to address ongoing discrimination. When research revealed entrenched discrimination in the paper industry, it helped organize the Black Association of Millworkers, which became an important force within the unions.

It is important to note that the Division's work was not limited to African-Americans. For example, it conducted an in-depth investigation of educational disparities affecting Native American children, and did significant research on issues affecting women and disabled people of all races. It worked on a wide array of issues from health-care delivery to hunger, regional planning and school-workplace linkages in local communities. Through all of these efforts, the Division served as a crucial tie between LDF, LDF's base and other groups.

Village under the plan.[16] What's more, the city encouraged rehabilitation in Bay Village by making available federally funded low-interest loans, opportunities not offered to Chinatown.[17] Another example of the disparate treatment between Bay Village and Chinatown was how the Plan handled traffic patterns in each neighborhood. The Plan specifically called for retaining the intimate character of Bay Village by blocking off outside traffic and orienting new construction away from major streets of Bay Village. On the other hand, similar street patterns in the Plan area outside of Bay Village were deemed wasteful, dangerous and incompatible for commercial, industrial and institutional use.[18]

Why was Chinatown treated worse than Bay Village? BRA believed Bay Village to be quaint and well-kept but Chinatown to be dilapidated and run-down,[19] even though the housing stock in the two neighborhoods was quite similar. Official documents also reveal that the BRA viewed Chinese-Americans as "self-sustaining," gainfully employed, off welfare, relatively healthy and with more male-headed households than whites. These sweeping generalizations had no empirical support. Instead, they were simply stock stereotypes of Chinese, as people who can and will endure great suffering, in silence, simply "taking care of themselves."[20]

Finally, notwithstanding numerous complaints about prostitution, drugs and violence associated with the Combat Zone businesses, Boston officials did nothing.[21] They retorted that "the police have more important things to do than to 'cover the combat zone like a tent'." The city recognized that coming down too hard on the Combat Zone would force X-rated businesses elsewhere, and it wanted to protect Back Bay and Beacon Hill from such encroachment.[22]

In short, since the 1950s, Chinatown has been forced to bear a disproportionate burden of the costs of urban renewal and highway construction. Its environment and its residents have suffered greatly while nearby neighborhoods and institutions either have been left untouched or have profited directly by the land stripped from Chinatown. The city of Boston has been willing to sacrifice Chinatown to benefit others, viewing its residents as politically docile and especially well suited to survive in a denigrated environment.

THE PARCEL C STRUGGLE

One of the last open Chinatown lots zoned for residential use, Parcel C is a piece of city-owned land, approximately 25,000 square feet. T–NEMC uses three small buildings on the northern edge of Parcel C as offices. Much of the space on Parcel C serves as a surface parking lot for T–NEMC patients and staff. The southeastern edge of Parcel C borders the Acorn Day Care Center operated by a nonprofit agency. The Acorn Day Care Center building serves as an adult-education facility at night. Parcel C is within 40 feet from a new family-housing development and one block from an elementary school, elderly housing and another low-income housing development.

[16] Stainton, at 70.

[17] See, e.g., Real Estate Research Corp., Urban Renewal Land Disposition Study, South Cove Urban Renewal Plan, at 196 (Washington, D.C., Dec. 1973) (hereinafter, Land Deposition Study); Stainton, at 70.

[18] Boston Redevelopment Authority, Information on the Proposed South Cove Urban Renewal Project and on the Bay Village Community, at 1-2 (Dec. 1965). See, also, Boston Redevelopment Authority, Back Bay–Beacon Hill–Bay Village: District Profile and Proposed 1979-1981 Neighborhood Improvement Program, at 8, 12, 14, 25 (Boston, 1979).

[19] Ibid.

[20] Land Disposition Study, at 185. See, also, Diagnostic Report of Residents. For more on the model-minority myth, see, Pat K. Chew, "Asian-Americans: The 'Reticent' Minority and Their Paradoxes," 36 Wm. and Mary L. Rev. 1 (1994); Frank H. Wu, "Neither Black Nor White: Asian-Americans and Affirmative Action," 15 B.C. Third World L. J. 225 (1995).

[21] Twenty years after the BRA relocated the Combat Zone next to Chinatown, a newspaper commentator noted, "The fact that a community lived there [in Chinatown] seems hardly to register in the public consciousness. In well over 100 **Boston Globe** stories on the area from 1960s and early 1970s, there is not one mention of the Asian community" (italics in original), Adrian Walker, "The Fight for Chinatown: Its Long-Overlooked Residents May Be the Ultimate Winners," **Boston Globe**, Oct. 23, 1994, A3, col. 1.

[22] Quoting Herbert P. Gleason, Boston City Corporation Counsel, Robert Jordan, "In the 'Zone,' It Will Be Business as Usual," Says Boston Counsel, **Boston Sunday Globe**, July 22, 1973, p. 27, col. 1.

Once home to Chinatown residents, the land that constitutes Parcel C was cleared of residential structures in the late 1950s to early 1960s during the planning for, and implementation of, urban renewal. The 1965 South Cove plan designated this area for urban renewal, but it was left undeveloped for 30 years, partly because no proposal was acceptable to the community. In 1986, T—NEMC proposed to build an 850-car garage on the property. At the time, the BRA recognized Chinatown's need for more housing and community facilities and rejected this proposal.

To address long-standing development conflicts, T—NEMC and Chinatown each produced a 10-year master plan in 1990, which unequivocally confirmed that Parcel C would be reserved for the community.[23] The BRA approved the plans and also zoned Parcel C as residential property, forbidding all institutional uses. In spite of this, less than three years later, T—NEMC submitted to BRA a proposal to acquire Parcel C to build an 8-story, 455-car garage. In exchange, T—NEMC would pay BRA $2 million, as well as build a smaller, 10,000 square-foot community center or pay $1.8 million in community benefits to the Chinatown Neighborhood Council (CNC), a community organization. Reneging on a prior promise, BRA heartily endorsed this plan.[24]

On May 17, 1993, with BRA's backing and assistance, T—NEMC presented its Parcel C garage proposal to the CNC. Despite the vocal opposition of more than 100 community members[25] attending this meeting, the CNC approved T—NEMC's proposal. BRA characterized this as unequivocal "community approval" of the T—NEMC project.

BRA then swiftly designated T—NEMC as the developer of Parcel C at a public hearing on June 10, 1993. The day before the hearing, more than 250 community members protested outside T—NEMC. At the hearing, the BRA was presented with a petition containing more than 2,500 signatures opposing the deal. Despite this overwhelming opposition, the BRA gave T—NEMC "tentative designation" to develop the Parcel C garage.[26]

After the hearing, community activists and residents formed the "Coalition to Protect Parcel C for Chinatown" (the Coalition). It was comprised of 21 community groups and hundreds of individuals. The Coalition's short-term goal was to defeat the garage proposal at all cost. Its long-term goal was to democratize community decision making by challenging the legitimacy of self-proclaimed Chinatown "leaders," such as CNC, which the city unjustifiably dubbed as the "voice" of Chinatown. Drawing upon lessons from previous struggles, the Coalition created six task-oriented committees and a steering committee.

Chinatown residents and organizational representatives sat on *The Steering Committee*. It developed four main strategies for the Parcel C struggle: 1) persuade hospital and city officials to withdraw the garage proposal; 2) organize the community to support any necessary legal action; 3) alert potential supporters within and outside Chinatown about the Parcel C fight; and 4) develop alternate plans for Parcel C.

[23] See, New England Medical Center, Master Plan 1990-2000, § I(B), at 5-9 (March, 1990). See, generally, Chinatown Community Plan, C.V, §§ C-D, at 50-70. T—NEMC's Master Plan affirmed the status of Parcel C as a community center no less than 11 times.

[24] See, Betsy Q. M. Tong, "N.E. Medical Garage Still on Table: Despite Protest, Officials Say Approval of Plan Probable," **Boston Sunday Globe**, June 13, 1993, City Section, p. 10, col. 1.

[25] The term "community" in this article generally refers to Asian-Pacific Americans and groups that supported the Coalition in its opposition to the proposed T—NEMC garage.

[26] Marie Gendron, "BRA OKs plans for Chinatown Garage," **Boston Herald**, June 11, 1993, p. 29, col. 1.

What to Do When You Just Can't Sue?

Whether a lawsuit ultimately will achieve clients' goals may be hard to determine in advance. The advisers considered what lawyers can contribute when faced with an issue in which litigation will likely be ineffective.

In many cases, the simple act of filing an action can result in adversaries sitting down at the table for fruitful negotiations. In some cases, a well-crafted demand letter from an attorney who has knowledge of the facts and the law can resolve a matter quickly. The ability of lawyers to understand the crafting of bills and passage of legislation, the functions and rules of administrative agencies, and their ability to use the tool of litigation, make them valuable allies in challenging unfair authority. Lawyers can apply their research skills to help trace sources of ownership, responsibility and authority in public documents and elsewhere.

Advice to clients about the possible legal consequences of their conduct is an invaluable legal service. Lawyers can counsel clients about how to conduct legal protests and how to avoid arrest, or minimize problems if the client—for example, Dr. Martin Luther King in Montgomery, Alabama—insists on getting arrested. In the Parcel C case, lawyers and community activists opted not to seize control of the disputed parcel, in order not to jeopardize the citizenship status of any residents. Instead, they obtained the appropriate permits and conducted an all-day street fair with a range of family amusements to demonstrate the potential of the site as a place for community recreation.

The Community Organizing Committee developed a threefold strategy: 1) educate the community about the garage proposal; 2) publicize the history of Parcel C and its significance to the community's long-term survival; 3) convince the community that it can make a difference by voicing its opinion.

The Legal Committee, a new entity that did not exist in previous community struggles in Boston's Chinatown, was comprised of legal-services lawyers, law students and college students. Its goal was to strengthen the community's position without reframing the community's struggle in narrow legal terms. The three attorneys on the committee, Zenobia Lai, Andrew Leong and Chi Chi Wu, were either current or former staff attorneys of Greater Boston Legal Services (GBLS). None of the members of the Legal Committee had substantial experience in land use, environmental or civil rights law. Originally, the Legal Committee intended to serve for a temporary period until another entity with more expertise could be found. However, the Legal Committee could find reduced-fee representation for only one aspect of the struggle—the city review process. Thus, the Legal Committee was thrust into the position of primary legal counsel for the Coalition to handle the *state* environmental review and any potential civil rights claims that may arise.

The Political Mobilization Committee sought to secure from mayoral candidates public statements against the garage. It made the future of Parcel C the rallying point for a Chinatown voter-registration drive. The committee made the fight against the garage a concrete example of democratic participation.

The Media Committee organized press conferences to publicize the Coalition's activities, coordinated letters to the editors and op-ed pieces and collaborated with Health Care for All (HCFA). HCFA is a coalition of unions, senior groups, religious organizations, community health centers, professional organizations and human service agencies that targeted T—NEMC for its perceived lack of community accountability and incessant expansion at the expense of Chinatown. This committee's work helped ensure the struggle's continuing visibility.

The External Outreach Committee was comprised of professionals from the health-care, union and environmental-health sectors. It framed the Parcel C struggle as a community control-and-survival issue.[27] It identified other Boston neighborhoods similarly besieged by unwanted developments and sought to form alliances with them to apply collective pressure on City Hall. Committee members also utilized their professional connections and brought in mainstream environmental justice and health groups[28] to support the Coalition in the environmental review process. Their support helped propel the Parcel C struggle into the mainstream, making it an important example of the burgeoning environmental-justice movement.

[27] The Coalition recognized that other communities of color might not immediately identify with the Parcel C struggle which, without more, could be looked upon as a local issue. When the Parcel C campaign was framed as a community-control issue, other neighborhoods in similar struggle for survival lent their support.

[28] These groups included: Environmental Diversity Forum, American Heart Association, Conservation Law Foundation, Sierra Club, Audubon Society, American Lung Association, Health Care For All and Boston University School of Public Health.

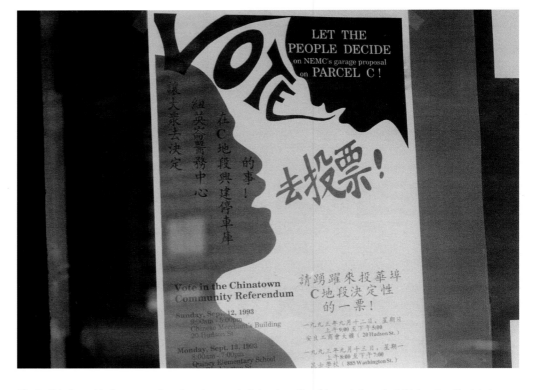

The Coalition's nonbinding community referendum, conducted and monitored by an independent third party, stimulated a very high turnout and established that Chinatown residents were opposed to parking-lot construction on Parcel C (above).

The Fund-Raising Committee, led by Coalition members with connections to private foundations, raised emergency-operating funds to supplement the time donated by member organizations. In addition to gathering outside financial support, the Coalition also realized that the community itself had to contribute financially. Not only would this produce additional funds, it would also raise awareness of the Parcel C struggle and encourage community ownership of the issue. To that end, the Fund-Raising Committee organized a variety show, collecting small donations and admission fees. It also took advantage of communitywide celebrations such as the August Moon and Dragon Boat festivals to raise money through T-shirt and button sales.

CENTRAL PRINCIPLES

The core principles of the Parcel C struggle were to ensure democratic decision making in Boston Chinatown by application of both conventional and innovative community-organizing techniques.

Democratic participation—letting the people decide—was the first principle of the Parcel C struggle. Actual residents of Chinatown, not self-proclaimed community "leaders" cutting self-interested deals with T–NEMC and City Hall, should decide whether a garage should be built on Parcel C. To get all residents involved, the Coalition conducted all meetings, demonstrations and rallies bilingually in both English and Chinese (Cantonese, Mandarin and Toisanese).[29] Community interpreters served at public meetings, negotiations, media interviews and speak-out sessions so that all residents could participate regardless of their English ability. Also, the community was asked to approve all major Coalition decisions in public meetings.

Pragmatism—doing what works—was the second principle. Instead of focusing on purely legal remedies, the Coalition organized the community and exerted political pressure as well. Even in terms of politics, the Coalition went beyond conventional strategies. To be sure, the Coalition engaged in highly visible and strategically-timed activities such as petition circulation, rallies, demonstrations and pickets.

But the Coalition tried unconventional tactics as well, such as holding a full-blown community referendum and taking over Parcel C for a Community Recreation Day.

The Campaign Begins: A Chronology

In the 18 months following the June 10, 1993, BRA hearing giving a tentative green light for garage construction, the Coalition pursued a relentless organizing campaign.

AUGUST 1993: REQUIRING FULL ENVIRONMENTAL REVIEW

As part of its building proposal, T–NEMC was required under state law to file an environmental notification form (ENF) with the state's Secretary of Environmental Affairs. This provided the first opportunity for the Legal Committee to intervene. Familiarizing itself quickly

[29] Meetings were conducted in either 1) English and Chinese (Cantonese and Toisanese), or 2) volunteers interpreted the entire meeting in Chinese or English to the minority linguistic members present. The Coalition published all its literature, including leaflets, newsletters and referendum question in both English and Chinese.

with complicated environmental law, the Legal Committee filed written comments with the state agency and demanded a full environmental review. In helping negotiate the various legal processes, the Legal Committee reiterated to the community that the environmental process alone could not stop the garage. Instead, it could only ensure that T–NEMC go through rigorous, expensive and time-consuming study and review. While attacking the garage by utilizing the state environmental-review law, the Legal Committee also closely monitored any public hearings concerning the Parking Freeze waiver, zoning amendments, master-plans amendments and the city's project review. It set up liaisons with environmental law experts, such as the Conservation Law Foundation, and contemplated a joint legal action in conjunction with other communities burdened by unwanted garages.

Native American Rights Fund (NARF)

For over 29 years, Oglala Sioux Tribe in South Dakota has labored under inadequate environmental protections and failed federal environmental-enforcement obligations. During this period, the Bureau of Indian Affairs and the Indian Health Service neglected to provide necessary facilities for delivery of adequate, safe drinking water and waste-water and solid waste-management services. Rather, they dumped raw sewage into the Tribe's creek, dumped hazardous medical wastes into open landfills and refused to finance removal of underground waste storage tanks that the agencies themselves had installed. These agencies also failed to provide protection for tribal land against illegal hazardous-waste dumping from outsiders.

Today, the Oglala Sioux's existing waste-water systems are overtaxed, resulting in raw sewage flowing into surface water and ground-water sources that are primary sources of drinking water for the reservation. In some cases, elementary schools and other venues where children are dependent on these sources, fail to meet even the federal standards.

Greatly adding to this dilemma is the paucity of enforceable tribal laws for the management and protection of these resources. Many of the existing codes, developed in the 1980s without involvement from either the tribal agencies responsible for environmental-resource management or the tribal community, have gone largely unimplemented.

To address this problem, attorneys at NARF developed a program to draft a new set of environmental codes and provisions that: 1) fit the resource needs of the tribe, 2) are acceptable to the tribal community, and 3) are capable of administration by the tribal agencies tasked with implementation.

As the first step in this process, NARF worked with the Tribe to create a mechanism to gather and catalog development activities and their potential impact on the reservation. Adopted almost two years ago, the Tribal Environmental Review Code (ERC) requires anyone proposing to engage in development activity on the reservation that may impact the environment to obtain an Environmental Review Permit from the Tribe. To date, the Tribe has processed 19 such permits. This process enables the Tribe to track placement of potential environmental hazards, monitor compliance with relevant tribal and federal laws, and ensure revenue collection for services. As a result of the process used for its adoption—a thoroughgoing consultation process with members of the Tribe, political and financial committees of the tribal government, council of elders, local political representatives of Tribe subdivisions, and private landowners on the reservation—the ERC has enjoyed widespread acceptance. There is growing compliance among people engaging in development activity on the reservation.

The next step is to unfold a similar process specifically for drafting a Safe Drinking Water Code and a Solid and Hazardous Waste Code for the Tribe.

Before the Office of Environmental Affairs issued its decision, it held a public hearing on August 31, 1993. In preparation for this hearing, the Coalition identified key spokespersons among residents and community-based organizations and presented oral and written testimony of more than 20 witnesses who addressed the topics of public health, safety, traffic, environmental justice, institutional-expansion history, historical and cultural preservation, and alternative land use and design. It also produced a new traffic study, based on research by Chinatown youths who counted and charted key intersections most likely to be affected by the T–NEMC garage. The study showed that the T–NEMC transportation study inaccurately predicted the rush-hour time in the community, counted only one half and in some instances one third of the actual automobile trips at the four major intersections most affected by the proposed garage and totally omitted the traffic impact of the impending construction of the Central Artery/Tunnel Project.[30] Finally, the Coalition garnered the support of mainstream environmental and health organizations.

The Coalition's forceful presentation convinced the Massachusetts Executive Office of Environmental Affairs to require T–NEMC to undergo a full environmental-impact review. This was the first big success for the Coalition. At the very least, it bought the Coalition some time.

August to September 1993: Community Referendum

While the Coalition was steeped in the environmental-review process, it also engaged in a high-risk political move: a referendum that would challenge the Chinatown Neighborhood Council's (CNC's) claim to be the sole voice of Chinatown.[31] It would also test the sincerity of T–NEMC's pledge to withdraw the garage proposal if the community truly opposed it. However, with little time to organize support and to educate the community, the Coalition might actually lose the election. Nevertheless, the Coalition thought the referendum was worth the risk.

The Coalition designed the election process carefully to pre-empt any potential CNC challenge of the vote's integrity. Instead of creating new voting-eligibility requirements, the Coalition adopted those of the CNC. In addition, the Coalition made various improvements to the CNC voting process, including prohibiting anyone affiliated with the Coalition or the CNC to "help" voters complete their ballots and contracting with an independent third party to conduct and monitor the balloting process.[32]

Held on Sept. 12 and 13, 1993, the referendum asked one simple question, which required a Yes or No answer. More than 1,700 individuals voted in the referendum, 654 of who were Chinatown residents. One thousand six hundred and ninety-two individuals voted No to the garage, only 42 voted Yes.[33] The referendum conclusively settled any claims by the CNC or the BRA that the community supported the garage proposal.

[30] Coalition to Protect Parcel C for Chinatown Comment to the Executive Office of Environmental Affairs, Attachment H, Aug. 25, 1993 (on file with authors). Although not scientifically rigorous, this community-collected data helped cast serious doubt on the overall validity of the T–NEMC project's impact report.

[31] Robert O'Malley, "What Is the Community and Who Represents It?" **Sampan**, June 4, 1993, p.1, col.1. During the three months leading up to the referendum, the BRA repeatedly refused to meet with the Coalition and referred to the CNC's overwhelming vote in support of the garage as dispositive. See, e.g., Paul L. Barrett, BRA letter to the Coalition to protect Parcel C for Chinatown, July 23, 1993 (on file with authors).

[32] Kevin Kempskie, "Chinatown Garage Heads to Referendum," **Boston Tab**, Aug. 31, 1993 p. 10, col. 1: "The referendum will be run by the American Friends Service Committee according to rules of the Chinatown Neighborhood Council."

[33] Marie Gendron, "Chinatown Vote Says No to Garage," **Boston Herald**, Sept. 15, 1993, p. 35, col. 1.

November 1993: CNC Election

Riding on its high-profile successes in the environmental-review process and referendum, the Coalition attempted to gain control of the CNC by running a Coalition slate for vacant seats on the 21-member elected body. The Coalition slate included two Chinatown residents, three community-based-organization representatives, and two business owners. Their platform was clear: stop the garage and ensure bilingual access to the CNC through democratic participation. Because CNC meetings were conducted only in English and because the leadership refused requests for interpreters, the CNC had effectively excluded the majority of its constituents from the process.

Bruised by their loss in the community referendum, the CNC vigorously organized its own supporters for the election. Although many elderly and grassroots people supported the Coalition, the business interests succeeded in turning out their workers in large numbers to vote in favor of the candidates supported by the CNC. Some even went so far as to bus their employees to the polling station, monitor and, in some cases, write in their ballots.[34] The Coalition's slate lost the election by a 2–1 margin.

August 1993 to August 1994: Designing a Concrete Alternative

The Coalition recognized that to show it was not merely obstructionist, it needed to offer a concrete redevelopment plan for Parcel C that would benefit and revitalize the community. The Coalition retained the pro bono service of an architect to design a community center and hired an architecture student to build a small-scale model.

February 1994: Responding to the Full Environmental-Impact Report

When T–NEMC completed the Draft Environmental-Impact Report on February 28, 1994, the Coalition's Legal Committee was again ready to respond. Believing that the "public comment" requirement under the Massachusetts Environmental Policy Act[35] required that the entire public—including non-English-speaking Chinatown residents who would be gravely affected by the proposal—should be able to participate, the Legal Committee demanded that T–NEMC translate the report into Chinese. In response, T–NEMC produced a seven-page Chinese summary of the almost 1,000-page document. Although the summary was partly incomprehensible because of technical jargon and incorrect Chinese translation, this was the first environmental-impact report that most community members had ever read.

In its lengthy Comment on the Draft Environmental-Impact Report, the Legal Committee provided specific criticisms framed in the historical context of Chinatown and the legacy of urban renewal.[36] The Comment also offered a concrete alternative that the Coalition had been developing since August 1993: a Parcel C community center, complete with architectural schematic drawings and construction-budget projection. Not only did the Coalition's response convince the state agency to require T–NEMC to revamp its environmental study; it also provided a thorough, well-documented account of institutional expansion within

[34] Since most of the restaurant workers tended to be new immigrants, they had no experience in voting in the United States or in their home country. The voting "booths" were set up on the teller counters in a bank, without partitions. Any voter could monitor how the others voted. Under such surveillance, employees voted as they were instructed. Andrew Leong, "Voting Irregularity or Sour Grapes?" **Sampan**, Dec. 17, 1993, p. 4-5.

[35] Massachusetts G.L.C. 30, §§ 61, 62; 301 C.M.R. § 11:00, et seq.

[36] The Comment challenged the sufficiency of the New England Medical Center environmental-impact report on 11 fronts. See, Zenobia Lai, Chi Chi Wu and Andrew Leong, "In re Comment to New England Medical Center Hospital Plan for Parking Garage on Parcel C," Clearinghouse Review, 49874, July 1994.

Chinatown. The community won another partial victory when the Secretary of Environmental Affairs required T–NEMC to translate meaningful portions of any subsequent environmental-impact report and suggested that T–NEMC meet with the Coalition to negotiate a solution.[37]

JULY 1994: SEEKING A 99-YEAR LEASE ON PARCEL C

When the Coalition unveiled the Parcel C community-center idea, it immediately drew criticism from City Hall, T–NEMC and other garage supporters on the grounds that the community could not afford such an undertaking.[38] To respond, the Coalition's Legal Committee researched the cost of buying Parcel C from the city. To its great surprise, the committee discovered that the BRA had let T–NEMC use Parcel C virtually rent-free. The land swap agreement between the BRA and T–NEMC allowed T–NEMC to continue to lease Parcel C (including the three office buildings) for four years, starting in September 1990, for one dollar per year.[39]

Outraged by this discovery, the Coalition decided to seek from the BRA a 99-year lease on Parcel C on identical terms. At the July 1994 press conference publicizing the Recreation Day (described below), the Coalition offered a stack of 99 one-dollar bills to the BRA. This embarrassing episode likely contributed to the BRA's decision finally to meet with Coalition delegates two weeks later.

AUGUST 1994: RECREATION DAY

Frustrated by the city's indifference, the Coalition considered occupying Parcel C for a weekend and converting it into a "shanty" town. This idea drew upon a historical effort in the African-American Community. In Boston's South End, in the late 1960s, a group of African-American activists occupied a parking lot that had once been the site of a vibrant African-American community. When 4,000 people converged on the lot in a three-day demonstration, building makeshift tents, they gave birth to a "tent city."

The idea of such a demonstration excited many of the younger activists who were largely unschooled in civil disobedience. This suggestion, however, made the Steering Committee uneasy because it could put unsuspecting community members in harm's way. An arrest, even if caused by justified civil disobedience, could affect the naturalization prospects of the many Chinatown residents who were not yet U.S. citizens. For them, arrest could mean deportation.

Instead of a shantytown takeover, the Coalition came up with the idea of a "Recreation Day," a creative demonstration that would violate no laws. Planned by the Coalition's youth team, Recreation Day was intended to regain the momentum and show what Parcel C could be, and how it could provide the desperately needed recreation space for children in Chinatown. A logo design competition and art-display contest gave the youth a way to join

[37] Trudy Coxe, Certificate of the Secretary of Environmental Affairs on the Draft Environmental-Impact Report of T–NEMC for a parking garage on Parcel C, April 29, 1994. Robert O'Malley, "State Rejects T–NEMC Environmental Report," **Sampan**, May 20, 1994, p. 1, col. 3. See, Andrew Leong, "The Struggle Over Parcel C: How Boston's Chinatown Won a Victory in the Fight Against Institutional Expansion and Environmental Racism," 21 Amerasia J., Winter 1995/1996, at 99, 112-113.

[38] See, e.g., Robert O'Malley, "Moy Says Yes," **Sampan**, Sept. 3, 1993, p. 1; Robert O'Malley, "Parcel C Coalition Continues Plan to Stop Hospital Garage," **Sampan**, April 1, 1994, p. 1, col. 2.

[39] Suffolk County Registry of Deeds, Book 16512 (Sept. 28, 1990), at 171, 226.

the struggle and taught them an early lesson in community service and participation. The Recreation Day drew more than 200 people, who participated in the games and activities set up just outside of Parcel C.

OCTOBER 1994: PREPARATION OF A CIVIL RIGHTS LAWSUIT LEADS TO VICTORY FOR THE COALITION

Notwithstanding the state Office of Environmental Affairs' order to T–NEMC to redo the environmental study, City Hall still refused to meet with the Coalition. This convinced the Legal Committee that a civil rights lawsuit had to be prepared. The Committee researched claims under the Equal Protection Clause of the 14th Amendment of the U.S. Constitution and the Federal Fair Housing Act.[40] Identifying T–NEMC's Parcel C garage proposal as the latest in a series of discriminatory public policies toward Chinatown, the Legal Committee incorporated 40 years of public acts and omissions by City Hall as the basis of the civil rights complaint.

After two months of intensive research, analysis and fact gathering, the Legal Committee felt confident about filing the complaint. It then set out to meet again with the named plaintiffs to answer questions and concerns and to ensure that they fully understood what filing this lawsuit meant. Although the Legal Committee could not guarantee that there would be no retaliation from the city, its promise to represent the plaintiffs against any such action reassured them.

The Coalition instructed the Legal Committee to file the lawsuit the day after a planned community rally. With the Coalition's approval, a week before the filing date, the Legal Committee informed the city's counsel of the Coalition's plan to sue. A few days later, City Hall struck a deal with T–NEMC, terminating the garage proposal and transferring the control of Parcel C to the Chinese Consolidated Benevolent Association. Instead of staging another protest, the community launched a victory rally on October 25, 1994, ending the 18-month struggle. Although the city did not formally involve the Coalition in its abrupt change of plans, all involved knew that it was the Coalition's efforts that stopped the T–NEMC garage and regained Parcel C for Chinatown.[41]

Epilogue

The success of Parcel C as a community movement and as a demonstration of good community-based lawyering grew out of a synergy of good fortune and good practice. It took place when the community was ready to fight and when a group of energetic, young, daring and committed lawyers, law students and activists were eager to assist.

The effectiveness of the struggle hinged on a combination of community empowerment, relationship building between lawyers and community, and opening communication between languages and cultures. These components paved the way for a pragmatic attainment of community goals. The lawyers were able to use the tremendous strengths of

[40] Title VIII of the Civil Rights Act of 1968, 42 U.S.C. §§ 3601, et seq.

[41] Even the representative of T-NEMC recognized the Coalition's role: "[T]he Coalition to Protect Parcel C for Chinatown effectively killed the garage with a skillfully orchestrated media campaign and a series of high-profile events that painted the plan as a sellout of the community." Adrian Walker, "Chinese Community Group Wins Say on Development of Parcel," **Boston Globe**, Oct. 22, 1994, p. 24, col. 2.

the community, utilize new areas of law and tap the resources within the legal services program. In the process, they also helped train law students to become the next generation of community lawyers.

Broader Implications

Land use and environmental issues will continue to plague Chinatowns and other old urban and heavily minority communities across the country. The pressures are likely to intensify as cities undergo rapid redevelopment in efforts to compete in global markets, and land becomes scarcer. In Philadelphia's Chinatown, a land-use case quite similar to that of Parcel C recently erupted. Local residents were pitted against the proposed construction of a major new stadium that will encroach upon the crowded neighborhood's limited space. The approaches developed in the Parcel C struggle may well provide important tools for the Philadelphia Chinatown community and others engaged in such struggles.

chapter 7

Chapter 7
Emerging Patterns and Lessons From the Field

The terrain of civil rights continues to shift along with the many social, economic and technological changes the country now faces. While there can be no fixed road map for future work, the case studies reveal clear patterns with important implications for lawyers, activists and funders. These patterns suggest that with careful investment to build capacity, meaningful change is possible. In the most promising examples:

- Community involvement and engagement with local governing institutions take high priority as a consistently reliable tool for solving pressing community problems and sustaining the struggle for justice;

- The attorney/client relationship is fluid, collaborative and multilateral, as the legal arena becomes one among several dynamically interrelated venues in which claims for justice are played out;

- Advocates on the national level are cognizant of the need to nurture and sustain local movements for justice, while maintaining and expanding the federal rights infrastructure upon which local work often builds; and

- Issues of race are defined and addressed in new ways. Popular discussion frames racial exclusion in terms of individual prejudice that causes whites to treat minorities differently. The cure is to treat everyone the same. By contrast, the racial-innovation approach seeks to reveal the deeper structural causes of racial exclusion and make connections between racial exclusion and broader kinds of institutional and social dysfunction.

COMMUNITY ENGAGEMENT
In the six case studies included in this report, the centrality of the lawyers' roles varied. However, the lawyer's focus on community participation significantly shaped how problems were defined, the methods used and the remedies sought.

CHANGING TERRAIN
Significant changes in the policy environment, such as devolution and privatization, have prompted many practitioners to prioritize community involvement. Devolution of federal functions to state and local governments could provide opportunities for local agencies to tailor policies and become more accountable to the specific needs and aspirations of their least powerful constituents. But the federal government has been the most reliable guarantor of racial justice, and greater state and local control could also undermine already weakened protections. Privatization could create new opportunities for greater self-sufficiency and wealth creation in some marginalized communities. However, it might also portend a lessening of racial-justice protection because traditional government regulation, due process and other constitutional guarantees become less effective against private actors. Marginalized minority communities will likely feel these impacts first. Widespread public participation is a hedge against all of these risks. An important task of racial-justice innovators is working to

reopen the space for public engagement with local democratic institutions. They focus their skills and specialized problem-solving efforts on challenging the systemic and institutional barriers that continue to produce inequities.

CREATING PUBLIC SPACE

Community participation can be fraught with difficulty in a society divided by racial and ethnic prejudice. Public space is needed for community deliberation on race matters. In several of the case studies, an organized constituency engaged lawyers as part of a comprehensive advocacy strategy played out in multiple local venues. The groups used these venues to publicly explore the meanings of racial fairness and justice. In Los Angeles, buses and bus shelters as well as public-agency hearings provided a staging area for raising community claims. As lawyers prepared thousands of pages of expert testimony and analysis to establish discriminatory transit-spending patterns, organizers made the analysis accessible by printing it on flyers and distributing it to riders on buses. They incorporated it into street theater and poster art. In Greensboro, churches, parking lots, Kmart-sponsored golf tournaments, op-ed and editorial pages of newspapers, and chamber-of-commerce meetings all became venues for struggle. Boston's Chinatown activists held a community referendum to enable residents to express their true opinions about the garage proposal.

THE CONTINUING IMPORTANCE OF STRATEGIC LITIGATION

Even with judicial cutbacks in legal protections for minorities and the poor, litigation—particularly when carried out in connection with a broader social movement—can effectively build communities' capacity to confront inequitable power structures. Community-linked litigation can function as "both symbolic and actual political activity: first, it can provide actual educational, participatory experiences for poor groups; second, it is the vehicle through which a community coheres and mobilizes."[1] Litigation can frame issues powerfully, influence public perceptions and, ultimately, restructure unfair institutions. The courtroom can be an important space for making public the often-hidden stories of marginalized people and for connecting those stories to disputed policies. A well-placed tactical intervention, be it a successful restraining order or discovery motion, can defend a movement against attack, keep it from closing down or remove obstacles that undercut its effectiveness.

In the Los Angeles MTA and the El Monte garment-worker struggles, the litigation process provided a platform for activism that helped marginalized people mobilize themselves. They developed a better understanding of the forces shaping their circumstances, of the heightened efficacy of group action, and of the ways that pressure can force local government and institutions to be more responsive. In each of these cases, through their participation, marginalized people actively shaped both the local government decision-making process and the outcomes that had fundamental impact on their lives.

MAKING USE OF THE ENTIRE ARRAY OF LEGAL TOOLS

In a 1992 report for the Rockefeller Foundation titled "Sustaining the Struggle for Justice," Professor Charles Lawrence concluded that minorities and the poor ought to have access to

[1] See, Lois H. Johnson, "The New Public Interest Law: From Old Theories to a New Agenda," 1 Public Interest Law Journal, at 169, 185 (1991).

"the full range of problem-solving tasks that lawyers traditionally employ to enhance the political and economic capacity of their paying clients." Lawyers possess key technical and transactional skills for building community capacity. They can advise clients about vehicles for structuring organizations and transactions. They can identify sources of capital, analyze regulatory schemes, negotiate on the client's behalf, structure relationships, draft agreements and navigate procedural obstacles.[2]

By defining problems in ways that target structural obstacles and providing research that highlights structural elements of exclusion, lawyers can also explore with community members the importance of democracy and engagement as a means of achieving more responsive policies. For example in the Boston Chinatown case, the attorneys researched and publicized, then challenged, the 34-year history of land-use decisions by the local, state and federal authorities that led to the virtual disappearance of open space in Chinatown. In Greensboro, activists focused on local incentives that were enacted to prevent corporate flight but rewarded companies that paid lower wages. In the Texas Ten Percent Plan case, the lawyers drafted creative legislation that targeted educational-system failure and provided research to demonstrate the linkages between systematic barriers and student performance.

Attorney/Client Relationships

Legal options are important tools in the fight for racial inclusion. But lawyers will be most effective if they are connected and responsive to constituencies. In the traditional representation model, lawyers are the chief problem solvers. They frame the claims and legal theories and generally neither cultivate nor rely on the problem-solving skills of their clients. They tell clients what is possible and give voice to client concerns through pleadings and formal proceedings that may marginalize or compartmentalize local knowledge and expertise. Clients can become dependent on lawyers as problem solvers. Leadership development within the community takes low priority. Legitimate protest may get discouraged in favor of "respectable" legal channels. Given the procedural nature of litigation, in the traditional representation model, high priority is placed on technical indicia of success. It is hard to assess impact on a community with the traditional tools of the lawyer.

By contrast, under a community-based approach, the particularized knowledge and skills of lawyers retains its critically important role. But when the ultimate goal is working with clients or a community to exercise their voice, changes occur in the nature of relationships, the definition of problems, the ways lawyers perform their tasks and the way they evaluate success. By drawing on local resources the attorneys can "bring together different fragments and patterns of local community know-how to bear on their work."[3]

Significantly, many of the best models of this approach first emerged within the civil rights movement, when lawyers were called to assist activists such as the Freedom Riders in local communities.

[2] See, e.g., Ann Southworth, "Taking the Lawyer Out of Progressive Lawyering," 46 Progressive Lawyering, at 213, 223 (1993). One of many practical examples of such transactional contributions is found in the creative argument by a Brooklyn Legal Services attorney that a New York statute governing tax-exempt bond financing for hospital expansion permitted a local medical clinic to utilize such bonds. See, "So Goes a Nation," supra.

[3] Gerald Lopez, Rebellious Lawyering: One Chicano's Vision of Progressive Law Practice, (Westview Press, 1992), at 53.

Many racial-justice innovators are driven to adopt more participatory approaches by the necessity of understanding changing forms of racial exclusion today. To protect against exploitation of low-wage and immigrant workers, to respond to the assault on affirmative action, to combat massive shifts of resources from cities to expanding suburbs, to halt environmental degradation in minority communities, and to win incorporation of increasingly diverse noncitizen populations requires thoroughgoing knowledge of the impacts on people's lives. Lawyers and clients must collaboratively engage in problem-solving efforts to make this knowledge available.

New approaches that stress engagement may build upon the traditional role of legal counselor/adviser by interpreting and applying legal standards. However, in the case studies, lawyers were most effective when they functioned as part of a broader problem-solving process, working to mediate between the role of the law and the goals of organized and cohesive community members. This is particularly important when community aspirations are not easily translated within the existing paradigms of justice. In this role, lawyers continuously ask how the law can be interpreted and applied to advance community goals. When possible, they reject abstract legal theories in favor of appeals to community values and for concrete practical needs. They also assist clients in drawing on their own problem-solving skills, demystifying the law and lawyering, and encouraging people to handle routine legal problems on their own.

It requires special attention to avoid a hasty resort to more structured and familiar legal procedures that can overtake the slower, less-scripted process of community-centered lawyering. Significantly different skills are needed than the litigation and transactional approaches taught in law school. The lawyer's inquiry begins by looking at the concrete needs and values of community members. The goal is to frame claims within a larger moral vision rather than principally in terms of a formal legal theory.

Thus, in Greensboro, the formal claim of the Kmart workers came under Title VII employment discrimination and several employees brought a successful lawsuit on these grounds. But the community-centered vision of the ministers was larger, putting the workers' claims for fair individual treatment within the larger context of a community struggling to defend its declining living standard against irresponsible corporate behavior. At the same time, the ministers connected their vision to legitimate local economic and business needs.

Kmart's motion for a restraining order to stop the protests might have silenced the ministers. The lawyers intervened at a critical moment in their struggle, converting the lawsuit from a device to stifle the community's voice to an additional opportunity to tell the workers' story. Attorney James Ferguson joined the ministers, union representatives and community members at press conferences and other public activities. Rather than present very tight legal arguments focused on specific procedural issues, they filed expansive papers to surface the underlying issues of racism and exploitation that concerned community members. They worked closely with community members, listening to what they were trying to accomplish. They involved them in the court proceedings so that community members could grasp the connections between the legal work and their struggles. The lawyers also measured their success in terms of community objectives, rather than in terms of procedural outcomes.

In the El Monte case, the attorneys had no guarantee that the enslaved workers could win their case. However, the workers gained a powerful voice after being silenced and isolated for years. Instead of focusing solely on winning, the attorneys used the workers' engagement with the legal system to help them learn how to navigate every aspect of the process. By helping to draft many of the pleadings, the workers ensured the accurate telling of their stories and it enabled them to better understand and come to terms with their experience. Similarly, in the Los Angeles MTA campaign, lawyers and activists worked hand in hand to present every detail of the transportation agency's failures to the court. The settlement specifically created an important role for the bus riders in monitoring overcrowding and on-time performance of the bus lines.

The case studies suggest that lawyers have the greatest success if they clearly understand the desires of the community members and involve them directly and meaningfully in the legal process—thus enabling the legal work to serve community interests in an integrated and holistic way. When they work as part of a comprehensive local effort, lawyers can play a role that may involve litigation or some other use of legal training. Such lawyers embed themselves in ongoing relationships with community members, going beyond their roles as counselors and advisers. They work with clients and other community members to determine whether and how much their help is needed. Through this process, lawyers can help their clients tailor and refine their goals and stay attuned to the ways the legal process can advance them. Where possible, participation in varied aspects of community life helps lawyers to stay focused on the community's goals and to better articulate those goals within formal legal constraints.

Lawyers can make their most important contributions to community struggles if they are prepared to listen and participate, to model just relationships in their own conduct, and to contribute their procedural and mediating skills. They must not allow their professional knowledge to crowd out other important forms of information and expertise. Says adviser Clyde Murphy, "I tell my lawyers that the most important thing they bring to a community meeting is their silence."[4] This type of lawyer/client relationship requires intensive communication and helps lawyers to "stop telling clients what they can or cannot do and begin asking them what they want to do."[5]

This is not to suggest that relationships between attorneys and their clients or the communities they serve are easy or conflict-free under a community-based model. In fact, they can often be the opposite. The lawyers and the community organizers in the Los Angeles MTA

[4] Adviser meeting, Oct. 17, 1999.

[5] Dayna Cunningham, telephone interview with James Ferguson, Dec. 1, 1999.

campaign clashed over whether to settle the case and on what terms. They were able to resolve most issues by persistent, and sometimes tense, negotiation. But when they could not come to terms on one question, the Bus Riders' Union and its lawyers agreed to separate counsel on a narrow issue. When the issue was resolved, interim counsel was dismissed, and the original attorneys resumed the representation. In part, this solution was possible because the attorneys in the MTA matter, as in other case studies, were able to recognize, support and communicate with local leadership—and vice versa.

DYNAMIC RELATIONSHIPS BETWEEN LOCAL AND NATIONAL GROUPS

With the increasing vitality of local efforts and with devolution increasingly shifting policy-making to the state and local levels, much attention in this report has rightly focused on local initiatives. However, local justice work is built on a scaffolding of racial-justice laws, policies and practices erected and maintained by the national civil rights organizations.

The Chicago Lawyer's Committee—Partnering With the Community

The transactional work of the Chicago Lawyers' Committee for Civil Rights Under Law, Inc. (CLC) includes assisting community organizations with incorporations, drafting leases, advice about liability, creation of business plans, and documentation for financing and loan agreements. CLC advises community-development and housing-development organizations about getting and managing tax-exempt status, zoning problems and joint ventures with for-profit entities. With their knowledge of technical aspects of organization, fiscal agency and employer-employee relations, CLC lawyers also assist community organizations with these matters.

Clyde Murphy, executive director of the CLC notes the crucial importance of setting the legal agenda "in consultation with [a] myriad of community organizations addressing the range of local issues—questions of community and economic development; the provision of affordable housing; opposition to racism; and the inclusion of people of color within local political, economic and social institutions."*

The CLC uses effective litigation as well as transactional legal assistance. For example, in 1996 the potential of a lawsuit by CLC contributed to the decision of the Chicago Housing Authority to adopt an innovative lead-abatement and prevention program affecting thousands of residents. CLC's efforts did not stop once the lawsuit became unnecessary. Its goal was to ensure effective implementation of the lead abatement program. CLC staff then worked with the Housing Authority to create a tracking system for monitoring children living in Housing Authority developments who had elevated blood lead levels (EBL). After completing random testing for lead hazards in several housing developments, the Housing Authority began an extensive notification process. It alerted all of the developments under its authority to the nature and extent of lead contamination in each of the housing developments. CLC assisted in this effort, also. Staff members helped to draft the Authority's Notification Package, which includes lead education materials and important contact numbers for unit testing and EBL testing.

*Clyde Murphy memorandum to P. Hair, Sept. 15, 1999.

Despite devolution, this is a nation closely knit together by media and communications links. Local efforts are greatly enhanced by the efforts of national groups dealing with Congress, federal administrative agencies and the media.

Many of the most visible efforts against racial equity have been mounted and/or orchestrated by a handful of national organizations as part of a coordinated nationwide offensive.[6] Such efforts necessitate a coordinated, nationwide response, which is best pursued by national organizations. For example, when the Office of Civil Rights released a new set of educational testing guidelines, a barrage of negative editorials and op-ed pieces were released in **The Wall Street Journal**, **The Washington Post** and other publications. No locally based legal or organizing effort could effectively and consistently respond to such attacks, which can have significant influence in national policy debates. However, because of working relationships between local litigators and national organizations, groups like the Leadership Conference on Civil Rights, LDF and others have effectively worked to counter attacks on the new guidelines.

Three basic elements comprise the civil rights legal scaffolding:

- The statutory and administrative framework of federal rights protection including Title VI,[7] the Voting Rights Act, Title I,[8] Title VII,[9] and a host of agency regulations and enforcement mechanisms. In an ongoing way, these structures provide a legal basis for creative and innovative racial-justice claims;

- The network of national organizations that monitor and respond to major national trends in civil rights and collaborate with local efforts to address rights violations;

- The national opinion leaders who provide an alternative to the majority narrative on public issues of interest to minorities.

Many legal controversies end up in the Supreme Court, the federal appellate courts or the U.S. Congress. Lawyers from national organizations specialize in dealing with issues in these national venues in a way that local lawyers cannot.

Activists and local lawyers in the Texas Ten Percent Plan case, the Los Angeles MTA case and the El Monte garment-workers case had partnerships with MALDEF, LDF and NAPALC— all national organizations that provided a range of resources to these local struggles. For many local organizations, partnership with a national organization gives them access to the Department of Justice and other national enforcement agencies, to members of Congress, national media, large law firms and other resources. All of this can heighten their leverage with local power structures. With their broader platforms and access, national organizations can help to highlight important local issues. Many local offenders fear the consequences of having a national spotlight thrown on them. Indeed, they rely on the invisibility of racial

[6] See, e.g., Alfred E. Ross, The Assault on Diversity: Behind the Challenges of Racial and Gender Remedies, Institute for Democratic Studies, Dec. 1999.

[7] Prohibition against racial descrimination by institutions that receive federal funding.

[8] Quality education protections for poor K–12 students.

[9] Prohibition against discrimination in employment.

injustice to ensure the continued marginalization of minority communities. The involvement of national groups can serve as an important prod to public officials who ignore or abandon the goals of equity and justice in their policies, programs and conduct.

Improvements in communication and accessibility of information, as well as advances in educational opportunity over the past several generations, have resulted in a dramatic surge in the number of advocates, organizers and attorneys "in the field." Many, while not formally on the staffs of national groups, have ongoing relationships with them. Particularly if these advocates and activists have adequate support on technical issues, they can be more effective in community capacity building and organizing than has traditionally been the case for national organization staff.

For both national and local groups there is growing understanding of the power of strategies that combine the strengths of local and national work. For example, NAACP LDF and the Lawyers' Committee for Civil Rights Under Law have supported amendments to strengthen Title VI, have monitored Supreme Court and lower-court decisions construing this statute, and have filed briefs in and litigated important cases—all to ensure that this law remains available to protect victims of discrimination. Without this work, lawsuits and settlements such as the MTA case would not be possible in the future. Some of the critical court rulings in Mississippi came in cases that were largely litigated by local attorneys, but the framework for that litigation and the precedents on which it relied arose from the sustained work of lawyers from the national organizations.

In recent years there have been repeated examples of local litigation that addresses specific violations or tests particular rules, being combined with national efforts to gain "legislative fixes" for bad judicial precedents. Often during the legislative battles, national groups will draw on local lessons to craft the strongest policy provisions and to explain the necessity of particular kinds of protection.

The national groups also play a critical role in evaluating and projecting upcoming threats to the infrastructure, in monitoring legislation, and looking for gaps in existing legislation that allow for blatant and subtle forms of discrimination to continue.

The Transition to New Approaches

Opportunities to infuse transformative approaches into current work will be difficult for activists working in high-pressure daily situations. Needed is an overarching vision to help practitioners identify promising possibilities for transformation. Such a vision may help practitioners avoid steps that seem to advance their immediate goals but undermine long-term objectives.

An affirmative vision can tie the work of lawyers to the ongoing quest for social justice and help to make it relevant to current debates about race and policy. It may prevent lawyers and activists from getting distracted or discouraged and serve as a reminder in the face of setbacks that the struggle is long term. A clear vision also can help advocates better understand that there are opportunities in losing as well as in winning. In many cases, strong wins are derived simply from engaging in the fight itself. In the process, advocates and activists gain experience and, perhaps, deny an adversary a clear mandate.

The advisers noted that the legal and moral claims of the 20th century have been based primarily on a vision of injustice. Professor Lani Guinier captured the change sought by the advisers when she proclaimed, "What we need is a vision of justice, not injustice."[10] Consistent with democratic values, the content of the vision must, in the words of adviser Susan Sturm, get forged in connection with community.

[10] Adviser Meeting, June 30, 1998.

The advisers considered an example from Haywood County, Tennessee, where injustice is symbolized by the fact that the railroad crossing in the African-American community is always broken. Guinier observes that getting the crossing fixed addresses the blatant injustice, so that with respect to the dangerous railroad tracks African-Americans are treated more like whites. But that is only a partial step toward justice. No one is worried about all the noisy trains that barrel through both communities. A fuller vision of justice would encompass safe and calm neighborhoods for all.[11]

[11] Adviser Meeting, Oct. 17, 1999.

The real-life experience of an African-American judge who was mistaken for a parking attendant provided another illustration. Adviser Brenda Wright probed the meaning of justice: "Is justice achieved when we fix things so that people who are judges are not mistaken for people who aren't," she asked..."and the duty of parking cars isn't confined just to one racial group, and...people in different racial groups can get to be judges? Or, is justice when the person who parks the car is...not invisible anymore?"[12] Professor Bill Quigley believes: "Concerns about the quality of public education, concerns about secure employment at a living wage and concerns about child care and health care, to name but a few, are fundamental matters of justice and must be a part of any true agenda for civil and human rights."[13]

[12] Adviser Meeting, Oct. 17, 1997.

[13] Bill Quigley, e-mail to P. Hair, Jan. 7, 1998.

The case studies examined in this report helped advisers powerfully glimpse elements of a positive vision of justice:

- Linking racial exclusion to broader structural exclusion while simultaneously drawing strength from the history and cultural resources of marginalized communities.

- Strengthening the institutions and assets available within marginalized communities to resist racism and to seek justice.

- Expanding participation of marginalized communities, and distributing resources more equitably across society.

- Promoting a community framework for justice that prioritizes social goods and collective interests.

These elements are more fully elaborated in the next chapter.

Chapter 8

Chapter 8
Renegotiating Issues of Race

This country's efforts to overcome its long history of racial exclusion are relatively recent and have suffered from constant resistance. Sometimes it seems as if the nation has grown weary of race. Over the past two decades a damaging and divisive campaign to undermine racial justice has been waged in the courts, legislatures and public discourse. It has strongly influenced public attitudes about racial-justice efforts. Its principal proponents assert that remedial measures to increase racial inclusion are no different morally than segregation and other mechanisms that have produced centuries of exclusion.

Even some friends of civil rights now express concern that a particularized focus on racial justice should be replaced with a more general campaign for class-based equity. Some argue that an economic approach would do more to improve the situation of racial minorities. This has led some progressives to avoid issues that have salience primarily for minority group members, such as bilingual education, immigration and affirmative action.

[1] Bill Quigley, e-mail to P. Hair, Jan. 7, 1998.

But the particular goal of racial justice must not be ignored for the goal of pursuing a broader mandate for social justice. While it is true that "the victims of injustice are not restricted to any race or ethnic group," a broad vision of justice recognizes that "people of color are victimized by racism and injustice"[1] in ways that require particular attention.

Dealing with issues of race directly and forcefully confronts issues of democracy. As a practical matter, when race has been ignored in the past, racial inequities remain intact. For example, Depression-era minimum-wage and collective-bargaining protections were considered universal policies when enacted although the legislation explicitly excluded agricultural and domestic workers. These categories were heavily dominated by Latino and African-American laborers. The wages and benefits in such jobs, still dominated by Latinos and African-Americans, continue to lag behind other sectors of the labor market. Failure to explicitly address issues of racial exclusion provides inadequate protection for marginalized groups and, in fact, legitimates the exclusion. To overcome the problem of race, it is necessary to understand it, probe it and develop solutions that specifically target the problem.

Ignoring race also denies marginalized communities the ability to draw on their positive history and culture, and the motivating power of the particularized injury. For example, in the Greensboro struggle, the racial dimensions of the problem tied the struggle to powerful civil rights history, from which the workers drew strategies, tactics, strength and hope.

Linking Race to Broader Structural Exclusion

Emerging practices provide clear and exciting evidence that racial issues can be addressed by multiracial and multiethnic coalitions, and in ways that strengthen, rather than undermine, multiracial cooperation. Advisers Susan Sturm and Lani Guinier posit that because racial minorities tend to be among the most vulnerable members of society and because race is highly visible, patterns of racial unfairness can serve as the "miner's canary,"[2] signaling a problem that affects other groups. In Texas after Hopwood, the harsh impact of the university admission system on African-Americans and Latinos did just that, pointing to unfairness for all in the admission system.

[2] When the canary died, it signaled that the air in the mine was bad, giving the miners time to get out. See, Susan Sturm, "From Gladiators to Problem-Solvers: Connecting Conversation About Women, the Academy and the Legal Profession," Duke Journal of Gender Law & Policy 119, 126 and N. 37 (1997).

In the Kmart-worker struggle, advocates also connected issues of racial unfairness to broader structural problems. Kmart paid its Greensboro employees (who were primarily African-American) $5.00 per hour less than those at 12 other facilities where the majority of employees were not black. An investigation of racial patterns revealed the financial discrepancy. However, white Greensboro workers also suffered from the low pay scale and came to understand that racial unfairness affects the entire community.

STRENGTHENING COMMUNITY CAPACITY TO RESIST RACISM

Strong, inclusive and accountable local institutions can help communities resist racial exclusion and build positive alternatives. These institutions can play critical roles because they function as the repositories of culture and resilience in marginalized communities. A better understanding of how local institutions enable communities to function can help racial-justice advocates identify residents' best chances for building healthy communities.

In Greensboro, rather than endure their employers' exploitative behavior, African-American Kmart workers approached church leaders, who rallied their congregations in support. The workers did not rely solely on government enforcement agencies, judicial intervention or other external forces to address their claims. During the Kmart fight, they congregated at the churches to reinforce their commitment, clarify their purpose, strengthen their spirits and build a sense of connectedness with other workers. Similarly, white Kmart workers relied on their trade union. They gathered at the union hall before rallies and other public actions, built their sense of community with other workers, and collectively grasped developments in the case.

Understanding the role of culture in bolstering the resilience of marginalized communities provides insight into why cultural sensitivity matters. It suggests that some problem-solving approaches are productive and successful *because* they draw upon cultural traditions and local social capital of racially and ethnically marginalized people and can leverage the inherent strengths of their communities. Because some dismiss minority cultures as "underclass," they neglect important ways in which the distinct values and practices that are rooted in minority cultures can enhance the struggle for justice.

In many cases, innovations based on distinct cultural strengths improve practices in an entire field. Examples of such innovations are being documented by groups such as the Harvard Project on American Indian Economic Development.[3] But the research has not systematically been brought to bear on the issues highlighted in this report. It is an area that deserves further exploration.

EXPANDING PARTICIPATION AND DISTRIBUTION OF RESOURCES

An affirmative vision of justice involves both the aspiration for greater participation by marginalized people and a significantly expanded concept of what participation is. At its core, expansive participation requires engagement in all aspects of political, economic, social and

[3] See, Stephen Cornell and Joseph P. Kalt, "Culture as Explanation in Racial and Ethnic Inequality: American Indians, Reservation Poverty and Collective Action," Harvard Project on American Indian Economic Development Project Report Series (April 1993), Malcolm Wiener Center for Social Policy, John F. Kennedy School of Government, Harvard University; Stephen Cornell, and Joseph Kalt, "Sovereignty and Nation Building: The Development Challenge in Indian Country Today," American Indian Culture and Research Journal, Vol. 22, No. 3, (1998), University of California, Los Angeles, American Indian Studies Center.

cultural systems that better life and livelihood. This idea of participation recognizes that communities and their members must decide for themselves what betterment means. Thus it demands revitalization of democratic institutions to make them more inclusive, responsive and accountable. It also requires building of community capacity to access and use information, and participate effectively in deliberation. As adviser Ceasar McDowell notes, such participation enables people in the context of communities their own voice and a hold on their own lives.

A focus on expanded participation may broaden the goals of traditional racial equity approaches under the law. Structural changes are sought to encourage community engagement. For example, in the Los Angeles case, an equity framework might require parity in funding between suburban and urban transit systems. Using a participation framework, the remedy might include reconfiguring the transportation policymaking processes to require broad public participation and a meaningful minority voice in transportation decision making—all to ensure equitable outcomes. In the schools context of Texas, an equity approach might require consistent standards for enforcing disciplinary measures or admitting students to preferred programs. A participation focus would maintain this demand for consistency, but also would urge school policies that provide opportunities for broad parent involvement in setting educational priorities and programs to develop citizenship skills among all students. In the context of voting in Mississippi, an equity framework might require sufficient

Using Cultural Strengths

An example effectively drawing on local cultural strengths can be found at the Navajo Nation, which has had tremendous success in developing a "mixed" judicial system that utilizes both Navajo and Western legal models. With its roots in Dine' Bibee Haz' annii, the traditional common law of the Navajo people, the Navajo Judicial Branch employs over 250 Peacemakers—respected community and spiritual leaders—to resolve many types of disputes, thereby enabling it to be more responsive to people, issues and traditional institutions. At the same time, the Western-looking, but self-designed, Navajo Supreme Court has both achieved a record of effective jurisprudence and established the independence it needs to fulfill a traditional function of holding the roles of political leaders to the service of the Navajo people.

In another example, the Nez Perce Tribe's Gray Wolf Recovery program has not only enabled the Tribe to take a lead role in managing the statewide recovery of an endangered species, but it is restoring the people's connection to wolves—a cultural factor that initiated the Tribe's involvement. Wolf legends that previously had been sequestered have come to light and are now shared widely in the Tribe; baby-naming ceremonies now include wolf names, and dancers with wolf pelts are reappearing for the first time in memory. Indeed, the program has refreshed a portion of Nez Perce culture, and is held up as a model for how other tribes can exercise their political sovereignty while strengthening their unique cultures.

numbers of safe majority-minority districts to ensure election of minority representatives. A participation focus would call for electoral mechanisms that provide a fair chance, and require broad electoral mobilization, for any candidate, including an African-American, to win.

Adviser Bill Quigley describes the current social system as intentionally creating a growing population of people who are not necessary anymore. Even in good times they are considered superfluous. Whether they're African-American, Hispanic, Asian-American or poor whites, that lack of need for people, or a sense of being unnecessary, is the foundation of injustice. An expanded conception of participation emphasizes the need to mediate the values of the marketplace with the moral relationships that tie peoples' fates to each other at the intimate scale of kinship, friendship and neighborly community. In this way, the personhood of those in the most marginalized communities, whether undocumented immigrants, low-wage workers or minority children in punitive school environments, will not be lost.

A concept of participation that incorporates lives and livelihoods has particular salience for racially marginalized groups, which have not benefited equally from the allocation of public resources and protections. As a starting point, it suggests more equitable distribution of resources. Thus, protection of low-wage workers, who are disproportionately immigrants and racial or ethnic minorities, becomes a more explicit focus of racial-justice concerns. In the case studies, efforts to gain protections for low-wage workers went far beyond demands for better wages and working conditions. In Greensboro and El Monte, with the support of ministers, community organizations and other partners, low-wage workers asserted the values and moral commitments that knit their communities together and successfully challenged exploitation by major global companies, powerfully demonstrating both the tools and the goals of an expanded conception of justice.

INCORPORATING RACE INTO A COMMUNITY FRAMEWORK OF JUSTICE

In the case studies, when issues are presented in terms of community interests, advocates define problems and propose solutions more broadly. In the Greensboro and the Texas Ten Percent case studies, the expansion of the focus marked a turning point. In Greensboro, workers protesting bad working conditions, came off the picket line and were replaced by some of the community's most respected ministers advocating for better corporate citizenship. In the Texas Ten Percent Plan, the focus of policy debate has begun to shift away from poor student performance and focus instead on poor school performance.

Yet, the law is not structured to encourage advocates to frame issues this way. The framework of individually based rights requires narrow definitions of problems so as to achieve tailored remedies. This process can obscure the broader interests at stake or the impact of individual claims on others within a community. The exclusive reliance on individual rights ignores the social dimension of human existence, the ways in which people define themselves and draw meaning from their relation to a group, and the compelling human need to be part of a community. It also forecloses important claims that might help elevate collective interests over narrow, polarizing or parochial interests, and it potentially forecloses useful remedial approaches grounded in collective action. A growing body of literature is helping to illuminate the tensions felt by practitioners between traditional legal advocacy and the broader goal of widespread community participation.[4]

Defining the scope of community—what constitutes a community? Who is included? Who decides what is in the interest of a community?—is an extremely complicated task. In the Parcel C case, for example, two neighborhood groups asserted competing claims to speak for the Chinatown community. One long-established group conducted meetings in English only, effectively excluding the majority of its constituents from participation. However, it was recognized as the official voice of the neighborhood by the city government and the media. The other group, which opposed the parking lot, was a recently formed coalition of neighborhood organizations. When the community referendum on the fate of the parcel was held an overwhelming majority of the voters in a significant turnout opposed the parking lot. This demonstrated that if organizing and advocacy are effective, the legitimacy of community activists will be made manifest.

An area needing further attention is the scope of possible legal claims under a community-based framework. Though the criminal law of conspiracy recognizes the possibility for heightened efficacy when individuals combine their efforts as a group, there is no parallel understanding of what is lost when communities or groups are diminished in their ability to act in this way. Under traditional rights jurisprudence, even in class actions, groups are seen as mere aggregations of like individuals. One promising area for exploration is environmental law, where new kinds of claims are being framed that capture and create rights to social goods.[5]

The Future

The innovations in racial-justice practice are energizing and promising, but for some they are also worrisome. If attorneys are routinely and deeply engaged in tasks that could also be done by nonlawyers, what is the essence of a lawyer? Similarly, if racial-justice advocacy is broadened beyond the traditional civil rights, black/white paradigm to encompass other minority groups and disadvantaged whites, how is the field defined, so that it is not simply an antipoverty or economic-development effort? The key question is how to frame a broad vision of justice, an "umbrella" under which a multitude of interests can gather, without losing the passion or diminishing the resources for battling the particular forms of racial discrimination and injustice that affect each individual racial group.

These case studies show that it is possible for lawyers to be problem solvers without losing their identity as members of the legal profession. Perhaps even more forcefully, they illustrate a vision of racial justice that simultaneously keeps the history and current status of each racial group at the forefront while broadening the constituency of social justice for all.

[4] See, William Quigley, "Reflections of Community Organizers: Lawyering for Empowerment of Community Organizations," 21 Ohio Northern Univ. L. Rev. 455 (1995); L. Johnson, supra; A. Southworth, supra; J. Calmore, "A Call to Context: The Professional Challenges of Cause Lawyering at the Intersection of Race, Space and Poverty," 67 Ford. L. Rev. 1927 (1999).

[5] For example, recent administrative rulings suggest that environmental amenities are goods held in common and that enforcement efforts must look at the cumulative impacts of pollutants, not simply the discrete effects of individual substances.

Recommendations for Funders

TAKE A FRESH LOOK AT RACIAL-JUSTICE LAWYERING
Include racial justice in funding guidelines:
Racial exclusion continuously reinforces poverty and disadvantage, weakens promising solutions to community problems, skews resource distribution and frustrates formation of broad coalitions. As a result, racial exclusion can undermine philanthropic efforts across a range of programs—from community revitalization to education reform, health and democratic participation.

Innovative racial-justice lawyering can help strengthen foundation and community efforts. Using creative problem-solving techniques, this work can help to harness minority communities' resources to address racial barriers. With fresh approaches that link racial exclusion to larger structural barriers, racial-justice lawyering potentially creates broader constituencies for equitable policies. Including racial-justice criteria within funding guidelines can help to focus grantee efforts on these issues.

Add legal advocacy to the social change tool kit:
For grantmakers seeking to expand community engagement, mobilize public will and promote policy change, innovative racial-justice lawyering provides a powerful, yet often overlooked, set of tools. Funders need not create new programs and initiatives to support innovative racial-justice litigation, policy analysis, legal advocacy and activism. Rather, they can add these tools to the array of approaches currently funded in established program areas. Funders can explore the ways that race is implicated in their ongoing programs and seek opportunities to integrate creative litigation and advocacy. Attention to race does not preclude concern for gender and economic inequities; rather, it may help to reveal the inextricable links among these related forms of exclusion.

Support the racial-justice infrastructure:
Combating racial justice requires a continuous web of activities at the local, regional and national level. Important and interdependent divisions of labor exist between groups working at these levels. New mechanisms are needed for sustained investment in local innovative racial-justice lawyering and legal problem solving. The local efforts have the advantage of directly impacting the lives of poor and marginalized groups. Through development of networks and coalitions, the best local innovation can have national significance. But in efforts to "go to scale," the resource needs of local efforts cannot be overlooked.

National foundations can enhance their capacity for strategic local funding by 1) creating advisory committees that include persons knowledgeable about racial issues within targeted locales, 2) setting up requests for proposal processes with reviewers including diverse local "experts," and 3) partnering with local and community foundations.

At the same time, many civil rights gains through the last century resulted from enforcement and advocacy efforts by national civil rights organizations. The work is not done: despite gains, racial-justice policies continue to be vigorously contested in the courts, legislatures and in public discourse. The need to maintain defensive action remains high. National civil rights groups continue to press for accountability of federal enforcement efforts. However, only a handful of philanthropic organizations support this crucial work. There is a need to strengthen and sustain the national civil rights organizations through flexible support that enables strategic deterrence and enforcement and rapid response to new civil rights challenges.

BUILD CAPACITY

Provide flexible, longer-term funding:

Narrowly tailored project support often undermines racial-justice institutions' ability to respond to unique or rapidly developing circumstances or to maintain relationships with local constituents. Capacity building, particularly among marginalized groups, can involve a range of intangible tasks that are difficult to anticipate in project designs. More flexible, longer-term support enables racial-justice advocates to build sustainable institutions and enhance their impact by increasing staff capacities, creating broad networks, developing advanced communication techniques, engaging in community mobilization and integrating the specialized knowledge of academics and researchers into their work.

Use participatory evaluation:

Rigid tools for evaluation are not appropriate to today's racial-justice lawyering. Litigation may be successful in strengthening community voice and engagement even if a lawsuit is lost. Community participation may grow even if a hoped-for policy change fails. These kinds of important changes may be missed using traditional measures of success. At the same time, racial-justice innovators, and the communities they serve, need to make frequent assessments of what has been accomplished and what has gone wrong, with a willingness to make appropriate midcourse adjustments. They need sensitive and responsive instruments to strengthen and inform their efforts, help members recognize and capture increases in democratic capacities, and alert themselves and funders to unproductive directions or misdirected efforts. Participatory methods and instruments can be established to monitor progress from the start of community efforts, rather than introduced midway through to determine future prospects for funding after efforts are in full swing.

Support training:

Some racial-justice lawyers may have little training and support for their approaches. Few materials exist to provide teaching and learning of the new methods of racial-justice legal work. Funding is needed to support legal training and the development of curricula for innovative racial-justice lawyering. For pathbreaking practitioners seeking to expand and disseminate their work, fellowship programs would also help to build the field. Promising mid-career professionals seeking to develop or enhance their community-practice skills could also benefit from such programs. A revolving fund to subsidize new legal practices would free innovative practitioners in the field from the constant financial strictures of building small firms, and would enable them to explore creative approaches to racial-justice legal work.

SUPPORT CONCEPTUAL WORK

The current racial-justice challenges are no less daunting than those faced by the original civil rights crusaders. Emerging issues include:

1) new labor grievances, particularly for low-wage and immigrant groups,
2) expanding conceptions of race and ethnicity due to profound demographic shifts,
3) massive shifts of resources from the cities to the ever-expanding suburbs,
4) environmental degradation in marginalized urban communities,
5) democratic incorporation and participation of racial minorities and an increasingly diverse noncitizen population, and
6) new methods to achieve inclusion and supplement affirmative action.

Even where not explicit, race is a factor in each of these issues.

The original civil rights strategies took years to plan. Support is needed now for efforts to understand the new challenges and to develop new conceptions of justice and practical approaches to addressing them. Such efforts could include:

1) strategic convenings and collaborations among lawyers, activists, organizers, clergy, academics, researchers and advocates,
2) research and analysis that bring the insights of different disciplines, institutions and racial groups to bear on key problems, and
3) fellowships and sabbaticals for racial-justice advocates to allow for reflection and deliberation.

HELP GALVANIZE PUBLIC WILL

Galvanizing public will to support policies for racial equity is a formidable task. Efforts must overcome both the general public's disbelief that racial exclusion persists *and* resignation among many communities that prospects for social transformation are dim. Foundation investment is urgently needed for developing sophisticated communication approaches to address both of these challenges. Such approaches must:

• Engage the majority—in the sound bites of popular debate as well as in sustained discourse—about the persistence of racial injustice and the continued need to remedy unfair disparities;

- Help marginalized communities to assess barriers to their full inclusion, voice policy preferences and seek practical ways to implement such policies;

- Encourage all communities to understand the high stakes of racial and social inequities and the policy options for addressing them;

- Promote promising examples of racial innovation and inspire hope in the prospects for social justice and racial transformation;

- Urge attitudinal and behavioral changes that overcome disenchantment and expand support for practical remedies; and

- Spark informed efforts to address racial issues.

With their bird's-eye view of change efforts, powerful links to key stakeholders in communities, broad convening power and financial resources, foundations have a critical role to play in advancing racial-justice innovation. The opportunity comes at a crucial moment in the nation's history when exploding racial and ethnic diversity challenge democratic institutions and provide a leverage point for change. With enlightened and persistent leadership, even small philanthropic investments could have decisive impact in the quest for greater racial and social justice and democratic inclusion.

Process

In 1997, the Rockefeller Foundation asked Penda D. Hair,[1] a veteran civil rights attorney, to lead an effort to find and document examples of successful advocacy in the struggle for justice. This report is the second stage in an effort by the Rockefeller Foundation to identify civil rights strategies that work. In 1992, Professor Charles Lawrence III produced a report on basic-rights advocacy entitled: "Sustaining the Struggle for Justice: A Program Review of the Basic Rights Portfolio." Professor Lawrence concluded that effective basic-rights advocacy must reclaim the moral high ground by stressing the universality of rights, finding areas of cooperation with new allies and emphasizing the importance of community. He also recognized that the landscape is changing and that advocates should strive to "generate new formulations and reconceptualizations of basic rights," integrating theory and practice. He stressed that "[a]dvocates must find ways to assist their clients in articulating shared interests, in forging common cause with others, and in creating the political will to renegotiate the social contract."

This report builds on Professor Lawrence's work. The Foundation sought to assess whether, and how well, the findings of the Lawrence Report had developed in the field. The Foundation also sought guidance from the field on steps that grantmakers could take to support and enhance effective advocacy and to promote wider knowledge and incorporation of the best practices.

We did not attempt to conduct a comprehensive mapping of the field, but instead sought suggestions from the advisers and from a broad group of advocates, policy experts, academics and foundation officials. From the many advocacy efforts uncovered, we initially selected approximately 10 for further investigation and later narrowed the group to six examples that could be examined in depth.

Hair and Rockefeller Foundation Program Officer Dayna L. Cunningham assembled a group of experienced advisers who gave generously of their time, their ideas and their insights. The diverse group of 15 advisers comprised a group of lawyers, advocates, scholars and funders, whose life work has been dedicated to the struggle for civil rights, human rights and justice.

The advisers gathered for 11 all-day meetings and spent countless hours probing the patterns that emerged from case studies. Their energy and their commitment to the report were extraordinary, inspiring and a testament to the vitality and importance of this field.

They examined the elements that might contribute to an updated vision of advocacy in the struggle for justice. Their goal was to reflect on the work in light of their considerable experience and to provide insights about the implications for practitioners, funders and opinion leaders. This report integrates the powerful insights, ideas and strategies that emerged from the adviser meetings with the experiences and lessons drawn from the case studies.

[1] Hair came to this project from her position as Director of the Washington, D.C., office of the NAACP Legal Defense and Educational Fund, Inc. She currently serves as Co-Director of the Advancement Project, a policy and legal-action organization.

Acknowledgments

The many lawyers, clients, community organizations and activists whose visionary work in the field is reflected herein generously shared their time, experiences, lessons and mistakes, as well as triumphs. This is their report. I have tried to be an accurate and thoughtful recorder.

Dayna L. Cunningham, Associate Director of the Rockefeller Foundation's Working Communities Division, conceived this project and brought together the people and the resources to bring it to fruition. Her penetrating ideas on race and lawyering infuse every page of the Report. As important, her strong belief in the project and her incredible determination inspired the author and the advisers, and pushed this work to completion. Susan P. Sturm, Professor of Law, Columbia Law School, and Lani Guinier, Professor of Law, Harvard Law School, were participants from the inception, helping to frame the project, identify case studies and put together the larger group of advisers.

Angela Glover Blackwell, then Vice President of the Rockefeller Foundation (now President of PolicyLink, a national organization working to identify, support and promote local policy innovation), played a critical role in initiating and supporting this project and provided many valuable insights.

Fifteen advisers guided the development of this report. Coming from national civil rights organizations, local public-interest law centers, universities and foundations, all of the advisers in their separate capacities have been deeply involved in the struggle for justice for many years. Their commitment to this project has been unwavering. The advisers are:

NATIONAL CIVIL RIGHTS LEGAL ORGANIZATIONS: Theresa Fay-Bustillos, currently Vice President of Global Community Affairs and Executive Director of the Levi Strauss Foundation, Levi Strauss & Co., served as Vice President of the Mexican American Legal Defense and Educational Fund during most of her tenure as an adviser; Karen K. Narasaki, Executive Director, National Asian Pacific American Legal Consortium; Mark Soler, President, Youth Law Center; Brenda Wright, Managing Attorney, National Voting Rights Institute, who previously served as staff attorney and Director of the Voting Rights Project of the Lawyers' Committee for Civil Rights Under Law; and Constance L. Rice, Co-Director of the Advancement Project, who began service as an adviser while Co-Director of the Western Regional office of the NAACP Legal Defense and Educational Fund, Inc.

LOCAL PUBLIC-INTEREST LAW ORGANIZATIONS: Clyde E. Murphy, Executive Director, Chicago Lawyers' Committee for Civil Rights Under Law, Inc.; Douglas I. Foy, President, Conservation Law Foundation, based in Boston.

THE ACADEMY—PROFESSORS WITH EXTENSIVE BACKGROUND IN RACIAL-JUSTICE ISSUES AND LEGAL PRACTICE: Lani Guinier, Professor of Law, Harvard Law School; Caesar McDowell, Associate Professor and Director, Center for Reflective Community Practice, Department of Urban Studies and

Planning, Massachusetts Institute of Technology; Susan Sturm, Professor of Law, Columbia Law School; William P. Quigley, Professor of Law, Loyola University, New Orleans, School of Law; and Gerald Torres, H.O. Head Centennial Professor of Real Property Law and Vice Provost, University of Texas at Austin, and Director, Texas, LEADS.

FOUNDATION OFFICERS WITH EXPERIENCE IN ADVOCACY FOR JUSTICE: Alan Jenkins, Deputy Director, Human Rights and International Cooperation, Ford Foundation; Geraldine P. Mannion, Chair, Special Projects, Carnegie Corporation of New York; Catherine Samuels, Director, Program on Law and Society, Open Society Institute.

The advisers consistently made time in crowded schedules for attending meetings, reviewing drafts and participating in consultations. Their sustained and intense engagement contributed tremendously to the vision and the ideas expressed in the Report. They eagerly delved into the most perplexing issues, challenging their own assumptions and spiritedly, but affectionately, debating and refining the analysis. Their devotion of time, energy and intellect is exceedingly valued and appreciated.

Several of the advisers played an even larger role. During the last year of the project, Susan Sturm and Bill Quigley provided critically important insights that helped structure the overview of Chapters 1 through 3. Their input gave the report clarity and focus that it would not otherwise have had. Clyde Murphy, Karen Narasaki and Mark Soler wrote text boxes that serve as "mini case studies" within the Report that help to explain the work of their institutions in light of the principles developed in this Report.

Additional text-box writers include: John Echohawk and Ray Ramirez of the Native American Rights Fund, Andrew Lee of the Harvard Indian Project, and David Balcom of the Lawyers' Committee for Civil Rights Under Law.

Several individuals assisted in the investigation and preparation of the case studies. While third-year law students in a seminar at Harvard Law School taught by Penda D. Hair and Professor Christopher Edley, Arianne Callender and Randall Kromm wrote papers on the El Monte garment-workers' advocacy and the Los Angeles MTA campaign, respectively. Their findings were incorporated into the case studies. Two other students in this class, Danielle Holley and Delia Spencer, produced a paper on the Texas Ten Percent Plan that was subsequently published in the Harvard Civil Rights Civil Liberties Law Review. The Ten Percent Plan case study draws on material from the early drafts of their paper, as well as the published article. Lincoln Mitchell, Ph.D., a consultant based in New York City, and Venu Gupta, a 1999 graduate of Harvard Law School, each conducted interviews and research for several of the case studies. The Parcel C case study is an adaption of a law review article written by Zenobia Lai, Andrew Leong and Chi Chi Wu, the lawyers who participated in that struggle.

Endless gratitude to Denise Gray-Felder, Vice President, Administration and Communications at the Rockefeller Foundation. Her contributions are too numerous to be listed here. Many thanks to Matt Rothschild, Editor of The Progressive, for his eleventh-hour edit of the entire manuscript.

Special thanks to Barbara Arnwine, Executive Director of the Lawyers' Committee for Civil Rights Under Law; Antonia Hernandez, President and General Counsel of the Mexican American Legal Defense and Educational Fund; and Elaine R. Jones, Director Counsel of the NAACP Legal Defense and Educational Fund, Inc. They reviewed early drafts and gave thoughtful comments that helped clarify the role of national organizations in the work documented by the Report.

Michael Damian, Project Assistant in the Working Communities Office of the Rockefeller Foundation, and Tujuana Tull, Office Manager for the Advancement Project, played multiple, critical roles, putting together many meetings and trips, revising countless drafts, and keeping the entire project organized and flowing.

Publicists Gwen McKinney and Leila McDowell of McKinney & McDowell brought enormous energy and skill to the task of garnering public attention to the issues raised in the Report.

George Soule and Andre Oliver, Associate Directors in the Rockefeller Foundation's Communications Office, gave much-appreciated wisdom and counsel.

Susan Muir, also from the Foundation's Communications Office, pushed relentlessly and thanklessly to meet production deadlines.

Graphic designer Robin Lynch of Negerkunst Studio made the report beautiful and accessible; her vision for the report also helped clarify some of the conceptual frameworks in the text.

With deep gratitude, Penda D. Hair, Washington, D.C., March 2001.

Photo and Art Credits

COVER: (left) ©Bettmann/CORBIS, (right) photo by Lewis A. Brandon III; INSIDE FRONT COVER: ©Liu Mei; FORWARD: page vi, Laurence Henry Collection, Photographs and Prints Division, Schomburg Center for Research in Black Culture, The New York Public Library, Astor, Lenox and Tilden Foundations; EXECUTIVE SUMMARY: page 8, ©Bettmann/CORBIS; INTRODUCTION: page 13, ©Hulton-Deutsch Collection/CORBIS; CHAPTER 1: page 15, Benson Latin American Collection, The University of Texas at Austin; page 16, Marsha Miller, Office of Public Affairs, The University of Texas at Austin; page 17, Archives of the St. Louis Post Dispatch; page 21, Prints and Photographs Collection, CN 00323, The Center for American History, The University of Texas at Austin; pages 26 and 27, ©2001 Alan Pogue, apogue@texas.net; page 35, Marsha Miller, Office of Public Affairs, The University of Texas, Austin; CHAPTER 2: page 39, UNITE Archives, Kheel Center, Cornell University, Ithaca, New York; pages 40 and 41, Los Angeles Times photo, Rick Meyer; page 45, Los Angeles Times photo, Bob Carey; pages 56, 57 and 59, photos courtesy of APALC; CHAPTER 3: page 61, ©Bettmann/CORBIS; pages 62, 63 and 77, photos by Southern Echo Staff; pages 66–68, Library of Congress; CHAPTER 4: page 83, ©Bettmann/CORBIS; page 84, Los Angeles Times photo, Clarence Williams; page 85, Los Angeles Times photo, Carolyn Cole; pages 87, 91 and 95 photos courtesy of the Strategy Center; CHAPTER 5: page 103, ©Bettmann/CORBIS; pages 104 through 113, photos by Lewis A. Brandon III; CHAPTER 6: page 121, ©Underwood and Underwood/CORBIS; page 122 ©David Robinson/CORBIS; page 123, Republished with permission of Globe Newspaper Company, Inc., from December 21 issue of The Boston Globe ©1993; pages 126–127, ©Richard Cummins/CORBIS; page 132, Republished with permission of Globe Newspaper Company, Inc., from September 4 issue of The Boston Globe ©1993; INSIDE BACK COVER, ©Liu Mei

Calligraphy: William Deere

Art Direction and Graphic Design: Robin Lynch, Negerkunst Studio, www.negerkunst.com